罗尔德·达尔短篇故事
品读及汉译探索
第5卷

An Interpretation of Short Stories by Roald Dahl
and an Exploration of Their Chinese Translations
Volume 5

闫宝华 王永胜 著
YAN Bao-hua, WANG Yong-sheng

哈尔滨工业大学出版社

内容提要

本书系对英国作家罗尔德·达尔"非儿童类"(个别篇章具有"儿童类"文学特点,但由于是罗尔德·达尔早期作品,也被收录进来,作为研究的对象)短篇故事(小说)进行研究所著系列图书中的第5卷,包括7部短篇小说。这些小说长短不一、难易各异,按照不同的主题分成三章加以编排,分别为"不堪回首""冤冤相报"和"意味深长"。除第三章外,每章收录两篇作品,先做引导性的介绍,名为"原作导读",再给出小说的原文供读者阅读或作为翻译的参考,同时给出语言点及文化层面上的注释,以辅助理解,名为"原作释读",最后给出探索性的汉语译文,名为"翻译探索"。

本书适合大学英语专业本科生及研究生阅读、研究、翻译之用(不少小说也可供高中生阅读、学习),也适合广大的文学爱好者阅读,更适合从事英汉翻译或外国文学研究的学者、教师、学生等阅读、参考。

图书在版编目(CIP)数据

罗尔德·达尔短篇故事品读及汉译探索. 第5卷/闫宝华,王永胜著. —哈尔滨:哈尔滨工业大学出版社,2015.5
 ISBN 978-7-5603-5388-3

Ⅰ.①罗… Ⅱ.①闫… ②王… Ⅲ.①短篇小说-小说研究-英国-现代②短篇小说-文学翻译-英国-现代 Ⅳ.①I561.074

中国版本图书馆CIP数据核字(2015)第102541号

策划编辑	田新华
责任编辑	田新华 常 雨
封面设计	思 华 高永利
出版发行	哈尔滨工业大学出版社
社　　址	哈尔滨市南岗区复华四道街10号 邮编150006
传　　真	0451-86414749
网　　址	http://hitpress.hit.edu.cn
印　　刷	哈尔滨市工大节能印刷厂
开　　本	880mm×1230mm 1/32 印张10 字数380千字
版　　次	2015年5月第1版 2015年5月第1次印刷
书　　号	ISBN 978-7-5603-5388-3
定　　价	39.00元

(如因印装质量问题影响阅读,我社负责调换)

前　言

对于罗尔德·达尔(Roald Dahl,1916—1990),中国读者耳熟能详的恐怕是他的一些儿童文学作品,国内外对他称呼最多的莫过于"儿童文学作家"。他的儿童文学作品的确十分畅销,已被翻译成多国文字出版发行,几乎家喻户晓。可以说,在儿童文学作家中,罗尔德·达尔是最为成功、最为知名的作家之一。达尔的儿童文学作品深受很多国家小朋友的喜爱,其中包括《詹姆斯与大仙桃》(James and the Giant Peach)、《查利与巧克力工厂》(Charlie and the Chocolate Factory)、《魔法手指》(The Magic Finger)、《查利与大玻璃升降机》(Charlie and the Great Glass Elevator)、《了不起的狐狸爸爸》(Fantastic Mr. Fox)、《特威特夫妇》(The Twits)、《女巫》(The Witches)、《好心眼儿巨人》(The BFG,1983 年获"惠特布雷德奖"——Whitbread Award)以及《玛蒂尔达》(Matilda)等儿童故事。

然而,作为英国儿童文学作家的罗尔德·达尔还写过其他类型的文学作品,特别是那些"非儿童类"短篇小说(个别篇章具有"儿童类"文学特点,但由于是罗尔德·达尔早期作品,也被收录进来,作为研究的对象,也可以说"成人类"短篇小说。也就是说,为成年人写的文学作品。当然,这些作品中有些具有"成人"色彩——含有色情内容,但达尔"成人"作品中的"成人"内容大多是比较"隐晦"的。这样的"成人"作品,基本收录在他的《迷情乱性》(Switch Bitch)一书中)也同样精彩。称之为"非儿童类",主要针对达尔"儿童类"作品耀眼的光环而言。其实,这些"非儿童类"短篇故事(小说)绝大多数是达尔转笔写儿童文学作品之前完成的,"儿童类"作品的耀眼光环或多或少掩盖了一些"非儿童类"作品的光芒,而在中国,这些"非儿童类"作品的"光芒"几乎没有散发出来,很少为中国广大读者所熟知。这些作品受到西方19世纪现实主义文学的影响,多数采用现实主义的创作手法。同时,达尔也从美国短篇小说家欧·亨利(O. Henry)那里汲取了一定的营养。就达尔作品本身对人物和景物的描写来看,可以说,他是"20世纪英国变形精神世界的一位工笔画家"①。同他的儿童文学作品一样,他早期的这些"非儿童类"作品同样具有结尾出奇、结局令人意想不到等特点,更进一步说,达尔的此类短篇小说这方面的特点尤为突出。这类作品充满奇思妙想,人物刻画细腻入微,其中不乏道貌岸然者、悲观主义者、心理变态者。此类作品也不乏荒谬、贪婪、邪恶、虚伪的成分,其中的人物大都在"机关用尽"之时,一不小心就"栽了跟头",或者在"聪明绝顶"之际,反而被自己的"聪明"所误。

罗尔德·达尔的父母是挪威人,但达尔本人1916年出生在英国格拉摩根郡的兰达夫(Llandaff, Glamorgan,格拉摩根原来是英国南威尔士的一个郡——著者注),并在雷普顿公学(Repton School)接受教育。第二次世界大战爆发,他应征入伍,加入英国皇家空军,驻扎在内罗毕。后来,他加入了驻利比亚的一个战斗机中队,受了重伤。之后,又作为一名战斗机飞行员到希腊和叙利亚参加战斗。1942年,达尔作为英国大使馆的空军助理专员去了华盛顿。华盛顿成为他人生的转折点,因为在那里他开始了自己的创作生涯。随后,他被调到情报部。战争结束的时候,他成为英国皇家空军中校。他的第一批短篇小说共有12篇,都是根据自己在战争期间的经历所写。这12篇作品首先发表在美国的一些主流杂志上,后来编撰成书出版,书名为《向你飞跃》(Over to You)。

罗尔德·达尔所有受到高度赞誉的作品都被译成多种文字,成为全世界的畅销书。安格利亚电视台(Anglia Television)将他的一些

---

① 参见"陈钰(1985)",这里只不过将其中的"二十世纪",规范性修改成"20世纪"。

短篇小说改编成电视系列剧,冠以标题《出乎意料的故事集》(*Tales of the Unexpected*)。他的作品还包括两本自传——《男孩时代》(*Boy*)和《独闯天下》(*Going Solo*),还有赢得很多赞誉的小说《我的叔叔奥斯瓦尔德》(*My Uncle Oswald*)以及《罗尔德·达尔倾心的鬼怪故事集》(*Roald Dahl's Book of Ghost Stories*)。最后一本是他自己编辑出版的。在生命的最后一年,他收集了一些奇闻轶事,并跟妻子弗利西蒂(Felicity)一起整理了一些烹饪食谱,汇编成一本书。这本书1996年由企鹅出版集团出版,书名为《罗尔德·达尔的烹饪书》(*Roald Dahl's Cookbook*)[①]。

罗尔德·达尔于1990年11月23日去世。英国《泰晤士报》(*The Times*)称其为"我们这一代人中最有影响力的作家之一,也是拥有极其广泛读者群的作家之一"(One of the most widely read and influential writers of our generation),并在写给他的讣告中写道:"孩子喜欢他写的故事,把他当成自己心目中最喜爱的人……他的作品将成为未来的经典之作"(Children loved his stories and made him their favourite... They will be classics of the future)。据报道,在2000年英国的"世界图书日"(World Book Day)投票中,罗尔德·达尔当选为"读者最喜爱的作家"(Favourite Author)[②]。

对于20世纪的英国作家罗尔德·达尔及其作品,《爱尔兰时报》(*Irish Times*)的一篇评论,可谓一语中的:"Roald Dahl is one of the few writers I know whose work can accurately be described as addictive. Through his tales runs a vein of macabre malevolence, the more effective because it springs from the slightest, almost inconsequential everyday things. The result is a black humour of the most sophisticated kind."(罗尔德·达尔是我所认识的为数不多的作家之一,可以准确无误地说,

---

① 参见"Roald Dahl. *The Best of Roald Dahl*. London:Penguin Books Ltd.,2006"。

② 参见"Roald Dahl. *The Collected Short Stories of Roald Dahl*. London:Penguin Books Ltd.,1992"。

其作品令人沉醉、上瘾。他的作品始终贯穿着一条主线,这条主线令人毛骨悚然,充满恶意和凶险,但却更加行之有效,因为其来源是一些不起眼的、几乎微不足道的日常事物。结果,最为错综复杂的黑色幽默便应运而生了)①。

  抛开后来"儿童类"作品的耀眼光环不说,罗尔德·达尔在20世纪中叶之所以蜚声世界,就是因为他所创作的这些"非儿童类"的短篇小说(当然,个别篇章具有"儿童类"文学特点,预示性地展露出达尔后来作为儿童文学作家的一丝"光芒")。但是,当时中国翻译出版业不是很发达,对他的作品译介得也不是很多。就算是有所译介,也处于零星的"散兵作战"状态,不成体系。在全球化浪潮滚滚而来的今天,研究罗尔德·达尔的这部分作品,并系统地加以翻译,如同打开尘封已久的大门,门内的景色依然会令当代中国读者惊喜不已。对于广大的英语学习者和文学爱好者来说,阅读达尔的这部分作品将会带来迥然不同的人生体验。其实,罗尔德·达尔这部分短篇小说的实质和绝妙,可以从英美主流媒体的评价窥见一斑:

"Roald Dahl is the prince of storytellers."   ——*Daily Mail*
"罗尔德·达尔是位讲故事的王子。" ——(英国)《每日邮报》

"The absolute master of the twist-in-the-tale"
  ——*The Observer*
"绝对的大师,其故事的结局出人意料。"
  ——(英国)《观察家报》

"These stories pack their punch."   ——*The Observer*
"这些故事蓄满了惊人之力。" ——(英国)《观察家报》

---

  ① 著者译自 Roald Dahl (1916—1990) 的 "*The Best of Roald Dahl*"(《罗尔德·达尔小说精品集》)一书的封底(back cover)。此书由英国"Penguin Books Ltd."出版公司于2006年出版发行。

"An unforgettable read, don't miss it."
——*Sunday Times*
"一次难忘的阅读体验,不可错过。"
——(英国)《星期日泰晤士报》

"Dahl is too good a storyteller to become predictable, so you never know whether the tyrant or the tyrannized will win in the end."
——*Daily Telegraph*
"达尔的故事讲得太精彩了,结局简直令人无法预测。因此,你永远都无法得知,最后的赢家是残暴的人,还是受到残暴对待的人。"
——(英国)《每日电讯报》

"Dahl has the mastery of plot and characters possessed by great writers of the past, along with a wildness and wryness of his own. One of his trademarks is writing beautifully about the ugly, even the horrible."
——*The Los Angeles Times*
"达尔拥有以往伟大作家的资质——善于营造情节、精于刻画人物,但达尔也拥有自己荒诞不经的一面,以及自己的一套挖苦讥讽的手段。其中的一个标志就是他对丑陋之人的精妙刻画,更有甚者是对恐怖之人的精妙刻画。"
——(美国)《洛杉矶时报》

"An ingenious imagination, a fascination with odd and ordinary detail, and a lust for its thorough exploitation are the…strengths of Dahl's storytelling."
——*The New York Times Book Review*
"达尔写作的影响力在于其独特的想象力,在于其对稀奇古怪和平淡无奇的细节的着迷程度,在于其对细节完完全全加以利用的欲望。"
——(美国)《纽约时报·书评》

"The mind of Roald Dahl is quintessentially nasty and wicked."
——*The Washington Post*

"罗尔德·达尔的思维具有典型的特点,那就是肮脏和邪恶。"
——(美国)《华盛顿邮报》

在此前提下,研究并翻译罗尔德·达尔的"非儿童类"短篇小说,将具有一定的学术价值和社会价值,会为中国文学的百花园增添一个品种,会为文学爱好者和翻译者提供一个可供参考的文本。

在历时三年多对罗尔德·达尔"非儿童类"短篇小说进行研究和翻译的过程中,共收集到长短不一的此类作品60篇,并站在一定的角度,根据著者个人的理解,细加编排,精心安排,详加注释,最终通过翻译,引介给中国读者。

本书在对罗尔德·达尔短篇小说的翻译探索中,采取了严谨的翻译态度,形成了以下基本的翻译思路:

(1)人名、地名按照一定的标准进行"异化"式处理(极个别人名作了"归化"式处理),主要依据《世界人名翻译大辞典》(新华社译名室编,中国对外翻译出版公司1993年第一版或2007年第二版)以及《世界地名翻译大辞典》(周定国主编,中国出版集团、中国对外翻译出版公司2008年第一版)等,个别的人名、地名的翻译兼顾了流行的译法。

(2)绝大多数非国际化的度量衡单位,特别是英制的度量衡单位,采用"同化"或"归化"的处理方法,以便汉语思维者能形象化地加以理解。

(3)每一篇的题目都采用汉语四字格来处理,以求汉语的工整,发挥汉语四字格表达的优势,但同时最大限度地兼顾原文题目的字面意义。

(4)就汉语译文整体而言,尽量杜绝"翻译腔",以保持汉语语言的纯洁性和规范性,但前提是确保对达尔小说原文的"忠实"。

(5)尽量完美地再现原文的风格,虽然做到这一点并不是轻而易举的事情。原文有些风格,在翻译中只能退其次而求之——基本上采用"归化"处理手法,照顾了汉语的通畅性。比如原文中很多非标准的英语表达,汉译时就没有在"风格"上充分得以体现,这也是以后有待继续探索的一个翻译问题。

当然,"金无足赤,人无完人",匆忙且蹒跚的步履必将会迈出"不和谐"的步伐。在对罗尔德·达尔的"非儿童类"短篇小说进行研究、翻译并成书的过程中,不当甚至错误之处在所难免,还望读者不吝赐教,多多批评,特别是多做文学翻译方面的批评。

需要特别声明的是,本系列书中所引用的罗尔德·达尔原著内容以及所做的翻译探索,旨在学术研究,不做商业用途。涉及相关版权的地方,已经做了引用和标注。

著者
闫宝华　王永胜
2015 年 3 月 31 日于渤海大学

目 录

第一章 不堪回首 ······ 1

第一节 《公学遗恨》Galloping Foxley ······ 3
一、原作导读 ······ 3
二、原作释读 ······ 5
三、翻译探索 ······ 30

第二节 《最后之举》The Last Act ······ 45
一、原作导读 ······ 46
二、原作释读 ······ 51
三、翻译探索 ······ 100

第二章 冤冤相报 ······ 134

第一节 《最后颂歌》Nunc Dimittis ······ 135
一、原作导读 ······ 136
二、原作释读 ······ 139
三、翻译探索 ······ 178

第二节 《复仇公司》Vengeance Is Mine Inc. ······ 202
一、原作导读 ······ 203
二、原作释读 ······ 205
三、翻译探索 ······ 235

第三章 意味深长 ·················· 255

第一节 《熏制奶酪》Smoked Cheese ·············· 256
一、原作导读 ·················· 257
二、原作释读 ·················· 258
三、翻译探索 ·················· 261

第二节 《倒立之鼠》The Upsidedown Mice ·············· 262
一、原作导读 ·················· 263
二、原作释读 ·················· 264
三、翻译探索 ·················· 267

第三节 《蛇毒解药》Poison ·············· 269
一、原作导读 ·················· 270
二、原作释读 ·················· 272
三、翻译探索 ·················· 289

参考文献 ·················· 301
后 记 ·················· 303

第一章 不堪回首

不堪回首的，当然，都是一些过往的事情。

由于唐末藩镇割据，再加上农民起义，大唐帝国走上了不可逆转的衰亡之路。这是中国历史上的一段特殊的混乱时期，自唐朝灭亡开始，至宋朝统一中国本土为止。这段时期分成"五代"（907—960）与"十国"。具体来说，"五代"是指从公元907年朱温建立梁朝开始的五十多年里，中原地区前后换了五个短暂的王朝——梁、唐、晋、汉、周。但是，为了和以前相同名称的朝代区别开来，历史上把它们称作后梁、后唐、后晋、后汉、后周。而在唐末、五代及宋初，中原地区之外存在过许多割据政权，其中前蜀、后蜀、吴、南唐、吴越、闽、楚、南汉、南平（荆南）、北汉十个割据政权被《新五代史》及后世史学家合称为"十国"。

在"十国"时期，江南以吴国最强，而后被李昇篡位，建国南唐。李煜就是盘踞在长江中下游地区的南唐国最后一个皇帝，也称"南唐后主"或"李后主"。做皇帝前的李煜不仅工词，而且善书画，晓音律；做了皇帝后的李煜仍醉心于书画，不把朝政放在首位。最终，李煜从尽情享乐的一国之君沦为一个异国他乡的"阶下囚"。从皇帝变成俘虏，巨大的反差令李煜伤感无比，不堪回首的往事也就不断涌上心头，于是，千古名篇《虞美人·春花秋月何时了》就诞生了。可以

说,这首词成了南唐后主的人生绝唱:

春花秋月何时了,往事知多少。小楼昨夜又东风,故国不堪回首月明中。

雕阑玉砌应犹在,只是朱颜改。问君能有几多愁,恰是一江春水向东流。①

是啊,不堪回首的是故国的往事。往事知多少?往事实在太多、太多,而不堪回首的,往往令人记忆深刻:

几年湖海挹馀芳,岂料兰摧一夜霜。
人世空传名耿耿,泉台杳隔路茫茫。
碧窗月落琴声断,华表云深鹤梦长。
最是不堪回首处,九泉烟冷树苍苍。②

古人的诗句中,不堪回首的往事频频可见,如"恩爱苦情抛未得,不堪回首步迟迟③""数里黄沙行客路,不堪回首思秦原④""不堪回首崎岖路,正是寒风皱错时⑤""惆怅不堪回首望,隔溪遥见旧书堂⑥"等。

当然,生活在当下的现代人,也有诸多往事是不堪回首的。那些落马的贪官对自己的"发迹史"不堪回首,少年囚犯对自己的"鲁莽"不堪回首……痛失爱情者,往事不堪回首;痛失亲人者,往事不堪回首;痛失青春年华者,往事不堪回首……诸如此类,不胜枚举。

---

① 李煜《虞美人》其二,转引自《全唐诗》第 889 卷第 026 首。
② 戴叔伦《哭朱放》,转引自《全唐诗》第 273 卷第 147 首。
③ 贯休《经弟妹坟》,转引自《全唐诗》第 835 卷第 005 首。
④ 周朴《春日秦国怀古》,转引自《全唐诗》第 673 卷第 032 首。
⑤ 贯休《送罗邺赴许昌辟》,转引自《全唐诗》第 835 卷第 010 首。
⑥ 邵谒《降巫诗》,转引自《全唐诗》第 865 卷第 025 首。

第一章 不堪回首 第一节 《公学遗恨》Galloping Foxley

不堪回首的,还有英国作家罗尔德·达尔笔下的往事。儿时的痛苦记忆,至今难忘,却不堪回首,这就是《公学遗恨》;突然之间想起了高中时期的恋人,忍不住要见上一面,却为未来留下了往事——不堪回首的往事,这就是《最后之举》。

第一节 《公学遗恨》Galloping Foxley

罗尔德·达尔的《公学遗恨》(Galloping Foxley)被收录在《罗尔德·达尔短篇故事集锦》(The Collected Short Stories of Roald Dahl)、《如你之人》(Someone like You)、《五部畅销书集》(5 Bestsellers)、《完全出人意料故事集》(Completely Unexpected Tales)、《罗尔德·达尔选集》(The Roald Dahl Omnibus)以及《罗尔德·达尔二十九篇成人故事集》(Twenty Nine Kisses from Roald Dahl)等书中。此外,这部小说也被改编成电视系列剧——1980年3月15日播映的《出乎意料的故事集》(Tales of the Unexpected)第二部中的第3集(Episode 2.3)[1],可见其影响力之大。

另外,这篇故事中主人公的个人经历,在达尔的另外一部作品《幸运开局》(Lucky Break)[2]以及自传作品《男孩时代》(Boy)也有所涉及,可见达尔对现实进行艺术加工的非凡功力。

一、原作导读

这是一部短篇小说,然而,读罢令人感觉颇具自传性质——达尔

---

[1] 这部分信息以及本书以后此类部分中的资料都借鉴了克里斯廷·霍华德(Kristine Howard)创建并维护的网站"Roald Dahl Fans.com"(罗尔德·达尔粉丝网)中的部分信息,网址为:http://www.roalddahlfans.com/,由著者翻译整理。以后各章的此部分信息,若没特殊标明,其出处同此。

[2] 关于这篇小说(严格来说,是一篇描述性的文章),读者可参阅本研究所成系列书的后续某卷。

的描写太细腻、太生动、太真实。这部作品中的一些"情景",虽然达尔小时候在英国公学就读时的确经历过,但这的确是一篇经过艺术加工的作品——虽然其情节谈不上有多么复杂。

这篇小说是以第一人称"我"(名叫"威廉·珀金斯")的视角展开的,但跟罗尔德·达尔其他很多作品中的"我"不同的是,本篇的叙述者"我"不是"隐身"的,而是具有举足轻重的地位,其作用不仅仅是"纽带"或者"桥梁",而是整部小说的主体。

威廉·珀金斯生活一直很安逸,是一个知足常乐的人,每天坐火车上下班。早晨赶 8:12 的火车,上车后就坐到火车一角靠窗的位置,伴着嘈杂的声音和火车的晃动,阅读《泰晤士报》,下车则步行一段距离到办公室,然后开始一天的工作……周而复始,他的这种生活已经形成了固定的节奏,变成了某种常规。但是,突然有一天,一个陌生人加入到早晨等车的行列中,威廉的常规性节奏就彻底被打乱了。

经过几天的接触,外加几句不情愿的交谈,威廉终于想起来了:这个不速之客就是小时候公学堂里的"头头",名叫布鲁斯·福克斯利,人称"奔腾的福克斯利"。上公学的时候,这个家伙无情地折磨包括威廉在内的低年级学生,给威廉的身心造成了极大的伤害。于是,公学时光那不堪回首的往事一下子涌上了心头……对,没错,这家伙就是当年折磨威廉的那个高年级的"头头"。这一点,威廉不会弄错的。

在认出这个令人生厌的陌生人就是小时候折磨自己的"学校霸王"的瞬间,痛苦的记忆顿时浮现在眼前,这令威廉十分震惊。但是现在,情况大不相同,眼前这个家伙不再"威风凛凛",威廉也不再是那个曾经备受折磨的威廉。于是,坐在通勤火车车厢中的威廉——故事的叙述者"我"——决定向坐在对面的家伙透露一下自己的身份,看对方有什么反应:

"打扰一下,真心希望你能原谅。我自我介绍一下吧。"我身体前倾,仔细地观察着,生怕错过任何一个精彩的瞬间。"我叫珀金斯——威廉·珀金斯。我曾就读于雷普顿公学,1907级学生。"

"I do hope you'll excuse me. I'd like to introduce myself." I was leaning forward watching him closely so as not to miss the reaction. "My name is Perkins—William Perkins—and I was at Repton in 1907."

"见到你,我很高兴,"他说,随即把报纸放到大腿上。"我叫福蒂斯丘——乔斯林·福蒂斯丘,我是伊顿公学1916级学生。"

"I'm glad to meet you," he said, lowering the paper to his lap. "Mine's Fortescue—Jocelyn Fortescue, Eton 1916."

这个家伙居然不是人称"奔腾的福克斯利"的布鲁斯·福克斯利?!

二、原作释读

这篇小说采用夹叙夹议的方式展开,中间是大量的插叙,阅读中要加以辨别,以便对这部小说在整体上有一个顺畅的理解。

Galloping[①] **Foxley**[②]

Five days a week, for thirty-six years, I have travelled the eight-twelve train to the City. It is never unduly[③] crowded, and it takes me right in to Cannon Street Station, only an eleven and a half minute walk from the door of my office in Austin Friars.

---

① gallop:*Verb* (of a person) run fast and rather boisterously(人快速地、喧闹地)奔跑

② 本部小说原文出自"DAHL, R. *The Best of Roald Dahl* . London:Penguin Books Ltd., 2006"。

③ unduly:*Adverb* immoderately; excessively 不适当地;过分地;过度地(e. g. We're not unduly worried. 我们并不过分担心。)

· 5 ·

I have always liked the process of commuting①; every phase of the little journey is a pleasure to me. There is a regularity about it that is agreeable and comforting to a person of habit, and in addition, it serves as a sort of slipway② along which I am gently but firmly launched into the waters of daily business routine.

Ours is a smallish country station and only nineteen or twenty people gather there to catch the eight-twelve. We are a group that rarely changes, and when occasionally a new face appears on the platform it causes a certain disclamatory③, protestant ripple, like a new bird in a cage of canaries④.

But normally, when I arrive in the morning with my usual four minutes to spare, there they all are, good, solid, steadfast people, standing in their right places with their right umbrellas and hats and ties and faces and their newspapers under their arms, as unchanged and unchangeable through the years as the furniture in my own living-room. I like that.

I like also my corner seat by the window and reading *The Times* to the noise and motion of the train. This part of it lasts thirty-two minutes

---

① commute: *Verb* [no obj.] travel some distance between one's home and place of work on a regular basis 通勤;经常在家和工作地点之间往返

② slipway: *Noun* a slope built leading into water, used for launching and landing boats and ships or for building and repairing them 船台;下水滑道

③ disclamatory: *Adjective* being in the nature of a disclamation 否认的;表示否认的(注:这个词算是个生僻词,很多有名的英文词典都没有收录。)

disclamation: *Noun* the act or an instance of disavowing; renunciation 不承认; 否认;放弃

④ canary: *Noun* a mainly African finch with a melodious song, typically having yellowish-green plumage. One kind is popular as a cage bird and has been bred in a variety of colours, especially bright yellow 丝雀;金丝雀

and it seems to soothe both my brain and my fretful old body like a good long massage. Believe me, there's nothing like routine and regularity for preserving one's peace of mind. I have now made this morning journey nearly ten thousand times in all, and I enjoy it more and more every day. Also (irrelevant, but interesting), I have become a sort of clock. I can tell at once if we are running two, three, or four minutes late, and I never have to look up to know which station we are stopped at.

The walk at the other end from Cannon Street to my office is neither too long nor too short—a healthy little perambulation① along streets crowded with fellow commuters all proceeding to their places of work on the same orderly schedule as myself. It gives me a sense of assurance to be moving among these dependable, dignified people who stick to their jobs and don't go gadding② about all over the world. Their lives like my own, are regulated nicely by the minute hand of an accurate watch, and very often our paths cross at the same times and places on the street each day.

For example, as I turn the corner into St Swithin's Lane, I invariably come head on with a genteel③ middle-aged lady who wears silver pin-

---

① perambulation: *Noun* a leisurely walk (usually in some public place)(通常指在公共场所)漫步;闲荡

② gad: *Verb* [no obj.] (informal) go around from one place to another, in the pursuit of pleasure or entertainment(非正式)闲逛;游荡;找乐子(e.g. He had heard gossip that I was gadding about with an airline stewardess. 他曾听到关于我的闲话,说我和一位空姐四处寻欢作乐。)

③ genteel: *Adjective* polite, refined, or respectable, especially in an affected or ostentatious way so as to appear upper class 彬彬有礼的;优雅的(尤指假装斯文)

ce-nez① and carries a black briefcase in her hand—a first-rate accountant, I should say, or possibly an executive in the textile industry. When I cross over Thread-needle Street by the traffic lights, nine times out of ten I pass a gentleman who wears a different garden flower in his buttonhole each day. He dresses in black trousers and grey spats② and is clearly a punctual and meticulous③ person, probably a banker, or perhaps a solicitor like myself; and several times in the last twenty-five years, as we have hurried past one another across the street, our eyes have met in a fleeting glance of mutual approval and respect.

At least half the faces I pass on this little walk are now familiar to me. And good faces they are too, my kind of faces, my kind of people—sound, sedulous④, businesslike folk with none of that restlessness and glittering eye about them that you see in all these so-called clever types who want to tip the world upside-down with their Labour Governments and socialized medicines and all the rest of it.

So you can see that I am, in every sense of the words, a contented commuter. Or would it be more accurate to say that I was a contented

---

① pince-nez: *Noun* [treated as sing. or pl.] a pair of eyeglasses with a nose clip instead of earpieces 夹鼻眼镜

② spat: *Noun* (often as "spats") (historical) a short cloth gaiter covering the instep and ankle(历史上的用法)布面鞋罩

③ meticulous: *Adjective* showing great attention to detail; very careful and precise 十分注意细节的;一丝不苟的(e.g. He had always been so meticulous about his appearance. 他一直以来都十分注意外表形象。)

④ sedulous: *Adjective* (of a person or action) showing dedication and diligence(人或行为)坚忍不拔的;勤勉的;一心一意的(e.g. He watched himself with the most sedulous care. 他照顾自己无微不至。)

commuter? At the time when I wrote the little autobiographical sketch[①] you have just read—intending to circulate it among the staff of my office as an exhortation[②] and an example—I was giving a perfectly true account of my feelings. But that was a whole week ago, and since then something rather peculiar has happened. As a matter of fact, it started to happen last Tuesday, the very morning that I was carrying the rough draft up to Town in my pocket; and this, to me, was so timely and coincidental that I can only believe it to have been the work of God. God had read my little essay and he had said to himself, "This man Perkins is becoming over-complacent. It is high time I taught him a lesson." I honestly believe that's what happened.

As I say, it was last Tuesday, the Tuesday after Easter[③], a warm yellow spring morning, and I was striding on to the platform of our small country station with *The Times* tucked under my arm and the draft of "The Contented Commuter" in my pocket, when I immediately became aware that something was wrong. I could actually *feel* that curious little

---

① sketch: *Noun* a rough or unfinished version of any creative work(任何作品的)粗样;初稿

② exhortation: *Noun* an address or communication emphatically urging someone to do something 劝告;规劝(e. g. exhortations to consumers to switch off electrical appliances 规劝消费者关掉电器的话)

③ Easter: *Noun* the most important and oldest festival of the Christian Church, celebrating the resurrection of Christ and held (in the Western Church) between 21 March and 25 April, on the first Sunday after the first full moon following the northern spring equinox. 复活节(基督教最重要、最古老的节日,庆祝"耶稣复活",西方教会在每年3月21日至4月25日之间北半球春分后的月圆后的第一个星期日庆祝。)

ripple of protest running along the ranks① of my fellow commuters. I stopped and glanced around.

The stranger was standing plumb② in the middle of the platform, feet apart and arms folded, looking for all the world as though he owned the whole place. He was a biggish, thickset③ man, and even from behind he somehow managed to convey a powerful impression of arrogance and oil. Very definitely, he was not one of us. He carried a cane instead of an umbrella, his shoes were brown instead of black, the grey hat was cocked at a ridiculous angle, and in one way and another there seemed to be an excess of silk and polish about his person. More than this I did not care to observe. I walked straight past him with my face to the sky, adding, I sincerely hope, a touch of real frost to an atmosphere that was already cool.

The train came in. And now, try if you can to imagine my horror when the new man actually followed me into *my own* compartment④! Nobody had done this to me for fifteen years. My colleagues always respect my seniority⑤. One of my special little pleasures is to have the place to

---

① rank: *Noun* (ranks) the people belonging to or constituting a group or class(属于或构成群体的)成员(e.g. the ranks of Britain's unemployed 英国的失业群体)

② plumb: *Adverb* (archaic) vertically(古旧用法)垂直地(e.g. Drapery fell from their human forms plumb down. 打褶的衣服从他们的人物模型上垂直掉了下来。)

③ thickset: *Adjective* (of a person or animal) heavily or solidly built; stocky (人或动物)体格(或体形)粗壮的

④ compartment: *Noun* division of a railway carriage marked by partitions 铁路客车的)隔间;车厢

⑤ seniority: *Noun* the state of being older than another or others or higher in rank than another or others 年长;老资格;资历深;职位高

myself for at least one, sometimes two or even three stations. But here, if you please, was this fellow, this stranger, straddling① the seat opposite and blowing his nose② and rustling the *Daily Mail* and lighting a disgusting pipe.

I lowered my *Times* and stole a glance at his face. I suppose he was about the same age as me—sixty-two or three—but he had one of those unpleasantly handsome, brown, leathery③ countenances④ that you see nowadays in advertisements for men's shirts—the lion shooter and the polo player and the Everest climber and the tropical explorer and the racing yatchsman⑤ all rolled into one; dark eyebrows, steely⑥ eyes, strong white teeth clamping⑦ the stem of a pipe. Personally, I mistrust all handsome men. The superficial pleasures of this life come too easily to them, and they seem to walk the world as though they themselves were personally re-

---

① straddle: *Verb* [with obj.] sit or stand with one leg on either side of 骑;跨;跨立于(e.g. He turned the chair round and straddled it. 他把椅子转过来,然后跨坐在上面。)

② blow one's nose: clear one's nose of mucus by blowing through it into a handkerchief(对着手帕)擤鼻子

③ leathery: *Adjective* having a tough, hard texture like leather 似皮革的;坚韧的(e.g. brown, leathery skin 褐色、像皮革似的皮肤)

④ countenance: *Noun* a person's face or facial expression 脸;面孔;表情

⑤ yatchsman: 此词疑为"yachtsman"之误。

yachtsman: *Noun* a man who sails yachts 快艇(或游艇)主人;驾驶快艇(或游艇)的人;帆船运动员

⑥ steely: *Adjective* (figurative) coldly determined; hard(比喻用法)坚定的;冷酷的;无情的(e.g. There was a steely edge to his questions. 他的问题带有冷酷的锐利。)

⑦ clamp: *Verb* hold (something) tightly against or in another thing 紧压;紧嵌(e.g. Maggie had to clamp a hand over her mouth to stop herself from laughing. 麦琪不得不用手紧捂住嘴,忍住笑声。)

sponsible for their own good looks. I don't mind a *woman* being pretty. That's different. But in a man, I'm sorry, but somehow or other I find it downright offensive. Anyway, here was this one sitting right opposite me in the carriage, and I was looking at him over the top of my *Times* when suddenly he glanced up and our eyes met.

"D'you① mind the pipe?" he asked, holding it up in his fingers. That was all he said. But the sound of his voice had a sudden and extraordinary effect upon me. In fact, I think I jumped. Then I sort of froze up and sat staring at him for at least a minute before I got hold of myself and made an answer.

"This is a smoker," I said, "so you may do as you please."

"I just thought I'd ask."

There it was again, that curiously crisp②, familiar voice, clipping③ its words and spitting them out very hard and small like a little quick-firing gun shooting out raspberry④ seeds. Where had I heard it before? And why did every word seem to strike upon some tiny tender spot far back in my memory? Good heavens, I thought. Pull yourself together. What sort of nonsense is this?

The stranger returned to his paper. I pretended to do the same. But by this time I was properly put out and I couldn't concentrate at all. In-

---

① d'you = do you

② crisp: *Adjective* (of a way of speaking) briskly decisive and matter-of-fact, without hesitation or unnecessary detail(说话方式)干脆的;干净利落的;简明的 (e. g. Her answer was crisp. 她的回答很爽快。)

③ clip: *Verb* speak (words) in a quick, precise, staccato manner 短促地说;简短地说

④ raspberry: *Noun* an edible soft fruit related to the blackberry, consisting of a cluster of reddish-pink drupelets 悬钩子属植物的浆果;悬钩子;覆盆子;木莓;山莓

stead, I kept stealing glances at him over the top of the editorial page. It was really an intolerable face, vulgarly, almost lasciviously① handsome, with an oily salacious② sheen③ all over the skin. But had I or had I not seen it before some time in my life? I began to think I had, because now, even when I looked at it I felt a peculiar kind of discomfort that I cannot quite describe—something to do with pain and with violence, perhaps even with fear.

We spoke no more during the journey, but you can well imagine that by then my whole routine had been thoroughly upset. My day was ruined; and more than one of my clerks at the office felt the sharper edge of my tongue, particularly after luncheon when my digestion started acting up on me as well.

The next morning, there he was again standing in the middle of the platform with his cane and his pipe and his silk scarf and his nauseatingly④ handsome face. I walked past him and approached a certain Mr. Grummitt, a stockbroker who has been commuting with me for over twenty-eight years. I can't say I've ever had an actual conversation with him before—we are rather a reserved lot on our station—but a crisis like this will usually break the ice.

---

① lasciviously: *Adjective* (of a person, manner, or gesture) feeling or revealing an overt and often offensive sexual desire(人、行为或姿势) 好色的;淫荡的 (e.g. He gave her a lascivious wink. 他淫荡的朝她眨了一眼。)

② salacious: *Adjective* (of writing, pictures, or talk) treating sexual matters in an indecent way and typically conveying undue interest in or enjoyment of the subject(文章、图画或言谈)诲淫的;淫秽的

③ sheen: *Noun* [in sing.] a soft lustre on a surface 光泽;光辉

④ nauseating: *Adjective* causing disgust, loathing, or revulsion 令人恶心的;使人厌恶的;令人反感的(e.g. Violence in movies is often nauseating. 电影里的暴力行为常常使人反感。)

"Grummitt," I whispered. "Who's this bounder[①]?"

"Search me[②]," Grummitt said.

"Pretty unpleasant."

"Very."

"Not going to be a regular, I trust."

"Oh God," Grummitt said.

Then the train came in.

This time, to my relief, the man got into another compartment.

But the following morning I had him with me again.

"Well," he said, settling back in the seat directly opposite. "It's a *topping*[③] day." And once again I felt that slow uneasy stirring of the memory, stronger than ever this time, closer to the surface but not yet quite within my reach.

Then came Friday, the last day of the week. I remember it had rained as I drove to the station, but it was one of those warm sparkling April showers that last only five or six minutes, and when I walked on to the platform, all the umbrellas were rolled up and the sun was shining and there were big white clouds floating in the sky. In spite of this, I felt depressed. There was no pleasure in this journey for me any longer. I knew the stranger would be there. And sure enough, he was, standing with his legs apart just as though he owned the place, and this time swinging his cane casually back and forth through the air.

---

① bounder: *Noun* (informal, dated, chiefly Brit.) a dishonourable man(主要为英国英语的非正式古旧用法)不道德的人(e.g. He is nothing but a fortune-seeking bounder. 他只不过是个不讲道德的投机者。)

② Search me: (Slang) used by a speaker to indicate that he or she does not have an answer to a question just asked(俚语表达)我(可)不知道;这可难住我了

③ topping: *Adjective* (Brit. informal, dated) excellent(英国英语的非正式古旧用法)极好的(e.g. That really is a topping dress. 那真是件好衣服。)

The cane! That did it! I stopped like I'd been shot.

"It's Foxley!" I cried under my breath. "Galloping Foxley! And still swinging his cane!"

I stepped closer to get a better look. I tell you I've never had such a shock in all my life. It was Foxley all right. Bruce Foxley or Galloping Foxley as we used to call him. And the last time I'd seen him, let me see—it was at school and I was no more than twelve or thirteen years old.

At that point the train came in, and heaven help me if he didn't get into my compartment once again. He put his hat and cane up on the rack, then turned and sat down and began lighting his pipe. He glanced up at me through the smoke with those rather small cold eyes and he said, "*Ripping*① day, isn't it. Just like summer."

There was no mistaking the voice now. It hadn't changed at all. Except that the things I had been used to hearing it say were different.

"All right, Perkins," it used to say. "All right, you nasty little boy. I am about to beat you again."

How long ago was that? It must be nearly fifty years. Extraordinary, though, how little the features had altered. Still the same arrogant tilt of the chin, the flaring nostrils, the contemptuous staring eyes that were too small and a shade② too close together for comfort; still the same habit of thrusting his face forward at you, impinging on you, pushing you into a corner; and even the hair I could remember—coarse and slightly wavy, with just a trace of oil all over it, like a well-tossed salad. He used to keep a bottle of green hair mixture on the side table in his study—when

---

① ripping: *Adjective*（Brit. informal, dated）splendid; excellent（英国英语非正式的古旧用法）极好的; 绝妙的; 令人愉快的（e.g. She's going to have a ripping time. 她将过得很愉快。）

② a shade...: a little... 有点; 略微（e.g. He was a shade hung-over. 他有点醉后头晕。）

you have to dust a room you get to know and to hate all the objects in it—and this bottle had the royal coat of arms① on the label and the name of a shop in Bond Street, and under that, in small print, it said "By Appointment—Hairdressers② To His Majesty King Edward VII." I can remember that particularly because it seemed so funny that a shop should want to boast about being hairdresser to someone who was practically bald—even a monarch③.

And now I watched Foxley settle back in his seat and begin reading the paper. It was a curious sensation, sitting only a yard away from this man who fifty years before had made me so miserable that I had once contemplated suicide. He hadn't recognized *me*; there wasn't much danger of that because of my moustache. I felt fairly sure I was safe and could sit there and watch him all I wanted.

Looking back on it, there seems little doubt that I suffered very badly at the hands of Bruce Foxley my first year in school, and strangely enough, the unwitting④ cause of it all was my father. I was twelve and a half when I first went off to this fine old public school. That was, let me see, in 1907. My father, who wore a silk topper⑤ and morning coat⑥,

---

① coat of arms: *Noun* the distinctive heraldic bearings or shield of a person, family, corporation, or country(个人、家族、公司或国家的)盾形纹章;盾徽

② hairdresser: *Noun* a person who cuts and styles hair as an occupation 美发师;理发师

③ monarch: *Noun* a sovereign head of state, especially a king, queen, or emperor 君主;国王;皇帝;女王;女皇

④ unwitting: *Adjective* (of a person) not aware of the full facts(人)不知晓的(e.g. an unwitting accomplice 不知情的从犯)

⑤ topper: *Noun* (informal) a top hat(非正式)高顶礼帽

⑥ morning coat: *Noun* a man's formal coat with a long back section cut into tails which curves up to join the waist at the front 男式晨燕尾服

escorted me to the station, and I can remember how we were standing on the platform among piles of wooden tuck①-boxes and trunks and what seemed like thousands of very large boys milling② about and talking and shouting at one another, when suddenly somebody who was wanting to get by us gave my father a great push from behind and nearly knocked him off his feet.

My father, who was a small, courteous, dignified person, turned around with surprising speed and seized the culprit③ by the wrist.

"Don't they teach you better manners than that at this school, young man?" he said.

The boy, at least a head taller than my father, looked down at him with a cold, arrogant-laughing glare, and said nothing.

"It seems to me," my father said, staring back at him, "that an apology would be in order."

But the boy just kept on looking down his nose at my father with this funny little arrogant smile at the corners of his mouth, and his chin kept coming further and further out.

"You strike me as being an impudent and ill-mannered boy," my father went on. "And I can only pray that you are an exception in your school. I would not wish for any son of mine to pick up such habits."

At this point, the big boy inclined his head slightly in my direction, and a pair of small, cold, rather close together eyes looked down into

---

① tuck: *Noun* [mass noun] (Brit. informal) food, typically cakes and sweets, eaten by children at school as a snack(英国英语非正式用法)食物(尤指小孩在学校当点心的糕点和糖果)(e.g. a tuck shop 一家小食品店)

② mill: *Verb* [no obj.] (mill about/around) (of people or animals) move around in a confused mass 无目的地乱转;绕圈子

③ culprit: *Noun* a person who is responsible for a crime or other misdeed 罪犯;犯人;导致过错的人

mine. I was not particularly frightened at the time; I knew nothing about the power of senior boys over junior boys at public schools; and I can remember that I looked straight back at him in support of my father, whom I adored and respected.

When my father started to say something more, the boy simply turned away and sauntered① slowly down the platform into the crowd.

Bruce Foxley never forgot this episode; and of course the really unlucky thing about it for me was that when I arrived at school I found myself in the same "house" as him. Even worse than that—I was in his study. He was doing his last year, and he was a prefect②—a "boazer"③ we called it—and as such he was officially permitted to beat any of the fags④ in the house. But being in his study, I automatically became his own particular, personal slave. I was his valet⑤ and cook and maid and errand-boy, and it was my duty to see that he never lifted a finger for himself unless absolutely necessary. In no society that I know of in the

---

① saunter: *Verb* [no obj., with adverbial of direction] walk in a slow, relaxed manner, without hurry or effort 闲逛;漫步(e.g. Adam sauntered into the room. 亚当悠闲地踱进房间。)

② prefect: *Noun* (chiefly Brit.) a senior pupil in some schools authorized to enforce discipline(主要为英国英语用法)(英国某些公立学校、美国某些私立学校负责维持秩序的)班长;级长

③ 在这篇小说中,作家罗尔德·达尔将雷普顿公学的"班长"(prefect)称作"boazer",而事实上,这可能是达尔本人误拼的一个词。根据"Answers"(http://wiki.answers.com/)的相关内容,雷普顿公学对"prefect"的称呼应该是"beausier"。

④ fag: *Noun* (Brit.) a junior pupil at a public school who works and runs errands for a senior pupil(英国英语)(英制公学里供高年级学生差遣的)低年级学生

⑤ valet: *Noun* a man's personal male attendant, responsible for his clothes and appearance(为男主人照料衣着和仪表的)贴身男仆;仆从

第一章 不堪回首 第一节 《公学遗恨》Galloping Foxley

world is a servant imposed upon to the extent that we wretched little fags were imposed upon by the boazers at school. In frosty or snowy weather I even had to sit on the seat of the lavatory (which was in an unheated outhouse①) every morning after breakfast to warm it before Foxley came along.

I could remember how he used to saunter across the room in his loose-jointed, elegant way, and if a chair were in his path he would knock it aside and I would have to run over and pick it up. He wore silk shirts and always had a silk handkerchief tucked up his sleeve, and his shoes were made by someone called Lobb (who also had a royal crest②). They were pointed shoes, and it was my duty to rub the leather with a bone for fifteen minutes each day to make it shine.

But the worst memories of all had to do with the changing room.

I could see myself now, a small pale shrimp of a boy standing just inside the door of this huge room in my pyjamas and bedroom slippers and brown camel-hair dressing-gown③. A single bright electric bulb was hanging on a flex④ from the ceiling, and all around the walls the black and yellow football shirts with their sweaty smell filling the room, and the

---

① outhouse：Noun an outside toilet 户外厕所

② crest：Noun (Heraldry) a distinctive device borne above the shield of a coat of arms (originally as worn on a helmet), or separately reproduced, for example on writing paper or silverware, to represent a family or corporate body. (纹章)(盾形纹章上方的)饰章(起先饰在头盔上)或单独印于信签或银器等之上作为家族或某团体的象征。

③ dressing-gown or dressing gown：a long loose robe, typically worn after getting out of bed or bathing(起床或洗澡后穿的)晨衣；浴袍

④ flex：Noun (chiefly Brit.) a flexible insulated cable used for carrying electric current to an appliance(主要为英国英语表达)花线；皮线

voice, the clipped, pip①-spitting voice was saying, "So which is it to be this time? Six with the dressing-gown on—or four with it off?"

I never could bring myself to answer this question. I would simply stand there staring down at the dirty floor-planks, dizzy with fear and unable to think of anything except that this other larger boy would soon start smashing away at me with his long, thin, white stick, slowly, scientifically, skilfully, legally, and with apparent relish, and I would bleed. Five hours earlier, I had failed to get the fire to light in his study. I had spent my pocket money on a box of special firelighters② and I had held a newspaper across the chimney opening to make a draught and I had knelt down in front of it and blown my guts out into the bottom of the grate③; but the coals would not burn.

"If you're too obstinate to answer," the voice was saying, "then I'll have to decide for you."

I wanted desperately to answer because I knew which one I had to choose. It's the first thing you learn when you arrive. Always keep the dressing-gown *on* and take the extra strokes. Otherwise you're almost certain to get cut. Even three with it on is better than one with it off.

"Take it off then and get into the far corner and touch your toes. I'm going to give you four."

Slowly I would take it off and lay it on the ledge④ above the boot-lockers. And slowly I would walk over to the far corner, cold and naked

① pip: *Noun* a small hard seed in a fruit 核；籽

② firelighter: *Noun*（Brit.）a piece of flammable material used to help start a fire（英国英语）引火物；点火器

③ grate: *Noun* the recess of a fireplace or furnace 壁炉（或熔炉）的炉膛

④ ledge: *Noun* a narrow horizontal surface projecting from a wall, cliff, or other surface 壁架或崖边突出落脚处

· 20 ·

now in my cotton pyjamas①, treading softly and seeing everything around me suddenly very bright and flat and far away, like a magic lantern② picture, and very big, and very unreal, and sort of swimming through the water in my eyes.

"Go on and touch your toes. Tighter—much tighter than that."

Then he would walk down to the far end of the changing-room and I would be watching him upside down between my legs, and he would disappear through a doorway that led down two steps into what we called "the basin-passage". This was a stone-floored corridor with wash basins along one wall, and beyond it was the bathroom. When Foxley disappeared I knew he was walking down to the far end of the basin-passage. Foxley always did that. Then, in the distance, but echoing loud among the basins and the tiles③, I would hear the noise of his shoes on the stone floor as he started galloping forward, and through my legs I would see him leaping up the two steps into the changing-room and come bounding④ towards me with his face thrust forward and the cane held high in the air. This was the moment when I shut my eyes and waited for the crack and told myself that whatever happened I must not straighten up.

① pyjamas or pajamas：*Plural Noun* a suit of loose trousers and jacket for sleeping in 睡衣裤

② magic lantern：(historical) a simple form of image projector used for showing photographic slides(历史上用法)幻灯机

③ tile：*Noun* a thin square slab of glazed pottery, cork, linoleum, or other material for covering floors, walls, or other surfaces(铺地、贴墙等用的)瓷砖；花砖；软木片；亚麻油地毡片

④ bound：*Verb* [no obj., with adverbial of direction] walk or run with leaping strides 跳动；跳跃着前进(e.g. Louis came bounding down the stairs. 路易斯蹦蹦跳跳地下了楼。)

Anyone who has been properly① beaten will tell you that the real pain does not come until about eight or ten seconds after the stroke. The stroke itself is merely a loud crack and a sort of blunt thud against your backside, numbing you completely (I'm told a bullet wound does the same). But later on, oh my heavens, it feels as if someone is laying a red hot poker② right across your naked buttocks and it is absolutely impossible to prevent yourself from reaching back and clutching it with your fingers.

Foxley knew all about this time lag, and the slow walk back over a distance that must altogether have been fifteen yards gave each stroke plenty of time to reach the peak of its pain before the next one was delivered.

On the fourth stroke I would invariably straighten up. I couldn't help it. It was an automatic defence reaction from a body that had had as much as it could stand.

"You flinched③," Foxley would say. "That one doesn't count. Go on—down you get."

The next time I would remember to grip my ankles.

Afterwards he would watch me as I walked over—very stiff now and holding my backside—to put on my dressing-gown, but I would always

---

① properly: *Adverb* [usu. as sub-modifier] (informal, chiefly Brit.) thoroughly; completely(主要为英国英语的非正式用法)彻底地；完全地(e.g. On the first day she felt properly well, Millie sat out on the front steps. 米莉在感觉自己彻底好了的第一天就到屋外门前的台阶上坐了坐。)

② poker: *Noun* a metal rod with a handle, used for prodding and stirring an open fire 拨火棒

③ flinch: *Verb* [no obj.] make a quick, nervous movement of the face or body as an instinctive reaction to fear or pain(因害怕或疼痛而)退缩；畏缩(e.g. She flinched at the acidity in his voice. 他尖刻的话音令她畏缩。)

try to keep turned away from him so he couldn't see my face. And when I went out, it would be, "Hey, you! Come back!"

I was in the passage then, and I would stop and turn and stand in the doorway, waiting.

"Come here. Come on, come back here. Now—haven't you forgotten something?"

All I could think of at that moment was the excruciating① burning pain in my behind.

"You strike me as being an impudent and ill-mannered boy," he would say, imitating my father's voice. "Don't they teach you better manners than that at this school?"

"Thank... you," I would stammer②. "Thank you... for the beating."

And then back up the dark stairs to the dormitory and it became much better then because it was all over and the pain was going and the others were clustering round and treating me with a certain rough sympathy born of having gone through the same thing themselves, many times.

"Hey, Perkins, let's have a look."

"How many d'you get?"

"Five, wasn't it? We heard them easily from here."

"Come on, man. Let's see the marks."

I would take down my pyjamas and stand there, while this group of experts solemnly examined the damage.

"Rather far apart, aren't they? Not quite up to Foxley's usual standard."

---

① excruciating: *Adjective* intensely painful 极痛苦的;难以忍受的(e. g. excruciating back pain 难以忍受的背痛)

② stammer: *Verb* [no obj.] speak with sudden involuntary pauses and a tendency to repeat the initial letters of words 结结巴巴地说话;结巴

"Two of them are close. Actually touching. Look these two are beauties!"

"That low one was a rotten① shot."

"Did he go right down the basin-passage to start his run?"

"You got an extra one for flinching, didn't you?"

"By golly②, old Foxley's really got it in for *you*, Perkins."

"Bleeding a bit too. Better wash it, you know."

Then the door would open and Foxley would be there, and everyone would scatter and pretend to be doing his teeth or saying his prayers while I was left standing in the centre of the room with my pants down.

"What's going on here?" Foxley would say, taking a quick look at his own handiwork③. "You—Perkins! Put your pyjamas on properly and get to bed."

And that was the end of a day.

Through the week, I never had a moment of time to myself. If Foxley saw me in the study taking up a novel or perhaps opening my stamp album, he would immediately find something for me to do. One of his favourites, especially when it was raining outside, was, "Oh, Perkins, I think a bunch of wild irises④ would look rather nice on my desk, don't you?"

---

① rotten: *Adjective* (informal) very bad(非正式) 蹩脚的;极差劲的(e. g. She was a rotten cook. 她是一个很差劲的厨师。)

② golly: *Exclamation* (informal, dated) used to express surprise or delight (非正式的古旧用法)啊;天呐(表示吃惊或高兴)

③ handiwork: *Noun* [mass noun] (one's handiwork) something that one has made or done(某人的)做的东西;作品(e. g. The dressmakers stood back to survey their handiwork. 裁缝退后几步,审视他们自己的作品。)

④ iris: *Noun* Genus Iris, many species and numerous hybrids. The iris family also includes the gladioli, crocuses, and freesias. 鸢尾;鸢尾属植物

Wild irises grew only around Orange Ponds. Orange Ponds was two miles down the road and half a mile across the fields. I would get up from my chair, put on my raincoat and my straw hat, take my umbrella—my brolly①—and set off on this long and lonely trek②. The straw hat had to be worn at all times outdoors, but it was easily destroyed by rain; therefore the brolly was necessary to protect the hat. On the other hand, you can't keep a brolly over your head while scrambling about on a woody bank looking for irises, so to save my hat from ruin I would put it on the ground under my brolly while I searched for flowers. In this way, I caught many colds.

But the most dreaded day was Sunday. Sunday was for cleaning the study, and how well I can remember the terror of those mornings, the frantic dusting and scrubbing, and then the waiting for Foxley to come in to inspect.

"Finished?" he would ask.

"I...I think so."

Then he would stroll over to the drawer of his desk and take out a single white glove, fitting it slowly on to his right hand, pushing each finger well home, and I would stand there watching and trembling as he moved around the room running his white-gloved forefinger along the picture tops, the skirting, the shelves, the window sills, the lamp shades. I never took my eyes off that finger. For me it was an instrument of doom. Nearly always, it managed to discover some tiny crack that I had overlooked or perhaps hadn't even thought about; and when this happened Foxley would turn slowly around, smiling that dangerous little smile that wasn't a smile, holding up the white finger so that I should see for myself

---

① brolly: *Noun* (Brit. informal) an umbrella(英国英语的非正式用法)伞

② trek: *Noun* a long arduous journey, especially one made on foot 长途跋涉（尤指步行）

the thin smudge① of dust that lay along the side of it.

"Well," he would say. "So you're a lazy little boy. Aren't you?"

No answer.

"Aren't you?"

"I thought I dusted it all."

"Are you or are you not a nasty, lazy little boy?"

"Y-yes."

"But your father wouldn't want you to grow up like that, would he? Your father is very particular about manners, is he not?"

No answer.

"I asked you, is your father particular about manners?"

"Perhaps—yes."

"Therefore I will be doing him a favour if I punish you, won't I?"

"I don't know."

"Won't I?"

"Y-yes."

"We will meet later then, after prayers, in the changing-room."

The rest of the day would be spent in an agony of waiting for the evening to come.

Oh my goodness, how it was all coming back to me now. Sunday was also letter-writing time.

Dear Mummy and Daddy—thank you very much for your letter. I hope you are both well. I am, except I have got a cold because I got caught in the rain but it will soon be over. Yesterday we played Shrewsbury and beat them 4 - 2. I watched and Foxley who you know is the head of our house scored one of our goals. Thank you very much for the

---

① smudge: *Noun* a blurred or smeared mark on the surface of something 污迹

cake. With love from William.

I usually went to the lavatory to write my letter, or to the boot-hole, or the bathroom any place out of Foxley's way. But I had to watch the time. Tea was at four-thirty and Foxley's toast had to be ready. Every day I had to make toast for Foxley, and on weekdays there were no fires allowed in the studies, so all the fags, each making toast for his own study-holder, would have to crowd around the one small fire in the library, jockeying① for position with his toasting-fork. Under these conditions, I still had to see that Foxley's toast was (1) very crisp, (2) not burned at all, (3) hot and ready exactly on time. To fail in any one of these requirements was a "beatable offence".

"Hey, you! What's this?"

"It's toast."

"Is this really your idea of toast?"

"Well..."

"You're too idle to make it right, aren't you?"

"I try to make it."

"You know what they do to an idle horse, Perkins?"

"Are you a horse?"

"Well—anyway, you're an ass—ha, ha so I think you qualify. I'll be seeing you later."

Oh, the agony of those days. To burn Foxley's toast was a "beatable offence". So was forgetting to take the mud off Foxley's football boots. So was failing to hang up Foxley's football clothes. So was rolling up Foxley's brolly the wrong way round. So was banging the study door when

---

① jockey: Verb [no obj.] struggle by every available means to gain or achieve something 不择手段地争取; 用尽一切办法获取(e. g. Both men will be jockeying for the two top jobs. 两人都将不择手段地争取这两个高层职务。)

Foxley was working. So was filling Foxley's bath too hot for him. So was not cleaning the buttons properly on Foxley's O. T. C.① uniform. So was making those blue metal-polish smudges on the uniform itself. So was failing to shine the *soles* of Foxley's shoes. So was leaving Foxley's study untidy at any time. In fact, so far as Foxley was concerned, I was practically a beatable offence myself.

I glanced out of the window. My goodness, we were nearly there. I must have been dreaming away like this for quite a while, and I hadn't even opened my *Times*. Foxley was still leaning back in the corner seat opposite me reading his *Daily Mail*, and through a cloud of blue smoke from his pipe I could see the top half of his face over the newspaper, the small bright eyes, the corrugated forehead, the wavy, slightly oily hair.

Looking at him now, after all that time, was a peculiar and rather exciting experience. I knew he was no longer dangerous, but the old memories were still there and I didn't feel altogether comfortable in his presence. It was something like being inside the cage with a tame tiger.

What nonsense is this? I asked myself. Don't be so stupid. My heavens, if you wanted to you could go ahead and tell him exactly what you thought of him and he couldn't touch you. Hey—that was an idea!

Except that—well—after all, was it worth it? I was too old for that sort of thing now, and I wasn't sure that I really felt much anger towards him anyway.

So what should I do? I couldn't sit there staring at him like an idiot.

At that point, a little impish② fancy began to take a hold of me.

---

① O. T. C.: abbreviation for (in the UK) Officers' Training Corps(英国)军官训练团

② impish: *Adjective* inclined to do slightly naughty things for fun; mischievous 淘气的;顽皮的(e.g. He had an impish look about him. 他脸上有种顽皮的表情。)

What I would like to do, I told myself, would be to lean across and tap him lightly on the knee and tell him who I was. Then I would watch his face. After that, I would begin talking about our schooldays together, making it just loud enough for the other people in the carriage to hear. I would remind him playfully of some of the things he used to do to me, and perhaps even describe the changing-room beatings so as to embarrass him a trifle. A bit of teasing and discomfort wouldn't do him any harm. And it would do me an awful lot of good.

Suddenly he glanced up and caught me staring at him. It was the second time this had happened, and I noticed a flicker① of irritation in his eyes.

All right, I told myself. Here we go. But keep it pleasant and sociable and polite. It'll be much more effective that way, more embarrassing for him.

So I smiled at him and gave him a courteous little nod. Then, raising my voice, I said, "I do hope you'll excuse me. I'd like to introduce myself." I was leaning forward watching him closely so as not to miss the reaction. "My name is Perkins—William Perkins—and I was at Repton② in 1907."

The others in the carriage were sitting very still, and I could sense that they were all listening and waiting to see what would happen next.

"I'm glad to meet you," he said, lowering the paper to his lap.

---

① flicker: *Verb* [no obj.] (of light or a source of light) shine unsteadily; vary rapidly in brightness(光或光源)闪烁

② Repton: *Noun* Here, it refers to the Repton School. It is a co-educational English independent school for both day and boarding pupils located in the village of Repton, Derbyshire, in the English Midlands. 这里的"Repton"指的是"雷普顿公学"。雷普顿公学是一所男女合校教育的独立学校，既招收走读生，又招收寄宿生。雷普顿公学位于英格兰中部地区德比郡的雷普顿村。

"Mine's Fortescue—Jocelyn Fortescue, Eton① 1916."

三、翻译探索

本篇小说的翻译中,虽然没有涉及过多专业方面的词汇,但会遇到英国英语中一些特有的表达,个别表达也许是作家本人的笔误,无从查找,只能硬着头皮根据上下文进行"创造性"翻译。从某种角度来看,翻译也是一个甄别原文"正误"的过程,也是一个剔除"糟粕"的过程,这也就是某些翻译理论家所说的翻译是一种"再创作"的体现吧。

公学遗恨

我一直乘坐 8:12 的火车进城上班,一周要坐五天,加起来坐了三十六年。车上从来都没有过于拥挤的时候。我一直坐到坎农大街站下车,然后步行到我的办公室门口,只需十一分半的时间。我的办公室位于奥斯汀弗赖尔斯。

我一直很喜欢上下班通勤这一过程。对我来说,这个短暂旅程的每一个阶段都其乐无穷。对于一个遵循习惯的人来说,这个周而复始的旅程令人心旷神怡,颇感安逸舒适。此外,这个旅程可以算作一段船下水试航的滑道,沿着这段滑道,我能够轻轻地、缓缓地,却也牢牢地、稳稳地滑进日常事务的海洋之中。

我们上下车是在一个乡村车站,规模稍小,只有十九或二十人聚集在那里,等着赶 8:12 那趟车。我们赶车的这些人几乎是一成不变的。所以嘛,偶尔有新面孔出现在月台上,就会激起一层抗议的涟漪,含有一层不加认可的意思,这就如同一只新来的小鸟飞进了一个满是金丝雀的笼子。

但是,正常情况下,我早晨到达车站时,通常离开车还有四分钟

---

① Eton:*Noun* a town in S England, near the River Thames: site of Eton College, a public school 伊顿(英格兰南部一个城镇,靠近泰晤士,是伊顿公学所在地)。

第一章　不堪回首　第一节　《公学遗恨》Galloping Foxley

的间隔时间。此时，大家也都到齐了。他们人都很不错，可以信赖，却一成不变。他们站的地方、撑的雨伞、戴的帽子、系的领带、面部表情，还有胳膊底下夹的报纸，这些年以来都始终如一，不曾变过，也不可能改变的，就像我自己家中起居室里的家具一样。这一点，我甚是喜欢。

我也喜欢车厢一角的靠窗的座位。我经常坐在那儿，伴着嘈杂的声音和火车的晃动，阅读《泰晤士报》。看报过程为三十二分钟，既放松大脑，又缓解我那疲惫的老身板，不亚于享受长时间按摩带来的效果。能让人保持心平气和的莫过于周而复始的日常事务了，这一点尽可相信我说的。现在，像今天早晨这样的旅程，我经历不下一万次，而且一天比一天更是乐在其中。我也说一句尽管跑题、但却很有意思的话，那就是，我已经变成了某种类型的钟表。我从来不用抬头看车停在哪个车站，就能立刻说出车晚点两分钟、三分钟，或者是四分钟。

在旅程的另一端，从坎农大街站下车步行到我的办公室，路程不算长，也不算短——属于健身路段：沿着大街行走，街上挤满了像我一样的通勤上班族。他们跟我一样步行到上班地点，日程安排也跟我的一样井井有条、一成不变。行走在这些令人信任的、体面的、有尊严的人中间，无形中给我增添了一种安全感。他们忠于职守，并不四处游荡、无所事事。跟我的生活一样，他们的生活也按照走时精准的手表上的分针做了恰到好处的调整。经常发生的情况是，每天在大街上同样的地点、同样的时间，我们的路径彼此交叉。

比如说吧，转过街角，进入圣斯威森巷，我总是会迎面遇见一位举止优雅的中年女士。她戴着一副夹鼻眼镜，一只手拎了个公文包。依这副打扮看，她若不是最优秀的会计，就可能是纺织行业的管理人员。走到针线大街交通灯那儿的时候，我十有八九会与一位绅士擦肩而过。他衣服的扣眼里会插上一朵花园里采摘的鲜花，花的品种一天一个样。他穿一条黑裤子，脚上绑了一副灰色的鞋套。看得出来，他是个严守时间、一丝不苟的人，或许是个银行家，或许跟我一样，是个小律师。在过去的二十五年时间里，我俩在大街上匆忙行走、擦肩而过的时候,虽然四目相对的时间极其短暂,但彼此眼里流露出的却是相互赞赏、彼此尊重的目光。

在这个短暂的步行旅程中,我现在熟悉至少一半跟我擦肩而过的面孔,都是一副副善意的面孔,跟我的面孔是一个类型。他们也都是跟我一个类型的同乡——思想健全、做事勤恳、求真务实。他们身上毫无焦躁不安的神态和飘忽不定的眼神。这样的神态和眼神在所谓的聪明人身上比比皆是,而这些聪明人一心要利用所有可以借助的力量——如工党政府、社会化医疗等,把这个世界上下颠倒过来。

所以,从我说的任何一层意义上都看得出来,我这个上下班跑通勤的是心安、知足了。或者说,我曾经心安、知足过,这样说会更加准确吗?我刚写完一个短小的自传概略——也就是上面你读到的,打算分发给办公室的人员阅读,以便把我作为榜样,起到劝诫的作用。因为在自传里,我完完全全、真实可靠地描述了自己的感受。但是,这只是整整一周前的想法了。自从有了那个想法,就发生了一件怪异的事情。实际上,这件怪事是上周二发生的。就是在那天早晨,我兜里揣着上述自传概略的草稿要乘车进城。这件事的发生巧就巧在跟我铁打不动的日常事务的时间相吻合。所以嘛,我只能相信,这件事儿是上帝的杰作——上帝读过我兜里的那篇小小的自传,就自言自语地说道:"这个叫珀金斯的家伙真是得意忘形啊。我要教训教训他。时间恰到好处。"说实话,我相信这件事儿就是这样发生的。

就像我刚才说的那样,那是星期二的事情,也就是复活节后的那个春天的星期二。那天早晨,天气暖洋洋的,天空呈黄色。我大步流星地走上我们那个小小的乡村车站的月台,胳膊底下夹着《泰晤士报》,兜里揣着我自传的草稿,还起了个名字叫《一个跑通勤人的心安与满足》。一到那儿,我就立即觉察到有什么地方不对劲了。事实上,我感觉到现场泛起了一层小小的涟漪——令人感到奇怪,这层涟漪正在跟我一样跑通勤的同乡队伍中间传播开来。于是,我停下脚步,扫视周围。

这位不速之客笔直地站在月台的中央位置,两脚分立、胳膊交叉,那眼神看起来就好像这里的地盘,非他莫属。这个家伙块头有点大，人很厚实。即使从后面瞅一眼，也看得出他总是能给人留下一种强势的印象，显得傲慢，满身油光光的。可以明确肯定的是，他不是我们当中的一员。他手里拿的是一根拐棍，而不是一把雨伞；穿的鞋是棕色的，却不是黑色的；灰帽子歪戴着，帽子歪的样子很是可笑；不管是横看也好，竖看也罢，他这个人都似乎过于招摇——穿戴整洁、光鲜照人。除此之外，我也懒得再看他一眼了。经过他身旁时，我把脸冲向天空，一直朝前走。与此同时，我诚心希望，我的这一举动会为周围已经凉爽的气氛再增添一丝寒意。

　　火车进站了。此时，要是能够想象，你就尽可能想象一下我惊恐的感觉吧——这个新来的家伙居然跟着我进入*我自己*经常乘坐的那节车厢的隔间。已经有十五年了，没有人胆敢这样对我。我的那些同事对我总是毕恭毕敬的，因为我是前辈，资历颇高。在车上，我的一个特权和自得其乐的事情就是，至少可以独享这个隔间一站地的距离，有时候是两站地的距离，甚至是三站地的距离。可是，说起来你也许不信，此时此刻在这个隔间里，多了这个新来的家伙。只见他两腿分开，跨坐在对面的座位上，擤着鼻涕，"哗啦哗啦"翻着《每日邮报》，还竟然点燃烟斗吸了起来，很令人讨厌。

　　我把《泰晤士报》压低一点，偷偷瞥了一下他的脸。我猜测，他的年龄跟我不相上下——六十二三的样子吧。面容帅气，却令人厌烦；面部呈棕褐色，有皮革般的质感。当今，他那副面孔在男士衬衫广告画面中看得到。看到他，就等于看到了猎杀狮子者、马球选手、珠峰攀登者、热带探险家、快艇赛手等，他的面孔是把这些人的面孔综合在一起的产物。他眉毛黑黑，双眼似钢铁般冰冷，牙齿白白的，显得强健有力，紧紧地咬住那烟斗的长柄。就我个人而言，任何一个帅气的男子，我都不信任。对帅气的男子来说，人生中浮华的快乐唾手可得，简直易如反掌。这样的男子似乎在世间游刃有余。就其个人而言，就好像是仅凭着自身英俊的长相，就非常吃得开。哪位女子长得漂亮悦目，我倒不介意，因为那不是一回事。但是无论怎么说，我认为，男子的帅气令人厌恶透顶。对这个看法，我感到十分抱歉。光说没用，看看坐在我正对面的这位男子吧。就在我压低《泰晤士报》看着他的时候,他却猛地抬起头,我们四目相对。

"我抽烟斗,你介意吗?"他用手指直直地夹住烟斗问道。他就说了这么一句话,可是他的声音却突然间在我身上产生了异乎寻常的反响。实际上,我想我当时一下子跳了起来。随即,我有点冻僵的感觉,然后坐下,两眼瞪了他足足一分钟,才控制住自己,做了回答。

"这不是禁烟车厢,"我说,"所以,你可以想吸就吸的。"

"刚刚想起来,最好问一下。"

又是*那样的*话语。那话语都不长,很是怪异,好像在哪儿听过。他说话时,把词做了大量的裁剪,然后狠狠地吐出来。吐出零星的几个词,就像一把枪在快速连射,但射出的却是一粒粒的木莓籽儿。在什么地方听到过这样的声音呢?为什么每一个词似乎都击打到我遥远记忆中的某个微小而脆弱的点上呢?我的天啊,怎么能想到那件事上啊。要镇定。那样想,不是等于胡扯吗?

这家伙继续看报。我假装也在看报,但是至此,我有些神不守舍、无法集中精力了。实际上,我手举着新闻评论版那页报纸,眼睛却不断地从报纸上方瞟着他。他那张脸真是让人忍无可忍:尽管帅气,却丑陋不堪、猥琐淫荡;脸上皮肤油腻腻的,闪动着淫秽的光泽。可问题是,我一生中的某个时刻,是否看到过这样一张脸?我开始认为,我看到过的。因为现在,即便是看一眼这张脸,我就会有一种奇特的、不舒适的感觉,这种感觉无法清楚地描述出来——与痛苦有关,与暴力有关,甚至或许还与恐惧有关。

这趟旅程中,我们再没说过话。但是,你不难想象,那时我的一切常规彻底被打乱了,甚至一整天也好不到哪里去。我办公室的职员,不止一个感觉到我言辞比以往尖刻、不中听,特别是午餐过后,我的胃也开始跟我过不去。

第二天早晨,他又来了,还是站在月台中间,拄着拐棍、叼着烟斗、围着丝巾,还是那张脸——帅气但令人生厌。我从他身旁走过,靠近了一个叫格拉米特的先生。这位先生是证券经纪人,我俩一起跑通勤二十八年有余,但是我还不能说,以前跟他有过实质意义上的对话。在上车的那个小站,我们彼此往往是缄默不语,可是在今天这个危急时刻,坚冰就会打破的。

"格拉米特,"我小声说。"那个新冒出来的是谁呢?"

"搜肠刮肚也不知道哇,"格拉米特说。

"相当惹人讨厌。"

"就是。"

"我相信,不会总是这样出现的。"

"噢,天呐,"格拉米特说。

接着,火车进站了。

这一次,这家伙钻进另一个隔间,我总算松了口气。

可是,紧接着一天的早晨,他又跟我坐一个隔间了。

"我说呀,"他坐到我正对面的座位后说道。"天气*好极*了。"我慢慢地变得不安起来,记忆又一次开始翻腾,这次翻腾比以前更强烈,眼看就要把那段记忆翻腾出来,结果还是没想起来。

一晃就是周五,也就是一周工作时间的最后一天。我记得,驱车到车站的时候,天已经下起了雨,只不过是四月里的一场阵雨,持续五六分钟而已,却洋溢着温暖的气息。走上月台时,所有雨伞都收起来了。太阳出来,闪闪发光,朵朵大块的白云在天空飘浮。虽是如此,我仍然心里压抑、神情沮丧。对我而言,这个旅程再也不会自得其乐了。我知道,那个家伙也在的,而且我十分肯定,他两腿分开站立在那里,就好像这里的地盘非他莫属似的。不仅如此,这次还在空中漫不经心地挥动着他的那根拐棍呢。

瞧,那根拐棍!就是那根拐棍!我翻腾的记忆戛然而止,好像被子弹击中了一样。

"是福克斯利!"我压低声音喊了起来。"奔腾的福克斯利!还是那样挥动着拐棍!"

我靠近一点,仔细看了看。我要说的是,一生中我从来没有如此的震惊。就是福克斯利了。我们那时常常称他布鲁斯·福克斯利或奔腾的福克斯利。最后一次看到他——让我想想——是在学校,当时我也就十二三岁的样子。

就在火车进站的那一刻,就像是上天的安排,他又一次钻进了我乘坐的车厢隔间。他摘掉帽子,用拐棍挑起来挂到支架上,随即转身坐下,开始点烟斗。他抬起头,两只冰冷的小眼睛透过烟雾看着我,说道:"很不错的天气,就像是夏天。"

现在就是听声音,也不会搞错的,声音根本没有多大变化。当然,现在他说的话跟我当时常常听到的比较起来,内容大不一样了。

"好吧,珀金斯,"那声音以前经常这样说。"好吧,你这个下贱的小孩,我要再抽你一下。"

时隔多久呢?一定是快五十年了。这么长时间过去了,他的那些特征竟然没有多大变化,真是超乎想象啊。下巴侧倾,还是那么傲慢无礼;鼻孔张开,呈喇叭形;两只眼睛太小了,盯人看时充满了轻蔑的目光,而且看人的时候凑得太近,让人感觉不舒服。他还是那个习惯:脸伸向你,把你抵住,推到一角;我甚至还记得他的头发,粗糙蓬乱、轻微带卷,满头只看到少许的油迹,就像一盘搅拌均匀的沙拉。他书房墙边的桌上经常放一瓶绿色的护发剂。要是被逼无奈去打扫一个房间,时间一长的话,你就会讨厌那房间里的一切。这个瓶子的标签上有一枚皇室盾形徽章,还有一行字,写的是邦德大街上一家商店的名字,名字下方印了一行小字:服务需预约——国王陛下爱德华七世的理发师。我特别记得这行字,是因为这太荒唐可笑了:竟然有这样的商店,吹嘘自己是某个实质上是秃头之人的美发师——甚至吹嘘是某个君主的美发师。

现在,我看到福克斯利坐到座位上,开始读报。这种感觉颇为怪异:五十年前认识的这个人就坐在那个地方,离我仅一步之遥,而这个人却把我折磨得如此悲惨,令我一度想到要自杀。当然,他没有认出*我是谁*,也不担心他会认出我,因为我留着小胡子。我相当有把握:我在明处,安安全全的;我大可坐在那儿,愿意怎么观察就怎么观察。

回首往事,我上学的第一年,在布鲁斯·福克斯利的手里,我被折磨得惨透了,这一点似乎毫无疑问。但是,奇怪得很,这一切背后不为人知的原因却在于我的父亲。当时我才十二岁半,第一次离家步入这所优秀的老牌公立学校。让我想想……对,那一年是1907

第一章 不堪回首 第一节 《公学遗恨》Galloping Foxley

年。我父亲一路送我到车站,父亲头戴一顶丝质高顶礼帽,身穿一件大燕尾服。我记得我俩站在月台上,周围堆放着木制的、装零食的箱子,还有装衣服的行李箱。一大群闹哄哄的、大块头的男孩子在周围绕着圈子瞎跑,相互说个不停、喊个没完。突然,有个家伙想从我俩身旁过去,结果却从后边使劲推了父亲一下,几乎把他推倒在地。

我父亲个子矮小,却是一个讲究客套、不失体面的人。他转过身,速度快得出奇,一下子抓住了罪魁祸首的手腕。

"年轻人,这所学校难道就没有教会你比这更文明的举止吗?"他说道。

这个撞人的男孩子至少比我父亲高出一头。他俯视着父亲,眼神冰冷,笑中带着傲气,但是什么也没说。

"对我来说,似乎,"父亲瞪了他一眼,说道,"道个歉是顺理成章的。"

但是,这个家伙却一直低着头,鼻子冲着父亲,嘴角微微露出傲慢的笑容,样子很好笑,下巴越来越向前伸出。

"看你这孩子,冒冒失失撞上了我,却粗鲁无礼,"父亲继续说。"我也只能祈求,你们学校你是个例外。我希望,我的儿子一个也别染上你这样的坏习惯。"

就在这时,这个大块头的家伙稍微把头倾斜一下,向我这边看来。于是,我跟他就四目相对了:他那双眼睛小小的,好像闭合到一起了,目光很是寒冷。当时,我倒不是特别地恐惧,因为对于公学里,大孩子欺负小孩子的那股势力,我一无所知。我还记得,我当时径直瞪了他一眼,为的是给父亲撑腰,因为我崇拜父亲,对父亲很敬重。

我父亲刚要再说点什么,这家伙干脆一转身,沿着月台溜溜达达走开,消失在人群之中。

布鲁斯·福克斯利永远忘不掉这段插曲。当然,对我来说,真正不幸的事情就是,到学校后我发现自己竟然跟这家伙"同居一室",而且糟糕透顶的是,我住的是他的书房。他还有一年就毕业,是年级长——我们一般称作"头头"。依他的身份,要揍房间里低年级中的哪一个,得他正式点头同意。但是,由于住在他的书房,我就自然而然变成了他特定的私人奴隶——男仆的活、厨师的活、女仆的活、跑腿的活,我都干。总之,我的义务就是确保他连手指头也不用抬一下,除非绝对必要非抬不可。据我所知,世界上没有一个社会里仆人被剥削的程度达到了公学里头头剥削我们这些可怜的低年级小学生那样的程度。不管是寒霜满地,还是大雪漫天,我每天早饭过后都必须坐到厕所的马桶座上,把马桶坐暖和了,福克斯利才能过来上厕所。要知道,厕所设在外屋,没有暖气的。

我还记得,他那时常常在屋子里大模大样、旁若无人地溜达来、溜达去,一副风度翩翩的样子。要是有一把椅子挡在前边,就一脚踢翻。我就立马跑过去,扶起椅子,再放好。他穿着丝绸衬衫,还总是把一块丝绸手绢掖到袖子里。他的鞋是一个叫洛布的人做的,这个人也有一枚皇室徽章。那是一双带尖儿的鞋。我的义务就是,每天花上十五分钟时间,用一根骨头蹭那鞋的皮革,直到蹭得油光锃亮为止。

但是,最为糟糕的记忆还得从更衣室说起。

此刻,我仿佛看到自己——脸色苍白、身材矮小如虾米般的一个男孩——站在这个偌大房间的房门里面,下身穿一条宽松的长睡裤,上身穿一件驼绒浴袍,脚穿一双轻便拖鞋。房间的天花板上垂下一根麻花状电线,电线头上接了一个电灯泡,明晃晃地亮着。四周的墙壁上挂满了足球衫,有黑色的、有黄色的,还散发出满屋子的汗臭味。屋子里有人在说话,声音很急促,边说边吐果核:"那么,这次选哪一样呢?浴袍不脱,打六下,但要是脱掉,就打四下。哪一样?"

这个问题我从没有回答过。我只是站在那儿,两眼盯着脏兮兮的地板,由于害怕而感到头昏眼花,什么也想不起来了。但是我知道,另一个更大块头的男孩子很快就会抽打我,用的是他那根长长的、细细的、白色的棍子,慢慢地、老练地、有条不紊地、理直气壮地抽打,还明显露出一副自得其乐的样子,接着我就会流血。五个小时以前,我在福克斯利的书房为他的壁炉生火,但没有点着。我花掉零用钱买了一盒特殊的引火物,甚至用报纸横在烟囱那儿以使通风良好,还跪在壁炉前,往炉膛的底部吹风,肚皮都要吹破了,但是煤就是烧

第一章 不堪回首　第一节　《公学遗恨》Galloping Foxley

不起来。

"要是你还倔到底,不回答的话,"那声音又说,"我可就替你决定了。"

我拼了命想回答的,因为我知道该选择哪一样,这是初来乍到要学会的第一件事情。要时时刻刻穿上浴袍,以承受额外的抽打。否则的话,几乎可以肯定,皮肤会给打开裂的。即使不脱掉浴袍给打三下,也比脱掉浴袍给打一下强得多。

"那就脱掉浴袍,到远处的角落,手触到脚趾。我要打你四下。"

我慢慢地脱掉浴袍,放到鞋柜上方的壁架上,然后慢慢地走到远处那个角落。现在,我踩着脚,下身只穿一条棉制的宽松睡裤,上身裸露着,感到寒冷。我看到周围的一切突然之间明亮起来,然后变得扁平,离我很远,就像幻灯机放出来的图像;周围的一切又变得很大、很不真实,就好像在我充满水的眼睛里游泳一样。

"赶快触到脚趾。太松弛了,触紧些。"

接着,福克斯利走到更衣室里离他远的那一头。我透过两腿间空隙看着他,这样看,他的头和脚是上下颠倒的。他穿过一道门,不见了。过了那道门,再下两个台阶,就走上了一条过道,我们称之为"脸盆过道"。实际上,这是一个走廊,地面用石头铺成,沿着一面墙摆满了洗脸盆,而走廊尽头就是浴室。看不见福克斯利的时候,我知道他正走向脸盆过道远处那端,这一点不会错的。接着,我就会听见他飞奔向前时,鞋在石头地面摩擦发出的噪声。虽然距离很远,但是声音在脸盆和墙砖之间反射发出的回声却很响。透过双腿,我看到他蹦上那两级台阶,进入更衣室,跳跃着奔我而来。他的脸向前伸出,拐棍高高举到空中。这时候,我只能闭上眼睛,等着听"啪啪"的抽打声,并对自己说,无论发生什么,千万不要挺直身体。

不管是谁,只要彻底挨过抽打,都会对你说,打的时候不疼,真正疼痛是在抽打完八到十秒后才开始的。抽打本身不过是"啪"的一记响亮的声音,感觉你背上发出沉闷的"嘭"的击声,致使你的那个部位完全麻木——我听说,子弹也会产生同样的效果。但是,过一会儿再看,我的天啊,疼得就好像有人拿一根红红的、滚烫的拨火棒径直戳向你裸露的屁股。这时候,你不想向后伸出手,不想用手指牢牢地抓住屁股,是绝对不可能的。

抽打后疼痛会延迟发作,对此福克斯利十分清楚。因此,他每次抽打完后,就向后慢慢退一段距离——将近十五米,留出足够的时间让疼痛达到顶峰。然后,再接着开始下一次抽打。

抽打到第四下的时候,我无法忍受,身体像以往一样,挺立起来。这是一种自然而然的防御性反应,因为身体已经忍受到无法容忍的程度了。

"你退缩了,"福克斯利当即说道。"刚才那个不算。接着打——弯下去。"

下一次抽打时,我就会记得抓牢踝关节。

打完后,他就看着我离开。现在,我身体僵直,后背挺着,随手穿上浴袍。但是,始终没有转身,怕他看到我的脸。走出屋子的时候,就会传来一声:"嘿,说你呢。回来!"

当时,我走在过道里,应声而停,转过身去,站到门口,等待着。

"过来,快过来,回到这里来。现在,你是否忘记点什么事儿呢?"

那一刻,我所能想起的就是我后部难以忍受的、灼烧般的疼痛。

"看你这孩子,冒冒失失撞上了我,却粗鲁无礼,"他就会模仿我父亲的声音说。"这所学校难道就没有教会你比这更文明的举止吗?"

"谢谢……你,"我就会结结巴巴地说。"谢谢……你……打了我。"

随后,我就登上黑暗的楼梯回到宿舍。回去后,情况就好多了,因为这一切总算结束了。虽然疼痛还在继续,但是其他人三五成群围过来,对我报以某种难过的同情,这种同情出于他们自身同样的经历,而且经历过很多次了。

"嘿,珀金斯,让我们看一下。"

"挨过多少下了?"

"五下,对吗?从这里很容易听见的。"

"好啦,伙计。给我们看看伤痕吧。"

我就脱下浴袍,站在那里,任由这组专家郑重其事地检查我的伤势。

"彼此隔得太远了,是不是呢?离福克斯利的正常水平,还差一点儿。"

"有两个靠得还挺近的,实质上碰到一起了。看呐,这两个就是赏心悦目啊!"

"低处的那个抽得太蹩脚了。"

"他是沿着脸盆过道开始助跑的吗?"

"由于退缩,你身上多了一个,对吧?"

"天呐,珀金斯,这一个真的是福克斯利这位老手为*你本人*量身定做的。"

"只是出了一点儿血。知道吗,最好洗一洗。"

紧接着,门就开了,福克斯利出现在门口。大家就四下散开,有的假装弄牙,有的假装祷告。只有我还站在屋子中间,裤子还没有提上。

"这里发生什么事情啦?"福克斯利就会问。然后,低头快速看了一眼我身上他的杰作。"你——珀金斯!浴袍穿利索点,上床睡觉。"

一天就这样结束了。

整个这一周里,我没有片刻属于我自己的时间。要是看见我在书房里拿起一本小说要读一读,或者看见我打开集邮册,他就会立刻找点事儿让我做。特别是外面下雨的时候,他最喜欢说的就是:"噢,珀金斯,我想啊,一束野生鸢尾花放到我的书桌上会相当漂亮的,你说是吧?"

野生鸢尾花只生长在橘塘的周围,而要到达橘塘,就得沿马路走六里多,再穿过田野走上一里地。于是,我就得从椅子上站起来,披起雨衣,戴上草帽,撑起雨伞——我自己那把小雨伞,就上了路,开始了漫长而孤独的艰苦跋涉。在外面,草帽不戴可不行,但大雨会轻而易举毁掉草帽。于是,为保护草帽,我那把小雨伞就是必需的。再者说,在树木茂盛的堤岸爬上爬下寻找鸢尾花,头顶也不能举一把雨伞的。所以,为了帽子不被雨水毁掉,找花的时候,我就把伞支到地面上,把草帽放到伞底下。这样的话,我感冒的次数就可想而知了。

然而,最恐怖的一天是星期天,那天要清理他的书房。我至今还清晰地记得每个星期天早晨那恐怖的场面:发疯似地扫,拼命地擦,完后就等着福克斯利进来检查。

"完事了?"他会这样问。

"完……完事了,我想。"

接着,他就溜达到自己书桌的抽屉那儿,从里面取出一只白白的手套,慢悠悠地套在右手上,把每一只手指都推捏到位。我就站在那里看着,浑身直哆嗦,特别是他绕着屋子转悠、用戴着白白手套的食指沿着图画表面、壁脚板、搁架、窗台、灯罩蹭来蹭去的时候。我的双眼紧紧跟着他那根手指,丝毫不敢溜号。对我来说,那根手指就是我命运的主宰。怪得很,那根手指次次不走空,总能千方百计蹭到某个细小的裂缝——恰巧是我忽略的、或者没有想到的所在。每当到了这个时候,福克斯利就会慢悠悠地转过身来,露出一丝恐怖、可怕的微笑——根本算不上什么微笑。随后,举起那根白白的、套在手套里的手指,让我把边上沾的那点薄薄的尘污看个清楚。

"啊,"他就会说。"看来,你这个小学生偷懒了。是不是?"

没有回答。

"是不是?"

"我想,我都打扫了。"

"你是不是又脏又懒呢?"

"是——是的。"

"可是,你的父亲不想让你长大成人还是这个样子,对不对?你的父亲很是讲究文明礼貌,对吧?"

没有回答。

"我问你呢。你的父亲是不是很讲究文明礼貌的?"

"或者——是的。"

"那么说来,我要是惩罚你,就算是帮了他一个忙,我说的对不对?"

"我不知道。"

"我说的对不对?"

"对——对的。"

"祷告完后,我们更衣室见。"

这一天的其余时间就会在无比痛苦的等待中度过,等待着傍晚的到来。

噢,我的天呐!现在,这一幕幕是多么令人记忆犹新啊!当然,星期天也是给家里写信的时间。

亲爱的爸爸、妈妈——十分感谢你们的来信。我希望你们都很好。我也很好,就是感冒了,因为被雨浇着了,但是很快就会好的。昨天我们学校队跟什鲁斯伯里队的比赛,我们赢了,比分是4:2。我去看了,福克斯利得了一分。这个人是我们寝室的年级长,你们认识的。蛋糕很好吃,十分感谢。爱你们的威廉敬上。

我一般要到厕所里写信,或者去衣帽间,或者去浴室——只要离开福克斯利的视线就行,但还要看着点时间。下午茶点时间是四点半,一定要把福克斯利的烤面包准备好。每天,福克斯利的烤面包我是一定要做好的。如果不是周末,所有的书房都是不允许生火的。因此,所有低年级学生都挤到图书馆里唯一的、小小的火炉周围,每个人都为自己所住书房的头头烤面包,大家都争着抢着要为自己烤面包的叉子在火炉上占据一席之地。即使有这么多艰苦的条件,给福克斯利烤的面包,我仍然要确保做到三点:(1)很松脆;(2)一点也不能烤焦;(3)热乎乎的,要十分准时地烤好。以上三点,哪怕有一点没有做到,就得遭受"抽打惩罚"。

"嘿,说你呢。这是什么呀?"

"是烤面包。"

"这真的是你心目中的烤面包吗?"

"呃……"

"你懒得连面包都烤不好,对不对?"

"我尽了力去烤的。"

"珀金斯,你知道马懒惰不干活,怎么办吗?"
"不知道。"
"你是马吗?"
"不是。"
"好吧——可怎么说,你算是一头驴。哈哈——所以嘛,我想你够资格的。过会再见。"

唉,那些日子巨大的痛苦啊。把福克斯利的面包烤焦,就得遭受"抽打惩罚"。遭受同样惩罚的情况还有:忘记把他足球靴子上面的泥巴去掉;卷起他的雨伞时把方向搞反了;"嘭嘭"敲书房的门,而他正好在里面学习;为他放的洗澡水太热;没有把他那件军官训练团制服的纽扣清理彻底;把蓝色的金属抛光剂溅落到那件制服上;未能把他的鞋底擦亮;不管什么时间把他的书房弄乱了。实际上,就福克斯利而言,我简直就是一块值得他"抽打惩罚"的料。

我向车窗外瞥了一眼。我的天啊,我们就要到站了。我一定是神情恍惚地回忆了好长时间,甚至连那份《泰晤士报》还没有打开。福克斯利仍然坐在我对面角落的那个座位上,阅读着《每日电讯报》。透过他烟斗里飘出的那股蓝色的烟雾,我看到了他报纸上方露出的上半部脸:小小的眼睛还很明亮,前额起了皱纹,卷曲的头发稍微泛着油光。

经过了那段时光,现在看着他,那种体验既怪异,又令人感到兴奋。我知道,他不再对我构成威胁,但过去的记忆犹在,在他面前,我不是完完全全感到舒适惬意的。这种感觉好似跟一头驯化了的老虎待在一只笼子里面一样。

我自己问自己:这是一种什么样的荒谬想法呢? 我的天,别自欺欺人了。要是你愿意,你不妨走上前去,一五一十告诉他你的想法,他也无法碰你一根手指头的。哇——这倒是一个好想法啊!

可是——且慢——说完后,值得吗? 现在,我已经过了做这种事的年龄了,况且,无论怎么说,我也不敢肯定,我对他真正有多少怒气。

那么,我该怎么办呢? 怎么也不能坐在那儿像傻子一样,直勾勾地看着他。

就在那时，我心里产生了一个小小的设想，如顽童般的一个设想。我对自己说，我接下来要做的就是，身体向前倾斜一下，轻轻一拍他的膝盖，然后告诉他我的名字。随后，我就可以观察他的脸，接着跟他谈谈我俩一起度过的学校时光，而且说话的声音要足够大，好让车厢里的人都听得见。我会当闹着玩似的提醒他，抖落出他那时对我的所作所为。或许呢，我甚至描述一下更衣室里那一次次的抽打，目的就是让他当众难堪一下。我的一点戏弄之意会令他稍感不安，但是对他无关大碍，对我却大有好处。

他猛地一抬头，发现我盯着他。这已经是第二次了。我注意到，他眼里闪出一丝的恼怒。

我对自己说，好吧，这就说吧。但，要说得轻松愉快、自然随和、彬彬有礼，才会更有效果、更加让他难堪。

想到这儿，我冲他微微一笑，随即轻轻地、客客气气地一点头。然后，抬高声音，说道："打扰一下，真心希望你能原谅。自我介绍一下吧。"我身体前倾，仔细地观察着，生怕错过任何一个精彩的瞬间。"我叫珀金斯——威廉·珀金斯。我曾就读于雷普顿公学，1907级学生。"

车厢里的其他人都一动不动地坐着，我感觉得出，他们都听到了，都观望着下面会发生什么情况。

"见到你，我很高兴，"他说，随即把报纸放到大腿上。"我叫福蒂斯丘——乔斯林·福蒂斯丘，我是伊顿公学1916级学生。"

第二节 《最后之举》The Last Act

罗尔德·达尔的《最后之举》(*The Last Act*)首次发表在《花花公子》(*Playboy*)杂志1966年1月号上，后又发表于《先锋派杂志》(*Avant Garde Magazine*)1969年1月号上。后来，这个故事又被收录到《罗尔德·达尔选集》(*The Roald Dahl Omnibus*)、《迷情乱性》

(*Switch Bitch*)、《五部畅销书集》(5 *Bestsellers*)以及《罗尔德·达尔短篇故事集锦》(*The Collected Short Stories of Roald Dahl*)等书中。

跟《外科医生》(*The Surgeon*)和《善本书商》(*The Bookseller*)①一样,这部小说也首发于美国的《花花公子》杂志,但不同的是,本篇结尾带有点儿"暴力"倾向和较为浓烈的"成人"色彩,这部小说与同样发表于这个杂志的《乱性香剂》(*Bitch*)②类似。

虽然本书着重研究的是罗尔德·达尔的"非儿童类"(个别篇章具有"儿童类"文学作品特点,但由于是罗尔德·达尔早期作品,也被收录进来,作为研究的对象)短篇小说,但是,这个"非儿童类"小说中的绝大部分还是适合儿童阅读的。本篇特别是结尾部分的情节具有"暴力"倾向和"成人"色彩,不建议儿童在没有指导的情况下阅读,中学生读者也应谨慎阅读。

一、原作导读

安娜·库珀得知心爱的丈夫埃德蒙·库珀死于车祸的消息时,几乎要疯掉了,甚至萌生了自杀的念头。他们十八岁结的婚,耳鬓厮磨,相亲相爱,难舍难分。

随着时间一年一年的逝去,他们之间的爱也变得越来越浓烈、越来越强大,到最后,达到了巅峰,简直到了荒唐可笑的程度:埃德蒙每天早晨离家去办公室上班,一天时间彼此见不到面,简直令他们都无法忍受……他们这种状态太完美了,完美到了令人简直是难以置信的程度,以至于人们几乎无法理解:在一个再也没有丈夫的世界中,她为什么没有一点儿欲望、没有一点儿心情继续活下去呢?

Every year that went by, their love became more intense and overwhelming, and toward the end, it had reached such a ridiculous peak

---

① 关于这两部小说,感兴趣的读者可以参阅《罗尔德·达尔短篇故事品读及汉译探索(第2卷)》第三章。

② 关于这部小说,感兴趣的读者可以参阅本系列研究后续某卷。

that it was almost impossible for them to endure the daily separation caused by Ed's departure for the office in the mornings... It was wonderful. It was so utterly unbelievably wonderful that one is very nearly able to understand why she should have had no desire and no heart to continue living in a world where her husband did not exist any more.

在这种状态下,安娜决定自杀,了断此生,追随丈夫而去,并且做好了一切准备。但是,还没等安娜实施自己的自杀计划,好友利兹来访,滔滔不绝说个不停,说自己开办的孩子领养协会的办公室缺人手,劝说安娜去帮忙。极不情愿的安娜在万般无奈的情况下答应去试试,这一试却彻底改变了安娜的生活状态。她发现,在这个社会上,自己还是有用的,于是,生活再次变得有意义起来。一年半的时间过去了,这种忙碌的工作使安娜再次融入这个社会,也不再像以前那样思念已故的丈夫,甚至记不清丈夫以前清晰的模样了。

就在这时,安娜奉命到德克萨斯州的达拉斯出一趟公差,去处理一起特别棘手的领养纠纷案。处理完公事回到宾馆,安娜开始感到恐惧和孤独,需要找朋友跟自己聊聊。可是,陌生的城市,到哪里寻找朋友? 突然之间,安娜记起了康拉德·克罗伊格,他是安娜高中时的同学,也是恋人。他俩当时都到了谈婚论嫁的阶段,却分道扬镳了,只因安娜遇见了埃德蒙而离开了康拉德,而康拉德最终娶了另一个名叫阿拉明蒂的女孩子。

安娜拨通了康拉德的电话。出乎意料的是,康拉德提议要在她入住的酒店一楼的酒吧跟她见面,喝酒叙旧。

她感觉有点紧张、慌乱,因为自从埃德蒙死后,她从未跟一个男人单独出去喝过什么东西。回去后,要是她将这件事告诉雅各布斯医生,他一定会很高兴的……他曾经不止一次对她说,除非她实际上用另一个男人在身体方面"替代"埃德蒙,否则,她的抑郁症状和自杀倾向永远都不会完全消失。

She felt mildly flustered. Not since Ed's death had she been out and had a drink alone with a man. Dr. Jacobs would be pleased when she told him about it on her return... and he had more than once told her that her depressions and suicidal tendencies would never completely disappear until she had actually and physically "replaced" Ed with another man.

  见到了康拉德,发现他还是那样英俊潇洒,她很开心。谈话期间,康拉德从医生的角度,对安娜点的酒、抽的烟进行了一番"专业性"的品头论足——这种酒对身体什么部位不好,那种烟对身体什么器官有影响,等等。安娜讲述了自己的遭遇,打听了康拉德的经历。其间,康拉德抱怨安娜当初撇下他不管,另寻新欢,而他却疯狂爱着安娜。闻听此言,安娜吃惊不小。

  他猛地将椅子往桌子跟前拉了一下,身体前倾。"你的心里是否曾经想过……?"
  他没往下说。
  她等待着。
  突然之间,他庄重地看着她,眼神是那么的热切,引得她向前靠了靠。
  "我的心里曾经想过什么?"她问。
  "想过这样一个事实:我和你……我们两个人……有点未尽事宜。"

He hitched① his chair closer to the table, and leaned forward. "Did it ever cross your mind..."
He stopped.
She waited.

---

  ① hitch:*Verb* [with obj., and adverbial of direction] move (something) into a different position with a jerk 急拉;猛推(e.g. She hitched the blanket around him. 她猛拉裹在他身上的羊毛毯。)

He was looking so intensely earnest all of a sudden that she leaned forward herself.

"Did what cross my mind?" she asked.

"The fact that you and I... that both of us... have a bit of unfinished business."

对于康拉德的这个"未尽事宜"的提议,安娜不知道是答应还是不答应,毕竟除了丈夫,她没有跟第二个男人上过床。

面对着康拉德,安娜说道:"这个提议不会碰巧是一个治疗学方面的方法吧,对不对?"

"一个什么?"

"一个治疗学方面的方法。"

"你到底想说什么呢?"

"这听起来,简直就像我的医生雅各布斯策划出来的一个情节啊。"

"听着,"他说。现在,他越过桌子向前倚去,一个手指尖触碰到她的左手。"以前与你相识的时候,我过于年轻、过于紧张,那样的提议未能说出口,尽管我很想说。当时,不管怎么说,我认为凡事不用操之过急,那样做没有任何的必要。我当时寻思着,我们前方还有整个一辈子的时间呢。可谁曾想,你会撇下我呢。"

To Conrad, Anna said, "This isn't by any chance a therapeutic[①] suggestion, is it?"

"A *what*?"

"A therapeutic suggestion."

"What in the world do you mean?"

---

① therapeutic：*Adjective* of or relating to the healing of disease(关于)治疗的;治疗学的(e.g. diagnostic and therapeutic facilities 诊断和治疗设施)

"It sounds exactly like a plot hatched① up by my Dr. Jacobs."

"Look," he said, and now he leaned right across the table and touched her left hand with the tip of one finger. "When I knew you before, I was too damn young and nervous to make that sort of proposition, much as I wanted to. I didn't think there was any particular hurry then, anyway. I figured we had a whole lifetime before us. I wasn't to know you were going to drop me."

几杯酒下肚之后,安娜感觉晕乎乎的,不知不觉间跟着康拉德"飘"回宾馆房间,彼此拥吻,安娜感到兴奋异常。其间,康拉德不断引用医学上的术语,而且行为古怪,这令快要进入"状态"的安娜开始反感,要求他离开,可他却开始粗鲁起来,动作也有点儿"暴力"起来……安娜开始歇斯底里般大喊大叫。

她慢慢地爬了起来,摇摇晃晃地走进浴室,边走边喊:"埃德蒙!……埃德蒙!……埃德蒙!……"声音很怪异,似乎是在乞求。浴室的门随即关上。

She climbed slowly to her feet, and as she staggered into the bathroom, she was crying "Ed!... Ed!... Ed!..." in a queer supplicating voice. The door shut.

就像是一个人蹑手蹑脚离开孩子正在里面睡觉的房间,他小心谨慎地跨出门,轻轻地将门随手带上,来到了走廊。

... and then, carefully, like a man who is tiptoeing from a room where a child is sleeping, he moved out into the corridor, closing the door softly behind him.

---

① hatch:[with obj.] conspire to devise (a plot or plan) 策划(阴谋或计划)(e.g. The little plot that you and Sylvia hatched up last night 你和西尔维亚昨天晚上想出来的小小阴谋)

二、原作释读

这篇小说的阅读难度不是很大,关键是要理解好一些专业性很强的医学词汇,同时还要体会好女主人公前后的微妙的心理变化。

The Last Act[①]

Anna was in the kitchen washing a head of Boston lettuce[②] for the family supper when the doorbell rang. The bell itself was on the wall directly above the sink, and it never failed to make her jump if it rang when she happened to be near. For this reason, neither her husband nor any of the children ever used it. It seemed to ring extra loud this time, and Anna jumped extra high.

When she opened the door, two policemen were standing outside. They looked at her out of pale waxen[③] faces, and she looked back at them, waiting for them to say something.

She kept looking at them, but they didn't speak or move. They stood so still and so rigid that they were like two wax figures somebody had put on her doorstep as a joke. Each of them was holding his helmet

---

① 本部小说原文出自 "DAHL, R. *The Collected Short Stories of Roald Dahl*. London: Penguin Books Ltd., 1992"。

② Boston lettuce: a type of cultivated lettuce forming a rounded head and having soft-textured, yellow-green inner leaves 波士顿莴苣

lettuce: *Noun* a cultivated plant of the daisy family, with edible leaves that are a usual ingredient of salads. Many varieties of lettuce have been developed with a range of form, texture, and colour 生菜;莴苣

③ waxen: *Adjective* having a smooth, pale, translucent surface or appearance like that of wax(像蜡一样)光滑的;苍白的;半透明的(e.g. a canopy of waxen, creamy blooms 顶上一片乳白凝脂般的花)

in front of him in his two hands.

"What is it?" Anna asked.

They were both young, and they were wearing leather gauntlets① up to their elbows. She could see their enormous motor-cycles propped up along the edge of the sidewalk behind them, and dead leaves were falling around the motor-cycles and blowing along the sidewalk and the whole of the street was brilliant in the yellow light of a clear, gusty② September evening. The taller of the two policemen shifted uneasily on his feet. Then he said quietly, "Are you Mrs. Cooper, ma'am③?"

"Yes, I am."

The other said, "Mrs. Edmund J. Cooper?"

"Yes." And then slowly it began to dawn upon her④ that these men, neither of whom seemed anxious to explain his presence, would not be behaving as they were unless they had some distasteful duty to perform.

"Mrs. Cooper," she heard one of them saying, and from the way he said it, as gently and softly as if he were comforting a sick child, she knew at once that he was going to tell her something terrible. A great wave of panic came over her, and she said, "What happened?"

"We have to inform you, Mrs. Cooper..."

---

① gauntlet: *Noun* a stout glove with a long loose wrist(结实带长臂套的)宽口手套

② gusty: *Adjective* characterized by or blowing in gusts 刮风的;一阵阵劲吹的(e.g. a gusty morning 一个刮风的早晨)

③ ma'am = madam: *Noun* a term of respectful or polite address used for 女士;夫人;太太;小姐

④ dawn on (upon) sb.: If an idea, the truth or a fact dawns on you, you realize it for the first time. 使开始明白;使渐渐领悟;使开始理解(e.g. It suddenly dawned on us that we were lost. 我们突然意识到我们迷路了。)

The policeman paused, and the woman, watching him, felt as though her whole body were shrinking and shrinking and shrinking inside its skin.

"... that your husband was involved in an accident on the Hudson River Parkway at approximately five forty-five this evening, and died in the ambulance..."

The policeman who was speaking produced the crocodile wallet she had given Ed on their twentieth wedding anniversary, two years back, and as she reached out to take it, she found herself wondering whether it might not still be warm from having been close to her husband's chest only a short while ago.

"If there's anything we can do," the policeman was saying, "like calling up somebody to come over... some friend or relative maybe..."

Anna heard his voice drifting away, then fading out altogether, and it must have been about then that she began to scream. Soon she became hysterical, and the two policemen had their hands full trying to control her until the doctor arrived some forty minutes later and injected something into her arm.

She was no better, though, when she woke up the following morning. Neither her doctor nor her children were able to reason with her in any way at all, and had she not been kept under almost constant sedation[①] for the next few days, she would undoubtedly have taken her own life. In the brief lucid[②] periods between drug-takings, she acted as though she

---

① sedation: *Noun* a state of calm or sleep produced by a sedative drug(镇静剂引发的)平静(或睡眠)状态

② lucid: *Adjective* showing ability to think clearly, especially in the intervals between periods of confusion or insanity 清醒的;神志清明的;头脑清楚的(e.g. He has a few lucid moments every now and then. 他不时会清醒一会儿。)

were demented①, calling out her husband's name and telling him that she was coming to join him as soon as she possibly could. It was terrible to listen to her. But in defence of her behaviour, it should be said at once that this was no ordinary husband she had lost.

Anna Greenwood had married Ed Cooper when they were both eighteen, and over the time they were together, they grew to be closer and more dependent upon each other than it is possible to describe in words. Every year that went by, their love became more intense and overwhelming, and toward the end, it had reached such a ridiculous peak that it was almost impossible for them to endure the daily separation caused by Ed's departure for the office in the mornings. When he returned at night he would rush through the house to seek her out, and she, who had heard the noise of the front door slamming, would drop everything and rush simultaneously in his direction, meeting him head on, recklessly, at full speed, perhaps halfway up the stairs, or on the landing, or between the kitchen and the hall; and as they came together, he would take her in his arms and hug her and kiss her for minutes on end as though she were yesterday's bride. It was wonderful. It was so utterly unbelievably wonderful that one is very nearly able to understand why she should have had no desire and no heart to continue living in a world where her husband did not exist any more.

Her three children, Angela (twenty), Mary (nineteen) and Billy (seventeen and a half), stayed around her constantly right from the start of the catastrophe. They adored their mother, and they certainly had no intention of letting her commit suicide if they could help it. They worked hard and with loving desperation to convince her that life could still be

---

① demented: *Adjective* (informal) driven to behave irrationally due to anger, distress, or excitement(非正式)疯狂的;狂怒的;行为失常的

worth living, and it was due entirely to them that she managed in the end to come out of the nightmare and climb back slowly into the ordinary world.

Four months after the disaster, she was pronounced① "moderately safe" by the doctors, and she was able to return, albeit② rather listlessly③, to the old routine of running the house and doing the shopping and cooking the meals for her grown-up children.

But then what happened?

Before the snows of that winter had melted away, Angela married a young man from Rhode Island④ and went off to live in the suburbs of Providence⑤.

A few months later, Mary married a fair-haired giant from a town

---

① pronounce: *Verb* [no obj.] (pronounce on) pass judgement or make a decision on 就……发表意见;表态(e.g. The Secretary of State will shortly pronounce on alternative measures. 国务卿不久将就其他替代措施发表意见。)

② albeit: *Conjunction* though 虽然;尽管(e.g. He was making progress, albeit rather slowly. 他那时在不断进步,虽然十分缓慢。)

③ listless: *Adjective* (of a person or their manner) lacking energy or enthusiasm(人或人的行为方式)无力的;无精打采的(e.g. bouts of listless depression 一阵阵无精打采的抑郁情绪)

④ Rhode Island: a state in the north-eastern US, on the Atlantic coast; pop. 1,003,460 (1990); capital, Providence. Settled from England in the 17th century, it was one of the original thirteen states of the Union (1776) and is the smallest and most densely populated. 罗得岛州(美国东北部一州,临大西洋,1990 年人口 1,003,460,首府普罗维登斯。17 世纪时英国人来此定居,是美利坚合众国最初的 13 个州之一[1776],是面积最小、人口最密集的州。)

⑤ Providence: *Noun* the state capital of Rhode Island, a port on the Atlantic coast; pop. 160,730 (1990). It was founded in 1636 as a haven for religious dissenters. 普罗维登斯(美国罗得岛州首府,大西洋沿岸港口;1990 年人口 160,730;1636 年创建时是宗教异见者的避难所。)

called Slayton, in Minnesota①, and away she flew for ever and ever and ever. And although Anna's heart was now beginning to break all over again into tiny pieces, she was proud to think that neither of the two girls had the slightest inkling② of what was happening to her. ("Oh, Mummy, isn't it wonderful!" "Yes, my darling, I think it's the most beautiful wedding there's ever been! I'm even more excited than you are!" etc., etc.)

And then, to put the lid on everything, her beloved Billy, who had just turned eighteen, went off to begin his first year at Yale③.

So all at once, Anna found herself living in a completely empty house.

It is an awful feeling, after twenty-three years of boisterous④, busy, magical family life, to come down alone to breakfast in the mornings, to sit there in silence with a cup of coffee and a piece of toast, and to wonder what you are going to do with the day that lies ahead. The room you are sitting in, which has heard so much laughter, and seen so many birthdays, so many Christmas trees, so many presents being opened, is

---

① Minnesota: *Noun* a state in the north central US, on the Canadian border; pop. 4,375,100 (1990); capital, St Paul. It became the 32nd state of the US in 1858. 明尼苏达州(美国中北部一州,与加拿大接壤,1990 年人口 4,375,100,首府圣保罗;1858 年成为美国第 32 州)。

② inkling: *Noun* a slight knowledge or suspicion; a hint 粗浅的认识;细微的感觉;暗示;提示(e. g. The records give us an inkling of how people saw the world. 这些记录让我们粗略地了解过去人们对世界的看法。)

③ Yale = Yale University: a university in New Haven, Connecticut 耶鲁大学(位于美国康涅狄格州纽黑文市)

④ boisterous: *Adjective* (of a person, event, or behaviour) noisy, energetic, and cheerful (人、事件或行为)喧闹的;吵吵嚷嚷的;兴高采烈的;尽情的(e. g. the children's boisterous behaviour 孩子们欢闹的举动)

· 56 ·

quiet now and feels curiously cold. The air is heated and the temperature itself is normal, but the place still makes you shiver. The clock has stopped because you were never the one who wound it in the first place. A chair stands crooked① on its legs, and you sit staring at it, wondering why you hadn't noticed it before. And when you glance up again, you have a sudden panicky feeling that all the four walls of the room have begun creeping in upon you very very slowly when you weren't looking.

In the beginning, she would carry her coffee cup over to the telephone and start calling up friends. But all her friends had husbands and children, and although they were always as nice and warm and cheerful as they could possibly be, they simply could not spare the time to sit and chat with a desolate② lady from across the way first thing in the morning. So then she started calling up her married daughters instead.

They, also, were sweet and kind to her at all times, but Anna detected, very soon, a subtle change in their attitudes toward her. She was no longer number one in their lives. They had husbands now, and were concentrating everything upon them. Gently but firmly, they were moving their mother into the background. It was quite a shock. But she knew they were right. They were absolutely right. She was no longer entitled to impinge upon their lives③ or to make them feel guilty for neglecting her.

---

① crooked: *Adjective* bent or twisted out of shape or out of place 弯曲的；歪曲的；扭曲的(e. g. His teeth were yellow and crooked. 他的牙齿又黄又不整齐。)

② desolate: *Adjective* feeling or showing misery, unhappiness, or loneliness 痛苦的；不幸的；孤独的(e. g. I suddenly felt desolate and bereft. 我突然产生了一种凄苦落寞的感觉。)

③ impinge upon sb./sth.: have an effect or impact, especially a damaging or negative one 对⋯⋯有重大(或严重)影响(尤指破坏性或负面的)(e. g. She didn't allow her personal problems to impinge on her work. 她没有让个人问题妨碍自己工作。)

She saw Dr. Jacobs regularly, but he wasn't really any help. He tried to get her to talk and she did her best, and sometimes he made little speeches to her full of oblique① remarks about sex and sublimation②. Anna never properly understood what he was driving at, but the burden③ of his song appeared to be that she should get herself another man.

She took to wandering around the house and fingering things that used to belong to Ed. She would pick up one of his shoes and put her hand into it and feel the little dents that the ball of his foot④ and his toes had made upon the sole. She found a sock with a hole in it, and the pleasure it gave her to darn that sock was indescribable. Occasionally, she took out a shirt, a tie, and a suit, and laid them on the bed, all ready for him to wear, and once, one rainy Sunday morning, she made an Irish stew⑤...

It was hopeless to go on.

So how many pills would she need to make absolutely sure of it this time? She went upstairs to her secret store and counted them. There were

---

① oblique: *Adjective* not explicit or direct in addressing a point(论述)不明晰的;不直截了当的;转弯抹角的;间接的(e.g. He issued an oblique attack on the President. 他对总统发出了转弯抹角的攻击之辞。)

② sublimation: *Noun* (psychology) modifying the natural expression of an impulse or instinct (especially a sexual one) to one that is socially acceptable(心理学)将意识上不能接受的(特别是指性方面的)本能和冲动转为可被个人和社会所接受的无意识的防御机制

③ burden: *Noun* (the burden) the main theme or gist of a speech, book, or argument(演讲、书或辩论的)主题;主旨(e.g. the burden of his views 他所提意见的主旨)

④ the ball of his foot: the rounded protuberant part of the foot at the base of the big toe 大脚趾球

⑤ Irish stew: *Noun* [mass noun] a stew made with mutton, potatoes, and onions 洋葱土豆煨羊肉

only nine. Was that enough? She doubted that it was. Oh, hell. The one thing she was not prepared to face all over again was failure—the rush to the hospital, the stomach-pump①, the seventh floor of the Payne Whitney Pavilion, the psychiatrists, the humiliation, the misery of it all...

In that case, it would have to be the razor-blade. But the trouble with the razor-blade was that it had to be done properly. Many people failed miserably when they tried to use the razor-blade on the wrist. In fact, nearly all of them failed. They didn't cut deep enough. There was a big artery② down there somewhere that simply had to be reached. Veins③ were no good. Veins made plenty of mess, but they never quite managed to do the trick. Then again, the razor-blade was not an easy thing to hold, not if one had to make a firm incision④, pressing it right home all the way, deep deep down. But *she* wouldn't fail. The ones who failed were the ones who actually *wanted* to fail. She wanted to succeed.

She went to the cupboard in the bathroom, searching for blades. There weren't any. Ed's razor was still there, and so was hers. But there was no blade in either of them, and no little packet lying alongside. That was understandable. Such things had been removed from the house on an earlier occasion. But there was no problem. Anyone could buy a packet

---

① stomach-pump or stomach pump: *Noun* a syringe attached to a long tube, used for extracting the contents of a person's stomach (for example, if they have taken poison)(洗胃用的)胃唧筒

② artery: *Noun* any of the muscular-walled tubes forming part of the circulation system by which blood (mainly that which has been oxygenated) is conveyed from the heart to all parts of the body 动脉

③ vein: *Noun* any of the tubes forming part of the blood circulation system of the body, carrying mainly oxygen-depleted blood towards the heart 静脉

④ incision: *Noun* a surgical cut made in skin or flesh(皮肤或肌肉的)切开;切开术(e.g. an abdominal incision 剖腹术)

of razor-blades.

She returned to the kitchen and took the calendar down from the wall. She chose September 23rd, which was Ed's birthday, and wrote r-b (for razor-blades) against the date. She did this on September 9th, which gave her exactly two weeks' grace① to put her affairs in order. There was much to be done—old bills to be paid, a new will to be written, the house to be tidied up, Billy's college fees to be taken care of for the next four years, letters to the children, to her own parents, to Ed's mother, and so on and so forth.

Yet, busy as she was, she found that those two weeks, those fourteen long days, were going far too slowly for her liking. She wanted to use the blade, and eagerly every morning she counted the days that were left. She was like a child counting the days before Christmas. For wherever it was that Ed Cooper had gone when he died, even if it were only to the grave, she was impatient to join him.

It was in the middle of this two-week period that her friend Elizabeth Paoletti came calling on her at eight thirty one morning. Anna was making coffee in the kitchen at the time, and she jumped when the bell rang and jumped again when it gave a second long blast.

Liz came sweeping in through the front door, talking non-stop as usual. "Anna, my darling woman, I need your help! Everyone's down with flu at the office. You've *got* to come! Don't argue with me! I know you can type and I know you haven't got a damn thing in the world to do all day except mope②. Just grab your hat and purse and let's get going.

---

① grace: Noun a period officially allowed for payment of a sum due or for compliance with a law or condition, especially an extended period granted as a special favour(付款或执行法律或符合条件的法定)期限(尤指宽限)

② mope: Noun (mopes) (dated) low spirits; depression(古旧用法)闷闷不乐;没精打采;消沉

Hurry up, girl, hurry up! I'm late as it is!"

Anna said, "Go away, Liz. Leave me alone."

"The cab is waiting," Liz said.

"Please," Anna said, "don't try to bully me now. I'm not coming."

"You are coming," Liz said. "Pull yourself together. Your days of glorious martyrdom① are over."

Anna continued to resist, but Liz wore her down, and in the end she agreed to go along just for a few hours.

Elizabeth Paoletti was in charge of an adoption society, one of the best in the city. Nine of the staff were down with flu. Only two were left, excluding herself. "You don't know a thing about the work," she said in the cab, "but you're just going to have to help us all you can..."

The office was bedlam②. The telephones alone nearly drove Anna mad. She kept running from one cubicle③ to the next, taking messages that she did not understand. And there were girls in the waiting room, young girls with ashen④ stony faces, and it became part of her duty to type their answers on an official form.

"The father's name?"

"Don't know."

---

① martyrdom: *Noun* [mass noun] the death or suffering of a martyr 殉难；受难

② bedlam: *Noun* [mass noun] a scene of uproar and confusion 喧嚣；喧闹混乱的场面(e.g. There was bedlam in the courtroom. 法庭上一片喧闹和乱哄哄的景象。)

③ cubicle: *Noun* a small partitioned-off area of a room, for example one containing a shower, toilet, or bed(分隔开的)小房间

④ ashen: *Adjective* of the pale grey colour of ash 灰白色的(e.g. the ashen morning sky 早晨灰白色的天空)

"You've no idea?"

"What's the father's name got to do with it?"

"My dear, if the father is known, then his consent has to be obtained as well as yours before the child can be offered for adoption."

"You're quite sure about that?"

"Jesus, I told you, didn't I?"

At lunchtime, somebody brought her a sandwich, but there was no time to eat it. At nine o'clock that night, exhausted and famished① and considerably shaken by some of the knowledge she had acquired, Anna staggered home, took a stiff② drink, fried up some eggs and bacon, and went to bed.

"I'll call for you at eight o'clock tomorrow morning," Liz had said. "And for God's sake be ready." Anna was ready. And from then on she was hooked.

It was as simple as that.

All she'd needed right from the beginning was a good hard job of work to do, and plenty of problems to solve—other people's problems instead of her own.

The work was arduous and often quite shattering emotionally, but Anna was absorbed by every moment of it, and within about—we are skipping right forward now—within about a year and a half, she began to feel moderately happy once again. She was finding it more and more difficult to picture her husband vividly, to see him precisely as he was when he ran up the stairs to meet her, or when he sat across from her at supper in the evenings. The exact sound of his voice was becoming less easy to recall, and even the face itself, unless she glanced at a photograph, was

---

① famished: *Adjective* (informal) extremely hungry(非正式)极度饥饿的

② stiff: *Adjective* (of an alcoholic drink) strong(酒)浓的;烈性的(e. g. a stiff measure of brandy 一杯很浓的白兰地)

no longer sharply etched① in the memory. She still thought about him constantly, but she discovered that she could do so now without bursting into tears, and when she looked back on the way she had behaved a while ago, she felt slightly embarrassed. She started taking a mild interest in her clothes and in her hair, she returned to using lipstick and to shaving the hair from her legs. She enjoyed her food, and when people smiled at her, she smiled right back at them and meant it. In other words, she was back in the swim once again. She was pleased to be alive.

It was at this point that Anna had to go down to Dallas② on office business.

Liz's office did not normally operate beyond state lines, but in this instance, a couple who had adopted a baby through the agency had subsequently moved away from New York and gone to live in Texas③. Now, five months after the move, the wife had written to say that she no longer wanted to keep the child. Her husband, she announced, had died of a heart attack soon after they'd arrived in Texas. She herself had remarried

---

① etch: *Verb* cause to stand out or be clearly defined or visible 使显露;使醒目(e.g. Joe watched the outline of the town etched against the sky. 乔望着在天空映衬下十分醒目的整个城镇。)

② Dallas: *Noun* a city in NE Texas, noted as a centre of the oil industry; pop. 1,006,900 (1990) 达拉斯(得克萨斯州东北部城市,石油工业中心,1990 年人口 1,006,900。)

③ Texas: *Noun* a state in the southern US, on the border with Mexico, with a coastline on the Gulf of Mexico; pop. 16,986,510; capital, Austin. The area formed part of Mexico until 1836, when it declared independence and became a republic. It became the 28th state of the US in 1845. 得克萨斯州(美国南部一州,与墨西哥接壤,位于墨西哥湾沿岸,首府奥斯丁,人口 16,986,510。1836 年从墨西哥脱离,宣布独立,成为共和国;1845 年成为美国第 28 个州。)

almost at once, and her new husband found it impossible to adjust to an adopted baby.

Now this was a serious situation, and quite apart from the welfare of the child itself, there were all manner of legal obligations involved.

Anna flew down to Dallas in a plane that left New York very early, and she arrived before breakfast. After checking in at her hotel, she spent the next eight hours with the persons concerned in the affair, and by the time she had done all that could be done that day, it was around four thirty in the afternoon and she was utterly exhausted. She took a cab back to the hotel, and went up to her room. She called Liz on the phone to report the situation, then she undressed and soaked herself for a long time in a warm bath. Afterwards, she wrapped up in a towel and lay on the bed, smoking a cigarette.

Her efforts on behalf of the child had so far come to nothing. There had been two lawyers there who had treated her with absolute contempt. How she hated them. She detested① their arrogance and their softly spoken hints that nothing she might do would make the slightest difference to their client. One of them kept his feet up on the table all the way through the discussion, and both of them had rolls of fat on their bellies, and the fat spilled out into their shirts like liquid and hung in huge folds over their belted trouser-tops.

Anna had visited Texas many times before in her life, but until now she had never gone there alone. Her visits had always been with Ed, keeping him company on business trips; and during those trips, he and she had often spoken about the Texans in general and about how difficult it was to like them. One could ignore their coarseness and their vulgari-

---

① detest: *Verb* [with obj.] dislike intensely 憎恶 (e. g. She really did detest his mockery. 她真的非常讨厌他的嘲弄。)

ty. It wasn't that. But there was, it seemed, a quality of ruthlessness still surviving among these people, something quite brutal, harsh, inexorable①, that it was impossible to forgive. They had no bowels of compassion, no pity, no tenderness. The only so-called virtue they possessed—and this they paraded② ostentatiously③ and endlessly to strangers—was a kind of professional benevolence. It was plastered④ all over them. Their voices, their smiles, were rich and syrupy⑤ with it. But it left Anna cold. It left her quite, quite cold inside.

"Why do they love acting so tough?" she used to ask.

"Because they're children," Ed would answer. "They're dangerous children who go about trying to imitate their grandfathers. Their grandfathers were pioneers. These people aren't."

It seemed that they lived, these present-day Texans, by a sort of eg-

---

① inexorable: *Adjective* of (a person) impossible to persuade by request or entreaty(人)不为恳求所动的;无动于衷的(e.g. The doctors were inexorable, and there was nothing to be done. 医生们不为恳求所动,我们无计可施。)

② parade: *Verb* [with obj.] display (something) publicly in order to impress or attract attention 炫耀;展示(e.g. He paraded his knowledge. 他炫耀自己的知识。)

③ ostentatious: *Adjective* characterized by vulgar or pretentious display; designed to impress or attract notice 炫耀的;卖弄的;讲究排场的;惹人注目的(e.g. a simple design that is glamorous without being ostentatious 富有魅力而又不豪华的朴实设计)

④ plaster: *Verb* (plaster something with/in) coat or cover something with (a substance), especially to an extent considered excessive(尤指过度地)涂满;盖满(e.g. a face plastered in heavy make-up 一张涂了厚厚一层化妆品的脸)

⑤ syrupy or sirupy: *Adjective* having the consistency or sweetness of syrup 糖浆般的(e.g. syrupy puddings 像糖浆般甜的布丁)

otistic① will, push and be pushed. Everybody was pushing. Everybody was being pushed. And it was all very fine for a stranger in their midst to step aside and announce firmly, "I will not push, and I will not be pushed." That was impossible. It was especially impossible in Dallas. Of all the cities in the state, Dallas was the one that had always disturbed Anna the most. It was such a godless city, she thought, such a rapacious②, gripped, iron, godless city. It was a place that had run amok③ with its money, and no amount of gloss and phony culture and syrupy talk could hide the fact that the great golden fruit was rotten inside.

Anna lay on the bed with her bath towel around her. She was alone in Dallas this time. There was no Ed with her now to envelop her in his incredible strength and love; and perhaps it was because of this that she began, all of a sudden, to feel slightly uneasy. She lit a second cigarette and waited for the uneasiness to pass. It didn't pass; it got worse. A hard little knot of fear was gathering itself in the top of her stomach, and there it stayed, growing bigger every minute. It was an unpleasant feeling, the kind one might experience if one were alone in the house at night and heard, or thought one heard, a footstep in the next room.

In this place there were a million footsteps, and she could hear them all.

She got off the bed and went over to the window, still wrapped in

---

① egotistic: *Adjective* characteristic of those having an inflated idea of their own importance; having an exaggerated sense of self-importance 自我本位的；自负的

② rapacious: *Adjective* aggressively greedy or grasping 贪婪的；掠夺的；强取的

③ run amok: behave in a wild or uncontrolled way 失去控制；发狂；狂暴肆虐 (e.g. The crowd ran amok through the city streets when they heard their leaders had been killed. 得知他们的头目被杀，这群人开始在城里大街上到处烧杀抢夺。)

her towel. Her room was on the twenty-second floor, and the window was open. The great city lay pale and milky-yellow in the evening sunshine. The street below was solid① with automobiles. The sidewalk was filled with people. Everybody was hustling home from work, pushing and being pushed. She felt the need of a friend. She wanted very badly to have someone to talk to at this moment. She would have liked a house to go to, a house with a family—a wife and husband and children and rooms full of toys, and the husband and wife would fling their arms around her at the front door and cry out, "Anna! How marvellous to see you! How long can you stay? A week, a month, a year?"

All of a sudden, as so often happens in situations like this, her memory went *click*, and she said aloud, "Conrad Kreuger! Good heavens above!" *He* lives in Dallas... at least he used to...

She hadn't seen Conrad since they were classmates in high school, in New York. They were both about seventeen then, and Conrad had been her beau②, her love, her everything. For over a year they had gone around together, and each of them had sworn eternal loyalty to the other, with marriage in the near future. Then suddenly Ed Cooper had flashed into her life, and that, of course, had been the end of the romance with Conrad. But Conrad did not seem to have taken the break too badly. It certainly couldn't have *shattered* him, because not more than a month or two later he had started going strong with another girl in the class.

Now what was *her* name?

---

① solid: *Adjective* not hollow or containing spaces or gaps 实心的; 没有空隙的(e.g. The shops were packed solid. 商店里被挤得水泄不通。)

② beau: *Noun* (dated) a boyfriend or male admirer(古旧用法)男友;(男性)追求者;情郎

A big handsome① bosomy② girl she was, with flaming red hair and a peculiar name, a very old-fashioned name. What was it? Arabella? No, not Arabella. Ara-something, though. Araminty? Yes! Araminty it was! And what is more, within a year or so, Conrad Kreuger had married Araminty and had carried her back with him to Dallas, the place of his birth.

Anna went over to the bedside table and picked up the telephone directory.

Kreuger, Conrad P. , M. D.

That was Conrad all right. He had always said he was going to be a doctor. The book gave an office number and a residence number.

Should she phone him?

Why not?

She glanced at her watch. It was five twenty. She lifted the receiver and gave the number of his office.

"Doctor Kreuger's surgery③," a girl's voice answered.

"Hello," Anna said. "Is Doctor Kreuger there?"

"The doctor is busy right now. May I ask who's calling?"

"Will you please tell him that Anna Greenwood telephoned him."

"Who?"

"Anna Greenwood."

"Yes, Miss Greenwood. Did you wish for an appointment?"

"No, thank you."

"Is there something I can do for you?"

---

① handsome: *Adjective* (of a woman) striking and imposing rather than conventionally pretty(女子)端庄健美的;气势不凡的

② bosomy: *Adjective* (of a woman) having large breasts(女人)乳房发达的

③ surgery: *Noun* (Brit.) a place where a doctor, dentist, or other medical practitioner treats or advises patients(英国英语)诊所

Anna gave the name of her hotel, and asked her to pass it on to Dr Kreuger.

"I'll be very glad to," the secretary said. "Goodbye, Miss Greenwood."

"Goodbye," Anna said. She wondered whether Dr. Conrad P. Kreuger would remember her name after all these years. She believed he would. She lay back again on the bed and began trying to recall what Conrad himself used to look like. Extraordinarily handsome, that he was. Tall... lean... big-shouldered... with almost pure-black hair... and a marvellous face... a strong carved face like one of those Greek heroes, Perseus① or Ulysses②. Above all, though, he had been a very gentle boy, a serious, decent, quiet, gentle boy. He had never kissed her much—only when he said goodbye in the evenings. And he'd never gone in for necking③, as all the others had. When he took her home from the movies on Saturday nights, he used to park his old Buick outside her house and sit there in the car beside her, just talking and talking about

---

① Perseus: *Noun* (Greek Mythology) the son of Zeus and Danae, a hero celebrated for many achievements. Riding the winged horse Pegasus, he cut off the head of the gorgon Medusa and gave it to Athene; he also rescued and married Andromeda, and became king of Tiryns in Greece. (希腊神话)珀尔修斯(宙斯和达那厄的儿子,功勋卓著的著名英雄,骑在有双翼的珀伽索斯马上,砍掉了怪物墨杜萨的头并把它献给雅典娜。他拯救并娶了安德洛墨达,而且成为希腊梯林斯的国王。)

② Ulysses: *Noun* (Roman Mythology) Roman name for Odysseus(罗马神话)尤利西斯(即希腊神话中的奥德修斯"Odysseus")

Odysseus: *Noun* the king of Ithaca and central figure of the Odyssey, renowned for his cunning and resourcefulness. Roman name Ulysses. (希腊神话)奥德修斯(伊萨卡岛的国王,《奥德赛》中的主人公,以狡猾机智闻名。罗马语名"Ulysses"。)

③ necking: *Noun* (informal) the act or practice of amorously kissing and caressing 激情拥吻

the future, his future and hers, and how he was going to go back to Dallas to become a famous doctor. His refusal to indulge in necking and all the nonsense that went with it had impressed her no end①. He respects me, she used to say. He loves me. And she was probably right. In any event, he had been a nice man, a nice good man. And had it not been for the fact that Ed Cooper was a super-nice, super-good man, she was sure she would have married Conrad Kreuger.

The telephone rang. Anna lifted the receiver. "Yes," she said. "Hello."

"Anna Greenwood?"

"Conrad Kreuger!"

"My dear Anna! What a fantastic surprise. Good gracious me. After all these years."

"It's a long time, isn't it."

"It's a lifetime. Your voice sounds just the same."

"So does yours."

"What brings you to our fair city? Are you staying long?"

"No, I have to go back tomorrow. I hope you didn't mind my calling you."

"Hell, no, Anna. I'm delighted. Are you all right?"

"Yes, I'm fine. I'm fine now. I had a bad time of it for a bit after Ed died..."

"What!"

"He was killed in an automobile two and a half years ago."

---

① no end: (informal) to a great extent; very much(非正式)很;非常(e.g. This cheered me up no end. 这使我很高兴。)

"Oh gee[①], Anna, I *am* sorry. How terrible. I...I don't know what to say..."

"Don't say anything."

"You're okay now?"

"I'm fine. Working like a slave."

"That's the girl..."

"How's...how's Araminty?"

"Oh, she's fine."

"Any children?"

"One," he said. "A boy. How about you?"

"I have three, two girls and a boy."

"Well, well, what d'you know[②]! Now listen, Anna..."

"I'm listening."

"Why don't I run over to the hotel and buy you a drink? I'd like to do that. I'll bet you haven't changed one iota[③]."

"I look old, Conrad."

"You're lying."

"I feel old, too."

"You want a good doctor?"

---

① gee: *Exclamation* (informal, chiefly N. Amer.) a mild expression, typically of surprise, enthusiasm, or sympathy(主要为北美非正式用法)(表示有些吃惊、热烈或同情)哟(e.g. Gee, Linda looks great at fifty! 哟,琳达50岁了看起来还很棒。)

② What do you know (about that): (informal, chiefly N. Amer.) used as an expression of surprise(主要为北美非正式用法)(表示吃惊)你看怪不怪;真想不到

③ iota: *Noun* [in sing.] [usu. with negative] an extremely small amount 极微小;一点儿;些微(e.g. Nothing she said seemed to make an iota of difference. 她所说的似乎没有起丝毫作用。)

"Yes. I mean no. Of course I don't. I don't want any more doctors. All I need is... well..."

"Yes?"

"This place worries me, Conrad. I guess I need a friend. That's all I need."

"You've got one. I have just one more patient to see, and then I'm free. I'll meet you down in the bar, the something room, I've forgotten what it's called, at six, in about half an hour. Will that suit you?"

"Yes," she said. "Of course. And... thank you, Conrad." She replaced the receiver, then got up from the bed, and began to dress.

She felt mildly flustered①. Not since Ed's death had she been out and had a drink alone with a man. Dr. Jacobs would be pleased when she told him about it on her return. He wouldn't congratulate her madly, but he would certainly be pleased. He'd say it was a step in the right direction, a beginning. She still went to him regularly, and now that she had gotten so much better, his oblique references had become far less oblique and he had more than once told her that her depressions and suicidal tendencies would never completely disappear until she had actually and physically "replaced" Ed with another man.

"But it is impossible to replace a person one has loved to distraction②," Anna had said to him the last time he had brought up the subject. "Heavens above, doctor, when Mrs. Crummlin-Brown's parakeet③

---

① fluster: *Verb* [with obj.] [often as adj. flustered] make (someone) agitated or confused 使慌张;使激动;使慌乱(e. g. Rosamund seemed rather flustered this morning. 罗莎蒙德今天早上似乎有些心神不宁。)

② to distraction: (in hyperbolic use) intensely(夸张用法)极度地(e. g. She loved him to distraction. 她爱他爱得发狂。)

③ parakeet or parakeet: *Noun* a small parrot with predominantly green plumage and a long tail 长尾小鹦鹉;鹦鹉;鹦哥

died last month, her *parakeet*, mind you, not her husband, she was so shook up about it, she swore she'd never have another bird again!"

"Mrs. Cooper," Dr. Jacobs had said, "one doesn't normally have sexual intercourse with a parakeet."

"Well...no..."

"That's why it doesn't have to be replaced. But when a husband dies, and the surviving wife is still an active and a healthy woman, she will invariably get a replacement within three years if she possibly can. And vice versa."

Sex. It was about the only thing that sort of doctor ever thought about. He had sex on the brain.

By the time Anna had dressed and taken the elevator downstairs, it was ten minutes after six. The moment she walked into the bar, a man stood up from one of the tables. It was Conrad. He must have been watching the door. He came across the floor to meet her. He was smiling nervously. Anna was smiling, too. One always does.

"Well, well," he said. "Well well well," and she, expecting the usual peck① on the cheek, inclined her face upward toward his own, still smiling. But she had forgotten how formal Conrad was. He simply took her hand in his and shook it once. "This is a surprise," he said. "Come and sit down."

The room was the same as any other hotel drinking-room. It was lit by dim lights, and filled with many small tables. There was a saucer of peanuts on each table, and there were leather bench-seats② all around

---

① peck: *Noun* a light or perfunctory kiss 轻轻的一吻;漫不经心的一吻,敷衍的一吻(e.g. a fatherly peck on the cheek 一个在脸颊上的父爱般的轻吻)

② bench-seat or bench seat：*Noun* a seat across the whole width of a car(横贯车厢的)统座;一体式长座椅

the walls. The waiters were rigged① out in white jackets and maroon② pants. Conrad led her to a corner table, and they sat down facing each other. A waiter was standing over them at once.

"What will you have?" Conrad asked.

"Could I have a martini③?"

"Of course. Vodka④?"

"No, gin⑤, please."

"One gin martini," he said to the waiter. "No. Make it two. I've never been much of a drinker, Anna, as you probably remember, but I think this calls for a celebration."

The waiter went away. Conrad leaned back in his chair and studied her carefully. "You look pretty good," he said.

"You look pretty good yourself, Conrad," she told him. And so he did. It was astonishing how little he had aged in twenty-five years. He was just as lean and handsome as he'd ever been—in fact, more so. His black hair was still black, his eye was clear, and he looked altogether like a man who was no more than thirty years old.

"You *are* older than me, aren't you?" he said.

"What sort of a question is that?" she said, laughing. "Yes Con-

---

① rig: Verb provide (someone) with clothes of a particular style or type 为……提供（特殊种类）服装(e. g. a cavalry regiment rigged out in green and gold 穿戴绿色和金色军服的骑兵团)

② maroon: Adjective of a brownish-crimson colour 栗色的; 褐紫色的

③ Martini: Noun a type of vermouth produced in Italy (意大利产) 马提尼酒, 也有人译作"马丁尼酒"。本书采用前一个翻译。

④ vodka: Noun [mass noun] an alcoholic spirit of Russian origin made by distillation of rye, wheat, or potatoes 伏特加酒

⑤ gin: Noun [mass noun] a clear alcoholic spirit distilled from grain or malt and flavoured with juniper berries 杜松子酒

rad, I am exactly one year older than you. I'm forty-two."

"I thought you were." He was still studying her with the utmost care, his eyes travelling all over her face and neck and shoulders. Anna felt herself blushing.

"Are you an enormously successful doctor?" she asked. "Are you the best in town?"

He cocked his head over to one side, right over, so that the ear almost touched the top of the shoulder. It was a mannerism① that Anna had always liked. "Successful?" he said. "Any doctor can be successful these days in a big city—financially, I mean. But whether or not I am absolutely first rate at my job is another matter. I only hope and pray that I am."

The drinks arrived and Conrad raised his glass and said, "Welcome to Dallas, Anna. I'm so pleased you called me up. It's good to see you again."

"It's good to see you, too, Conrad," she said, speaking the truth.

He looked at her glass. She had taken a huge first gulp, and the glass was now half empty. "You prefer gin to vodka?" he asked.

"I do," she said, "yes."

"You ought to change over."

"Why?"

"Gin is not good for females."

"It's not?"

"It's very bad for them."

"I'm sure it's just as bad for males," she said.

"Actually, no. It isn't nearly so bad for males as it is for females."

---

① mannerism: *Noun* a habitual gesture or way of speaking or behaving; an idiosyncrasy 言谈举止;习惯;习性;癖好(e. g. Learn the great man's speeches and studying his mannerisms. 学习伟人的演讲,研究伟人的举止。)

"Why is it bad for females?"

"It just is," he said. "It's the way they're built. What kind of work are you engaged in, Anna? And what brought you all the way down to Dallas? Tell me about you."

"Why is gin bad for females?" she said, smiling at him.

He smiled back at her and shook his head, but he didn't answer.

"Go on," she said.

"No, let's drop it."

"You can't leave me up in the air like this," she said. "It's not fair."

After a pause, he said, "Well, if you really want to know, gin contains a certain amount of the oil which is squeezed out of juniper[①] berries[②]. They use it for flavouring."

"What does it do?"

"Plenty."

"Yes, but what?"

"Horrible things."

"Conrad, don't be shy. I'm a big girl now."

He was still the same old Conrad, she thought, still as diffident[③], as scrupulous[④], as shy as ever. For that she liked him. "If this drink is

---

① juniper: *Noun* an evergreen shrub or small tree which bears berry-like cones, widely distributed throughout Eurasia and North America. Many kinds have aromatic cones or foliage 刺柏属植物

② juniper berry: the berrylike cone of a juniper 杜松子；杜松果

③ diffident: *Adjective* modest or shy because of a lack of self-confidence 谦卑的；害羞的；缺乏自信的

④ scrupulous: *Adjective* very concerned to avoid doing wrong 过度谨慎的(e. g. She's too scrupulous to have an affair with a married man. 她非常谨慎，不会和已婚男子发生恋情。)

第一章 不堪回首 第二节 《最后之举》*The Last Act*

really doing horrible things to me," she said, "then it is unkind of you not to tell me what those things are."

Gently, he pinched the lobe of his left ear with the thumb and forefinger of his right hand. Then he said, "Well, the truth of the matter is, Anna, oil of juniper has a direct inflammatory① effect upon the uterus②."

"Now come on!"

"I'm not joking."

"Mother's ruin," Anna said. "It's an old wives' tale."

"I'm afraid not."

"But you're talking about women who are pregnant."

"I'm talking about all women, Anna." He had stopped smiling now, and he was speaking quite seriously. He seemed to be concerned about her welfare.

"What do you specialize in?" she asked him. "What kind of medicine? You haven't told me that."

"Gynaecology③ and obstetrics④."

"Ah-ha!"

"Have you been drinking gin for many years?" he asked.

"Oh, about twenty," Anna said.

"Heavily?"

---

① inflammatory: *Adjective* relating to or causing inflammation of a part of the body 炎症性的;引起炎症的

② uterus: *Noun* the womb (as a bodily organ, especially in medical and technical contexts) 子宫(尤见于医学技术文章)

③ gynaecology or gynecology: *Noun* [mass noun] the branch of physiology and medicine which deals with the functions and diseases specific to women and girls, especially those affecting the reproductive system 妇科学;妇科

④ obstetrics: *Plural Noun* [often treated as sing.] the branch of medicine and surgery concerned with childbirth and midwifery 产科学

"For heaven's sake, Conrad, stop worrying about my insides. I'd like another martini, please."

"Of course."

He called the waiter and said, "One vodka martini."

"No," Anna said, "gin."

He sighed and shook his head and said, "Nobody listens to her doctor these days."

"You're not my doctor."

"No," he said. "I'm your friend."

"Let's talk about your wife," Anna said. "Is she still as beautiful as ever?"

He waited a few moments, then he said, "Actually, we're divorced."

"Oh, no!"

"Our marriage lasted for the grand total of two years. It was hard work to keep it going even that long."

For some reason, Anna was profoundly shocked. "But she was such a beautiful girl," she said. "What happened?"

"Everything happened, everything you could possibly think of that was bad."

"And the child?"

"She got him. They always do." He sounded very bitter[①]. "She took him back to New York. He comes to see me once a year, in the

---

① bitter: *Adjective* (of a conflict, argument, or opponent) full of anger and acrimony 怒不可遏的;激烈的;尖酸刻薄的(e.g. a bitter five-year legal battle 一场持续五年的激烈的诉讼争斗)

summer. He's twenty years old now. He's at Princeton①."

"Is he a fine boy?"

"He's a wonderful boy," Conrad said. "But I hardly know him. It isn't much fun."

"And you never married again?"

"No, never. But that's enough about me. Let's talk about you."

Slowly, gently, he began to draw her out② on the subject of her health and the bad times she had gone through after Ed's death. She found she didn't mind talking to him about it, and she told him more or less the whole story.

"But what makes your doctor think you're not completely cured?" he said. "You don't look very suicidal to me."

"I don't think I am. Except that sometimes, not often, mind you, but just occasionally, when I get depressed, I have the feeling that it wouldn't take such a hell of③ a big push to send me over the edge."

"In what way?"

"I kind of start edging toward the bathroom cupboard."

"What do you have in the bathroom cupboard?"

"Nothing very much. Just the ordinary equipment a girl has for shaving her legs."

---

① Princeton: Noun a historic borough in west central New Jersey, home to Princeton University 普林斯顿(美国新泽西州中西部一个享有自治权的历史名城,是普林斯顿大学所在地。)

② draw someone out: gently or subtly persuade someone to talk or become more expansive 引(某人)开口(或畅谈)(e.g. She drew me out and flattered me. 她引我说话,还恭维我。)

③ a (one) hell of a...: (informal) used to emphasize something very bad or great(非正式)(用以强调某物很坏或很大)非常;极其(e.g. It cost us a hell of a lot of money. 这花了我们很多钱。)

"I see. " Conrad studied her face for a few moments, then he said, "Is that how you were feeling just now when you called me?"

"Not quite. But I'd been thinking about Ed. And that's always a bit dangerous. "

"I'm glad you called. "

"So am I," she said.

Anna was getting to the end of her second martini. Conrad changed the subject and began talking about his practice. She was watching him rather than listening to him. He was so damned handsome it was impossible not to watch him. She put a cigarette between her lips, then offered the pack to Conrad.

"No thanks," he said. "I don't. " He picked up a book of matches from the table and gave her a light, then he blew out the match and said, "Are those cigarettes mentholated①?"

"Yes, they are. "

She took a deep drag②, and blew the smoke slowly up into the air. "Now go ahead and tell me that they're going to shrivel③ up my entire reproductive system," she said.

He laughed and shook his head.

"Then why did you ask?"

"Just curious, that's all. "

---

① mentholated: *Adjective* treated with or containing menthol 用薄荷醇处理的;含薄荷醇的(e.g. mentholated shaving creams 薄荷剃须膏)

② drag: *Noun* (informal) an act of inhaling smoke from a cigarette(非正式)抽烟的一吸;一抽;一口(e.g. He took a long drag on his cigarette. 他深深吸了一口烟。)

③ shrivel: *Verb* wrinkle and contract or cause to wrinkle and contract, especially due to loss of moisture(尤指由于失去水分而)(使)枯萎;(使)收缩(e.g. The flowers simply shrivelled up. 那些花只是枯萎凋零了。)

"You're lying. I can tell it from your face. You were about to give me the figures for the incidence of lung cancer in heavy smokers."

"Lung cancer has nothing to do with menthol①, Anna," he said, and he smiled and took a tiny sip of his original martini, which he had so far hardly touched. He set the glass back carefully on the table. "You still haven't told me what work you are doing," he went on, "or why you came to Dallas."

"Tell me about menthol first. If it's even half as bad as the juice of the juniper berry, I think I ought to know about it quick."

He laughed and shook his head.

"Please!"

"No, ma'am."

"Conrad, you simply cannot start things up like this and then drop them. It's the second time in five minutes."

"I don't want to be a medical bore," he said.

"You're not being a bore. These things are fascinating. Come on! Tell! Don't be mean."

It was pleasant to be sitting there feeling moderately high on two big martinis, and making easy talk with this graceful man, this quiet, comfortable, graceful person. He was not being coy②. Far from it. He was simply being his normal scrupulous self.

"Is it something shocking?" she asked.

"No. You couldn't call it that."

---

① menthol: *Noun* [mass noun] a crystalline compound with a cooling minty taste and odour, found in peppermint and other natural oils. It is used as a flavouring and in decongestants and analgesics 薄荷醇;薄荷脑

② coy: *Adjective* reluctant to give details, especially about something regarded as sensitive(尤指对敏感问题)含糊其辞的;不愿表态的(e.g. He is coy about his age. 他避而不谈他的年龄。)

"Then go ahead."

He picked up the packet of cigarettes lying in front of her, and studied the label. "The point is this," he said. "If you inhale menthol, you absorb it into the bloodstream. And that isn't good, Anna. It does things to you. It has certain very definite effects upon the central nervous system. Doctors still prescribe it occasionally."

"I know that," she said. "Nose-drops and inhalations①."

"That's one of its minor uses. Do you know the other?"

"You rub it on the chest when you have a cold."

"You can if you like, but it wouldn't help."

"You put it in ointment and it heals cracked lips."

"That's camphor②."

"So it is."

He waited for her to have another guess.

"Go ahead and tell me," she said.

"It may surprise you a bit."

"I'm ready to be surprised."

"Menthol," Conrad said, "is a well-known anti-aphrodisiac③."

"A what?"

"It suppresses sexual desire."

"Conrad, you're making these things up."

"I swear to you I'm not."

"Who uses it?"

---

① inhalation: *Noun* [count noun] (Medicine) a preparation to be inhaled in the form of a vapour or spray(医学)吸入药剂

② camphor: *Noun* [mass noun] a white volatile crystalline substance with an aromatic smell and bitter taste, occurring in certain essential oils 樟脑；莰酮

③ aphrodisiac: *Noun* a food, drink, or drug that stimulates sexual desire 催欲剂；春药

第一章 不堪回首 第二节 《最后之举》*The Last Act*

"Very few people nowadays. It has too strong a flavour. Saltpetre① is much better."

"Ah yes. I know about saltpetre."

"What do you know about saltpetre?"

"They give it to prisoners," Anna said. "They sprinkle it on their cornflakes every morning to keep them quiet."

"They also use it in cigarettes," Conrad said.

"You mean prisoners' cigarettes?"

"I mean all cigarettes."

"That's nonsense."

"Is it?"

"Of course it is."

"Why do you say that?"

"Nobody would stand for it," she said.

"They stand for cancer."

"That's quite different, Conrad. How do you know they put saltpetre in cigarettes?"

"Have you never wondered," he said, "what makes a cigarette go on burning when you lay it in the ashtray? Tobacco doesn't burn of its own accord②. Any pipe smoker will tell you that."

"They use special chemicals," she said.

"Exactly; they use saltpetre."

"Does saltpetre burn?"

---

① saltpetre or saltpeter: *Noun* another term for potassium nitrate 意义同"potassium nitrate"

potassium nitrate: [mass noun] a white crystalline salt which occurs naturally in nitre and is used in preserving meat and as a constituent of gunpowder 硝酸钾；钾硝

② of one's own accord: voluntarily or without outside intervention 自愿地；自动地(e.g. He would not seek treatment of his own accord. 他不会主动去求医的。)

· 83 ·

"Sure it burns. It used to be one of the prime ingredients of old-fashioned gunpowder. Fuses①, too. It makes very good fuses. That cigarette of yours is a first-rate slow-burning fuse, is it not?"

Ann looked at her cigarette. Though she hadn't drawn on it for a couple of minutes, it was still smouldering② away and the smoke was curling upward from the tip in a slim blue-grey spiral.

"So this has menthol in it and saltpetre?" she said.

"Absolutely."

"And they're both anti-aphrodisiacs?"

"Yes. You're getting a double dose."

"It's ridiculous, Conrad. It's too little to make any difference."

He smiled but didn't answer this.

"There's not enough there to inhibit③ a cockroach④," she said.

"That's what you think, Anna. How many do you smoke a day?"

"About thirty."

"Well," he said, "I guess it's none of my business." He paused, and then he added, "But you and I would be a lot better off today if it

---

① fuse or fuze: *Noun* a length of material along which a small flame moves to explode a bomb or firework, meanwhile allowing time for those who light it to move to a safe distance 导火线;导火索

② smoulder or smolder: *Verb* [no obj.] burn slowly with smoke but no flame (有烟而无火苗地)阴燃(e. g. The bonfire still smouldered, the smoke drifting over the paddock. 篝火仍有余烬,烟雾萦绕在牧场上空。)

③ inhibit: *Verb* [with obj.] hinder, restrain, or prevent (an action or process) 阻碍;制止;防止(动作或过程)(e. g. Cold inhibits plant growth. 寒冷抑制植物生长。)

④ cockroach: *Noun* a beetle-like insect with long antennae and legs, feeding by scavenging. Several tropical kinds have become established worldwide as pests in homes and catering establishments 蟑螂

was."

"Was what?"

"My business."

"Conrad, what do you mean?"

"I'm simply saying that if you, once upon a time, hadn't suddenly decided to drop me, none of this misery would have happened to either of us. We'd still be happily married to each other."

His face had suddenly taken on a queer sharp look.

"Drop you?"

"It was quite a shock, Anna."

"Oh dear," she said, "but everybody drops everybody else at that age, don't they?"

"I wouldn't know," Conrad said.

"You're not cross with me still, are you, for doing that?"

"Cross!" he said. "Good God, Anna! Cross is what children get when they lose a toy! I lost a wife!"

She stared at him, speechless.

"Tell me," he went on, "didn't you have any idea how I felt at the time?"

"But Conrad, we were so *young*."

"It destroyed me, Anna. It just about destroyed me."

"But how..."

"How what?"

"How, if it meant so much, could you turn right around and get engaged to somebody else a few weeks later?"

"Have you never heard of the rebound?" he asked.

She nodded, gazing at him in dismay.

"I was wildly in love with you, Anna."

She didn't answer.

"I'm sorry," he said. "That was a silly outburst. Please forgive me."

There was a long silence.

Conrad was leaning back in his chair, studying her from a distance. She took another cigarette from the pack, and lit it. Then she blew out the match and placed it carefully in the ashtray. When she glanced up again, he was still watching her. There was an intent, far look in his eyes.

"What are you thinking about?" she asked.

He didn't answer.

"Conrad," she said, "do you still hate me for doing what I did?"

"Hate you?"

"Yes, hate me. I have a queer feeling that you do. I'm sure you do, even after all these years."

"Anna," he said.

"Yes, Conrad?"

He hitched his chair closer to the table, and leaned forward. "Did it ever cross your mind..."

He stopped.

She waited.

He was looking so intensely earnest all of a sudden that she leaned forward herself.

"Did what cross my mind?" she asked.

"The fact that you and I... that both of us... have a bit of unfinished business."

She stared at him.

He looked back at her, his eyes as bright as two stars. "Don't be shocked," he said, "please."

"Shocked?"

"You look as though I'd just asked you to jump out of the window with me."

The room was full of people now, and it was very noisy. It was like being at a cocktail party. You had to shout to be heard.

Conrad's eyes waited on her, impatient, eager.

"I'd like another martini," she said.

"Must you?"

"Yes," she said, "I must."

In her whole life, she had been made love to by only one man—her husband, Ed.

And it had always been wonderful.

Three thousand times?

She thought more. Probably a good deal more. Who counts?

Assuming, though, for the sake of argument, that the exact figure (for there has to be an exact figure) was three thousand six hundred and eighty...

... and knowing that every single time it happened it was an act of pure, passionate, authentic lovemaking between the same man and the same woman...

... then how in heaven's name could an entirely new man, an unloved stranger, hope to come in suddenly on the three thousand, six hundred and eighty-*first* time and be even halfway acceptable?

He'd be a trespasser①.

All the memories would come rushing back. She would be lying there suffocated by memories.

She had raised this very point with Dr. Jacobs during one of her sessions a few months back, and old Jacobs had said, "There will be no nonsense about memories, my dear Mrs. Cooper. I wish you would forget

---

① trespasser: *Noun* someone who intrudes on the privacy or property of another without permission 侵入者; 未经许可进入者

that. Only the present will exist."

"But how do I get there?" she had said. "How can I summon up enough nerve suddenly to go upstairs to a bedroom and take off my clothes in front of a new man, a stranger, in cold blood...?"

"Cold blood!" he had cried. "Good God, woman, it'll be boiling hot!" And later he had said, "Do at any rate try to believe me, Mrs. Cooper, when I tell you that any woman who has been deprived of sexual congress after more than twenty years of practice—of uncommonly frequent practice in your case, if I understand you correctly—any woman in those circumstances is going to suffer continually from severe psychological disturbances until the routine is reestablished. You are feeling a lot better, I know that, but it is my duty to inform you that you are by no means back to normal..."

To Conrad, Anna said, "This isn't by any chance a therapeutic[①] suggestion, is it?"

"A *what*?"

"A therapeutic suggestion."

"What in the world do you mean?"

"It sounds exactly like a plot hatched[②] up by my Dr. Jacobs."

"Look," he said, and now he leaned right across the table and touched her left hand with the tip of one finger. "When I knew you before, I was too damn young and nervous to make that sort of proposition, much as I wanted to. I didn't think there was any particular hurry then, anyway. I figured we had a whole lifetime before us. I wasn't to know you

---

① therapeutic: *Adjective* of or relating to the healing of disease(关于)治疗的;治疗学的(e.g. diagnostic and therapeutic facilities 诊断和治疗设施)

② hatch: [with obj.] conspire to devise (a plot or plan) 策划(阴谋或计划)(e.g. the little plot that you and Sylvia hatched up last night 你和西尔维亚昨天晚上想出来的小小阴谋)

were going to drop me."

Her martini arrived. Anna picked it up and began to drink it fast. She knew exactly what it was going to do to her. It was going to make her float. A third martini always did that. Give her a third martini and within seconds her body would become completely weightless and she would go floating around the room like a wisp of hydrogen gas.

She sat there holding the glass with both hands as though it were a sacrament①. She took another gulp. There was not much of it left now. Over the rim of her glass she could see Conrad watching her with disapproval as she drank. She smiled at him radiantly②.

"You're not against the use of anaesthetics③ when you operate, are you?" she asked.

"Please, Anna, don't talk like that."

"I am beginning to float," she said.

"So I see," he answered. "Why don't you stop there?"

"What did you say?"

"I said, why don't you stop?"

"Do you want me to tell you why?"

"No," he said. He made a little forward movement with his hands as though he were going to take her glass away from her, so she quickly put it to her lips and tipped it high, holding it there for a few seconds to allow the last drop to run out. When she looked at Conrad again, he was

---

① sacrament: *Noun* a thing of mysterious and sacred significance; a religious symbol 具有神秘性质和神圣意义的事物;宗教的象征

② radiant: *Adjective* (of a person or their expression) clearly emanating great joy, love, or health(人或表情)喜气洋洋的;洋溢着爱的;光华照人的(e.g. She gave him a radiant smile. 他对她粲然一笑。)

③ anaesthetic or anesthetic: *Noun* a substance that induces insensitivity to pain 麻醉剂

placing a ten-dollar bill on the waiter's tray, and the waiter was saying, "Thank *you*, sir. Thank you indeed," and the next thing she knew she was floating out of the room and across the lobby of the hotel with Conrad's hand cupped lightly under one of her elbows, steering her toward the elevators. They floated up to the twenty-second floor, and then along the corridor to the door of her bedroom. She fished the key out of her purse and unlocked the door and floated inside. Conrad followed, closing the door behind him. Then very suddenly, he grabbed hold of her and folded her up in his enormous arms and started kissing her with great gusto①.

She let him do it.

He kissed her all over her mouth and cheeks and neck, taking deep breaths in between the kisses. She kept her eyes open, watching him in a queer detached sort of way, and the view she got reminded her vaguely of the blurry close-up view of a dentist's face when he is working on an upper back tooth.

Then all of a sudden, Conrad put his tongue into one of her ears. The effect of this upon her was electric. It was as though a live② two-hundred-volt plug had been pushed into an empty socket, and all the lights came on and the bones began to melt and the hot molten sap③ went run-

---

① gusto: *Noun* [mass noun] enjoyment or vigour in doing something; zest 津津有味;兴致勃勃;充沛的精力;热情(e. g. She sang it with gusto. 她充满热情地演唱了这首歌曲。)

② live *Adjective* (of a wire or device) connected to a source of electric current (线路或仪器)带电的;通电的

③ sap: *Noun* [mass noun] the fluid, chiefly water with dissolved sugars and mineral salts, which circulates in the vascular system of a plant(植物的)汁;液

第一章　不堪回首　第二节 《最后之举》The Last Act

ning down into her limbs and she exploded into a frenzy①. It was the kind of marvellous, wanton②, reckless, flaming frenzy that Ed used to provoke in her so very often in the olden③ days by just a touch of the hand here and there. She flung her arms around Conrad's neck and started kissing him back with far more gusto than he had ever kissed her, and although he looked at first as though he thought she was going to swallow him alive, he soon recovered his balance.

Anna hadn't the faintest idea how long they stood there embracing and kissing with such violence, but it must have been for quite a while. She felt such happiness, such... such *confidence* again at last, such sudden overwhelming confidence in herself that she wanted to tear off her clothes and do a wild dance for Conrad in the middle of the room. But she did no such foolish thing. Instead, she simply floated away to the edge of the bed and sat down to catch her breath. Conrad quickly sat down beside her. She leaned her head against his chest and sat there glowing all over while he gently stroked her hair. Then she undid one button of his shirt and slid her hand inside and laid it against his chest. Through his ribs④, she could feel the beating of his heart.

"What do I see here?" Conrad said.

"What do you see where, my darling?"

---

① frenzy: *Noun* [usu. in sing.] a state or period of uncontrolled excitement or wild behaviour 狂乱;狂热;极度激动;狂热的行为(或举动)(e. g. Doreen worked herself into a frenzy of rage. 多琳使自己陷入一阵狂怒之中。)

② wanton: *Adjective* (especially of a woman) sexually immodest or promiscuous(尤指妇女)淫荡的;淫乱的

③ olden: *Adjective* [attrib.] (archaic) of or relating to former times(古旧用法)过去的;从前的(e. g. the olden days 过去的时光)

④ rib: *Noun* each of a series of slender curved bones articulated in pairs to the spine (twelve pairs in humans), protecting the thoracic cavity and its organs 肋骨

"On your scalp①. You want to watch this, Anna."

"You watch it for me, dearest."

"Seriously," he said, "you know what this looks like? It looks like a tiny touch of androgenic alopecia②."

"Good."

"No, it is not good. It's actually an inflammation③ of the hair follicles④, and it causes baldness. It's quite common on women in their later years."

"Oh shut up, Conrad," she said, kissing him on the side of the neck. "I have the most gorgeous hair."

She sat up and pulled off his jacket. Then she undid his tie and threw it across the room.

"There's a little hook on the back of my dress," she said. "Undo it, please."

Conrad unhooked the hook, then unzipped the zipper and helped her to get out of the dress. She had on a rather nice pale-blue slip⑤. Conrad was wearing an ordinary white shirt, as doctors do, but it was

---

① scalp: *Noun* the skin covering the head, excluding the face 头皮

② androgenic alopecia: a condition of hair loss in women similar to male pattern baldness, but beginning later in life and less severe 雄激素性脱发症

③ inflammation: *Noun* [mass noun] a localized physical condition in which part of the body becomes reddened, swollen, hot, and often painful, especially as a reaction to injury or infection 发炎；炎(症) (e.g. chronic inflammation of the nasal cavities 慢性鼻腔炎)

④ follicle: *Noun* (also as "hair follicle") the sheath of cells and connective tissue which surrounds the root of a hair 毛囊

⑤ slip: *Noun* a loose-fitting garment, typically a short petticoat 宽松衣服 (尤指短衬裙) (e.g. a silk slip 真丝衬裙)

now open at the neck, and this suited him. His neck had a little ridge① of sinewy② muscle running up vertically on either side, and when he turned his head the muscle moved under the skin. It was the most beautiful neck Anna had ever seen.

"Let's do this very very slowly," she said. "Let's drive ourselves crazy with anticipation."

His eyes rested a moment on her face, then travelled away, all the way down the length of her body, and she saw him smile.

"Shall we be very stylish and dissipated③, Conrad, and order a bottle of champagne④? I can ask room service to bring it up, and you can hide in the bathroom when they come in."

"No," he said. "You've had enough to drink already. Stand up, please."

The tone of his voice caused her to stand up at once.

"Come here," he said.

She went close to him. He was still sitting on the bed, and now, without getting up, he reached forward and began to take off the rest of her clothes. He did this slowly and deliberately. His face had become suddenly rather pale.

---

① ridge: *Noun* a narrow raised band running along or across a surface 脊状突起带;隆起部(e.g. Buff your nails in order to smooth ridges. 打磨指甲,让隆起部分平滑。)

② sinew: *Noun* a piece of tough fibrous tissue uniting muscle to bone; a tendon or ligament 肌腱;筋

③ dissipated: *Adjective* (of a person or way of life) overindulging in sensual pleasures(人或生活方式)浪荡的;沉迷于酒色的(e.g. dissipated behaviour 放荡之举)

④ champagne: *Noun* [mass noun] a white sparkling wine from Champagne, regarded as a symbol of luxury and associated with celebration 香槟酒

"Oh, darling," she said, "how marvellous! You've got that famous thing! A real thick clump of hair growing out of each of your ears! You know what that means, don't you? It's the absolutely positive sign of enormous virility①!" She bent down and kissed him on the ear. He went on taking off her clothes—the bra, the shoes, the girdle②, the pants, and finally the stockings, all of which he dropped in a heap on the floor, The moment he had peeled off her last stocking and dropped it, he turned away. He turned right away from her as though she didn't exist, and now he began to undress himself.

It was rather odd to be standing so close to him in nothing but her own skin and him not even giving her a second look. But perhaps men did these things. Ed might have been an exception. How could she know? Conrad took off his white shirt first, and after folding it very carefully, he stood up and carried it to a chair and laid it on one of the arms. He did the same with his undershirt. Then he sat down again on the edge of the bed and started removing his shoes. Anna remained quite still, watching him. His sudden change of mood, his silence, his curious intensity, were making her a bit afraid. But they were also exciting her. There was a stealth③, almost a menace in his movements, as though he were some splendid animal treading softly toward the kill. A leopard.

---

① virility: *Noun* masculine vigor; potency 男子气概;男性生殖力

② girdle: *Noun* a woman's elasticated corset extending from waist to thigh; a belt or sash worn around the waist (自腰部至大腿的女用)松紧裤;紧身褡

③ stealth: *Noun* [mass noun] cautious and surreptitious action or movement 秘密行动;背人的活动(e.g. the silence and stealth of a hungry cat 一只饥饿的猫默不作声和悄悄地活动)

第一章　不堪回首　第二节　《最后之举》The Last Act

She became hypnotized① watching him. She was watching his fingers, the surgeon's fingers, as they untied and loosened the laces of the left shoe, easing it off the foot, and placing it neatly half under the bed. The right shoe came next. Then the left sock and the right sock, both of them being folded together and laid with the utmost precision across the toes of the shoes. Finally the fingers moved up to the top of the trousers, where they undid one button and then began to manipulate the zipper. The trousers, when taken off, were folded along the creases②, then carried over to the chair. The underpants followed.

Conrad, now naked, walked slowly back to the edge of the bed, and sat. Then at last, he turned his head and noticed her. She stood waiting...and trembling. He looked her slowly up and down. Then abruptly, he shot out a hand and took her by the wrist, and with a sharp pull he had her sprawled across the bed.

The relief was enormous. Anna flung her arms around him and held on to him tightly, oh so tightly, for fear that he might go away. She was in mortal fear that he might go away and not come back. And there they lay, she holding on to him as though he were the only thing left in the world to hold on to, and he, strangely quiet, watchful, intent, slowly disentangling③ himself and beginning to touch her now in a number of dif-

---

① hypnotize or hypnotise: *Verb* capture the whole attention of (someone); fascinate 深深吸引(某人); 使着迷(e. g. The barman seemed hypnotized by the pub's female singer. 酒吧男招待似乎被这位酒吧歌女深深吸引了。)

② crease: *Noun* a line or ridge produced on paper or cloth by folding, pressing, or crushing it(纸或布的)折痕; 褶皱; 折缝(e. g. khaki trousers with knife - edge creases 折缝笔挺的卡其裤)

③ disentangle: *Verb* [with obj.] free (something or someone) from something that they have become entangled with 使摆脱(e. g. It became more and more difficult to disentangle fact from prejudice. 要分清事实和偏见越来越难了。)

ferent places with those fingers of his, those expert surgeon's fingers. And once again she flew into a frenzy.

The things he did to her during the next few moments were terrible and exquisite. He was, she knew, merely getting her ready, preparing her, or as they say in the hospital, prepping her for the operation itself, but oh God, she had never known or experienced anything even remotely like this. And it was all exceedingly quick, for in what seemed to her no more than a few seconds, she had reached that excruciating point of no return where the whole room becomes compressed into a single tiny blinding speck of light that is going to explode and tear one to pieces at the slightest extra touch. At this stage, in a swift rapacious parabola①, Conrad swung his body on top of her for the final act.

And now Anna felt her passion being drawn out of her as if a long live nerve were being drawn slowly out of her body, a long live thread of electric fire, and she cried out to Conrad to go on and on and on, and as she did so, in the middle of it all, somewhere above her, she heard another voice, and this other voice grew louder and louder, more and more insistent, demanding to be heard:

"I said are you *wearing* something?" the voice wanted to know.

"Oh darling, what is it?"

"I keep asking you, are you *wearing* something?"

"Who, me?"

---

① parabola: *Noun* a symmetrical open plane curve formed by the intersection of a cone with a plane parallel to its side. The path of a projectile under the influence of gravity follows a curve of this shape 抛物面;抛物线

"There's an obstruction① here. You must be wearing a diaphragm② or some other appliance."

"Of course not, darling. Everything's wonderful. Oh, do be quiet."

"Everything is not wonderful, Anna."

Like a picture on the screen, the room swam back into focus. In the foreground was Conrad's face. It was suspended above her, on naked shoulders. The eyes were looking directly into hers. The mouth was still talking.

"If you're going to use a device, then for heaven's sake learn to introduce it in the proper manner. There is nothing so aggravating as careless positioning. The diaphragm has to be placed right back against the cervix③."

"But I'm not wearing anything!"

"You're not? Well, there's still an obstruction."

Not only the room but the whole world as well seemed slowly to be sliding away from under her now.

"I feel sick," she said.

"You what?"

"I feel sick."

"Don't be childish, Anna."

"Conrad, I'd like you to go, please. Go now."

---

① obstruction: *Noun* [count noun] a thing that impedes or prevents passage or progress; an obstacle or blockage 障碍物;妨碍物(e. g. The tractor hit an obstruction. 拖拉机撞上了一个障碍物。)

② diaphragm: *Noun* a thin contraceptive cap fitting over the cervix(避孕用的)子宫帽

③ cervix: *Noun* the narrow neck-like passage forming the lower end of the womb 子宫颈

"What on earth are you talking about?"

"Go away from me, Conrad!"

"That's ridiculous, Anna. Okay, I'm sorry I spoke. Forget it."

"*Go away*!" she cried, "*Go away*! *Go away*! *Go away*!"

She tried to push him away from her, but he was huge and strong and he had her pinned.

"Calm yourself," he said. "Relax. You can't suddenly change your mind like this, in the middle of everything. And for heaven's sake, don't start weeping."

"Leave me alone, Conrad, I beg you."

He seemed to be gripping her with everything he had, arms and elbows, hands and fingers, thighs and knees, ankles and feet. He was like a toad the way he gripped her. He was exactly like an enormous clinging toad, gripping and grasping and refusing to let go. She had seen a toad once doing precisely this. It was copulating① with a frog on a stone beside a stream, and there it sat, motionless, repulsive②, with an evil yellow gleam in its eye, gripping the frog with its two powerful front paws and refusing to let go...

"Now stop struggling, Anna. You're acting like a hysterical child. For God's sake, woman, what's eating you?③"

"You're hurting me!" she cried.

"*Hurting* you?"

"It's hurting me terribly!"

---

① copulate: *Verb* [no obj.] have sexual intercourse 交媾;交配

② adjective: *Adjective* arousing intense distaste or disgust 使人厌恶的;令人反感的

③ What's eating you (him or her)?: (informal) What is worrying or annoying you (him or her)? (非正式)你(他、她)在担心什么? 你(他、她)在为什么事烦恼?

She told him this only to get him away.

"You know why it's hurting?" he said.

"Conrad! Please!"

"Now wait a minute, Anna. Allow me to explain."

"No!" she cried. "I've had enough explaining!"

"My dear woman..."

"No!" She was struggling desperately to free herself, but he still had her pinned.

"The reason it hurts," he went on, "is that you are not manufacturing① any fluid. The mucosa② is virtually dry..."

"Stop!"

"The actual name is senile③ atrophic vaginitis④. It comes with age, Anna. That's why it's called *senile* vaginitis. There's not much one can do..."

At that point, she started to scream. The screams were not very loud, but they were screams nevertheless, terrible, agonized stricken screams, and after listening to them for a few seconds, Conrad, in a single graceful movement, suddenly rolled away from her and pushed her to one side with both hands. He pushed her with such force that she fell on to the floor.

She climbed slowly to her feet, and as she staggered into the bath-

---

① manufacture: *Verb* (of a living thing) produce (a substance) naturally(有生命的东西)分泌

② mucosa: *Noun* a mucous membrane 黏膜

③ senile: *Adjective* (of a person) having or showing the weaknesses or diseases of old age, especially a loss of mental faculties(人)老年的;高龄的;衰老的(e. g. She couldn't cope with her senile husband. 她无法应付年迈的丈夫。)

④ vaginitis: *Noun* [mass noun] inflammation of the vagina 阴道炎

room, she was crying "Ed!... Ed!... Ed!..." in a queer supplicating① voice. The door shut.

Conrad lay very still listening to the sounds that came from behind the door. At first, he heard only the sobbing of the woman, but a few seconds later, above the sobbing, he heard the sharp metallic click of a cupboard being opened. Instantly, he sat up and vaulted② off the bed and began to dress himself with great speed. His clothes, so neatly folded, lay ready at hand, and it took him no more than a couple of minutes to put them on. When that was done, he crossed to the mirror and wiped the lipstick off his face with a handkerchief. He took a comb from his pocket and ran it through his fine③ black hair. He walked once round the bed to see if he had forgotten anything, and then, carefully, like a man who is tiptoeing④ from a room where a child is sleeping, he moved out into the corridor, closing the door softly behind him.

三、翻译探索

本篇小说中，作家罗尔德·达尔充分"炫耀"了自己在医学方面所掌握的知识，特别是生理学方面的知识，这方面的词汇也就构成了翻译的障碍。在翻译过程中，译者还需站在"内行"的角度来处理这

---

① supplicate: *Verb* [no obj.] ask or beg for something earnestly or humbly 恳求；哀求；祈求

② vault: *Verb* [no obj., with adverbial of direction] leap or spring while supporting or propelling oneself with one or both hands or with the help of a pole 用手（或杆）支撑跳跃(e.g. He vaulted over the gate. 他用手一撑，跃过大门。)

③ fine: *Adjective* (of a thread, filament, or person's hair) thin(线、丝或头发)纤细的(e.g. I have always had fine and dry hair. 我的头发总是又细又干。)

④ tiptoe: *Verb* [no obj., with adverbial of direction] walk quietly and carefully with one's heels raised and one's weight on the balls of the feet 踮起脚走；蹑手蹑脚地走(e.g. Liz tiptoed out of the room. 利兹踮着脚走出房间。)

方面的词汇,以突出男主人的性格特点。

最后之举

安娜正在厨房里洗一棵波士顿莴苣,要为家人做晚饭。恰在此时,门铃响了。门铃就安装在水槽的正上方。每次门铃响起,而此时她也恰巧在门铃旁边,那铃声就会吓她一跳。为了这一缘由,不管她的丈夫,还是她的每一个孩子,回家时从不按门铃。这一次,门铃的声音格外响亮,因而,安娜这一跳也是格外高。

打开门时,她看见两名警察站在门外。这两名警察的脸都很光滑,脸色苍白,眼睛都看着她,而她也看向他们,等待他们俩发话。

她一直盯着他俩看,可是,他俩谁都不说话,也没有动弹一下。两个人一动不动地站在那儿,笔直地站立着,犹如两尊蜡像——不知什么人开的什么玩笑,将其放到了她家门外的台阶前。两名警察每人的双手都将头盔举到胸前。

"有什么事儿吗?"安娜问。

这两名警察都很年轻,都戴着皮革制的宽口手套,手套很长,一直延伸到胳膊肘部位。她发现,两辆大个头摩托车停放在这两个人身后的人行道边上,摩托车周围的地面上到处都是枯干的树叶,被风一吹,顺着人行道飘走了。整条大街沐浴在九月傍晚的金黄之中,天空清澈,强风一阵阵吹过。个头高一些的那名警察不安地交换着双脚的位置,然后安静地问:"夫人,你是库珀太太吗?"

"是的,我就是。"

另一名警察接着问:"是埃德蒙·J·库珀太太吗?"

"没错。"说完,她慢慢地开始弄明白了:这两名警察,似乎没有一名想要迫不及待地解释到场的原因,而且,他俩要执行的任务若不是前来告知某种灾难性的事件的话,就不会有这样的状态了。

"库珀太太,"她听到其中一名警察说道。他说话时,声音很小,语气温柔,好似安慰一个生病的孩子。由此,她立刻断定,他要跟她说的,是某件可怕的事情。于是,一阵惊恐之感袭上心头,她问:"发生什么事了?"

"库珀太太,我们不得不通知你……"

这名警察暂停一下,而这名女子则看着他。她感到,自己整个身体在衣服里开始收缩起来,收缩得越来越小、越来越小。

"……今天傍晚大约五点四十五分的时候,在哈德孙河帕克韦路上,你的丈夫发生了车祸。在抢救过程中,死在救护车里……"

说话的这名警察拿出一个鳄鱼皮钱夹,那是两年前她跟丈夫埃德蒙结婚二十周年纪念日的时候,她送给埃德蒙的礼物。她伸手接过钱夹的时候,不禁浮想联翩:就在刚才,钱夹还揣在她丈夫胸前的兜子里,现在是否仍然带着他的体温呢。

"要是有什么事情我们能帮得上的话,"这名警察说,"诸如打电话叫什么人过来……某个朋友,或者亲戚,或许……"

安娜听到自己的声音逐渐飘散开来,最后完全消失。一定就在那时,她开始大叫起来,很快就进入了歇斯底里状态。两名警察手忙脚乱地按住她,力图将她控制住,一直忙活了四十多分钟,直到医生赶了过来。医生随即往她的胳膊里面注射了什么东西。

尽管如此,第二天早晨醒来的时候,她并没有改进多少。不管是医生,还是哪个孩子,用什么方法都劝不了她。余下那几天,要持续地给她注射镇静剂的话,她就会了结此生,这点毋庸置疑。在两次用药的间隙——她暂时神志清醒的短暂时刻,她就如同着了魔一般,呼喊着丈夫的名字,告诉他,她会尽可能快地随他而去。这话听着就令人揪心。她的这一举止立竿见影地说明,她刚刚失去的可不是什么普普通通的丈夫。

安娜·格林伍德和埃德蒙·库珀两个人结婚的时候都是十八岁。长期以来,他们耳鬓厮磨,越来越亲近,越来越相互依赖,那种程度简直是无以复加。随着时间一年一年地逝去,他们之间的爱也变得越来越浓烈、越来越强大,到最后,达到了巅峰,简直到了荒唐可笑的程度:埃德蒙每天早晨离家去办公室上班,一天时间彼此见不到面,简直令他们俩都无法忍受。晚上下班一回到家,他就会冲进屋子,对她千呼万唤。而她呢,一听到正门发出"砰"的一声响,就会扔掉手里的一切,立马朝他的方向奔去,不顾一切地奔过去,能跑多快

第一章 不堪回首 第二节 《最后之举》The Last Act

就跑多快,跟他撞个满怀。相撞的地点或许在楼梯中间,或许在楼梯平台处,或许在厨房与大厅之间。一旦相遇,他就用两只胳膊搂住她,拥抱她,亲吻她,一吻就是好几分钟不停歇,就好像他们俩昨天刚刚结完婚似的。他们这种状态太完美了,完美到了令人简直是难以置信的程度,以至于人们几乎无法理解:在一个再也没有丈夫的世界中,她为什么没有一点儿欲望、没有一点儿心情继续活下去呢?

从这个飞来横祸的开始,她的三个孩子就一直围绕在她的左右。三个孩子分别是二十岁的安杰拉,十九岁的玛丽,还有十七岁半的比利。这几个孩子爱母亲,也敬重母亲。除了竭尽全力做点什么,他们还要确保不让母亲做出自杀的举动。他们辛辛苦苦、用尽爱心去劝说母亲:生活美好,活下来仍然是值得的。最后,完全归功于孩子们的良苦用心,她总算摆脱了梦魇,慢慢地爬了出来,回到了正常的现实世界之中。

这次灾难发生四个月后,医生们纷纷表态,认为她"还算安全",基本上也算恢复到了常态——虽然还是做着以前常做的事情:操持家务、上街购物、为长大成人的孩子煮饭做菜,但是整个人变得无精打采的。

可是,接下来,情况如何呢?

那年冬天的积雪还没有融化的时候,安杰拉远嫁到罗德岛,跟她年轻的丈夫一起生活在首府普罗维登斯市的郊区。

几个月过后,玛丽嫁给了明尼苏达州斯莱顿市的一位金发大高个。她这一出嫁,就永远、永远、永远地飞走了。现在,尽管安娜的心再度破碎成一块儿、一块儿的,但一想到自己的两个女儿没有因为她身上发生的事情而受到丝毫的影响,她就很是自豪。("哦,妈咪,简直是棒极了!""是的,我亲爱的孩子。我想呢,这是世上所有婚礼中最棒的婚礼,我甚至比你还要兴奋啊!"以及诸如此类的话。)

接着,归结到最后,她喜欢得不得了的儿子比利,刚到十八岁,就离开家去耶鲁大学读一年级了。

至此,安娜一下子发现,家中空空荡荡,只剩下她一个人了。

度过了长达二十三年欢闹、忙碌、富于魔力的家庭生活之后,每天早晨独自一人吃饭,静默地坐在那儿喝咖啡、吃吐司面包,同时还不知道即将开始的一天里要干些什么,这种感觉糟糕透顶。独坐的房间里,曾经听到过那么多的欢笑,庆祝过那么多的生日,看到过那么多的圣诞树,打开过那么多的礼物,可是现在,一点声息都没有。说来奇怪的是,她感觉屋子里寒冷起来。尽管里面屋子已经加热,室温也正常,但是,屋子里仍然令人不寒而栗。时钟已经停止转动,因为你从来都不是第一个想到要给时钟上弦的人。一把椅子立在那儿,变了形,而你却坐在原地呆呆地看着,心里纳闷:以前怎么没有注意到那把椅子呢。你再次抬起头向上看去,头脑中突然产生一种恐慌的感觉:一旦收回眼神,房间的四壁开始蹑手蹑脚地向你慢慢地、慢慢地爬了过来。

刚开始的时候,她就端着咖啡走到电话那儿,一个一个地给朋友打电话,可问题是,她所有的朋友都有丈夫和孩子。尽管所有的朋友都尽可能一直对她好言好语、热情洋溢、兴高采烈,但是,早晨什么都不做,大老远赶来跟一位孤独、凄苦的女士一起坐着聊天,她们怎么都抽不出那样的时间。所以嘛,她就转而给嫁出去的女儿拨电话。

安娜的两个女儿也一直对她甜甜蜜蜜、亲切友好,但是,她很快就察觉出她俩态度的微妙变化:她们的生活中,她不再占据第一的位置。现在,她们各自有了丈夫,一切围着丈夫这个中心轴旋转,于是,她俩虽是轻柔却也坚决地将母亲挪到了背景的位置上。知道了这一点,她十分震惊,但是,她清楚,她们做得没错,甚至做得绝对正确。她不再有权去干预她们的生活,也不能让她们感到因为忽略了她而内疚。

她定期去看雅各布医生,但他也确实帮不上什么忙。他尽量让她多多交谈,她也尽力做到。有的时候,他稍微对安娜说教一番,话语里转弯抹角地提到了性以及让性得到升华等方面的事情,可是,她从未能完全理解他话中的用意,依稀觉得他的主要意思是让她再找一个丈夫。

她喜欢上在房间里转悠,触摸着曾经属于埃德蒙的东西。她会抓起他的一只鞋,将手伸进去,摸着他的大脚趾和其他脚趾在鞋底磨出的浅浅的凹痕。她找出一只磨出了洞的袜子,开始织补起来,从中得到的快乐无以言表。偶尔有的时候,她拿出一件衬衫、一条领带、一套衣服,在床上摆放整齐,就等他来穿戴。有一次,那是一个星期天的早晨,外面下着雨,她烹饪了一份洋葱、土豆焖牛肉……

继续活下去,毫无希望。

这一次,吞下多少药片才能绝对地有把握呢?她上楼,来到她的秘密储藏室,数着药片,可是,只剩下九片了。九片足够了吗?对此,她表示怀疑。哦,真见鬼。唯一的一件她没有准备好可能再次面对的事情,就是服药自杀失败——被紧急送到佩恩惠特尼医院,送到那里的七楼隔离室,然后洗胃,紧接着,会有精神病专家的询问,羞愧难当,以及诸如此类的悲惨状况……

要是那样的话,还不如用剃须刀片呢。可是,剃须刀片的麻烦是,用起来要干净利落,而很多人用它来割腕的时候,都悲惨地以失败告终。事实上,几乎所有人都没有成功过,因为他们割得不够深。手腕皮肤以下某个地方有一条大动脉血管,要是割不到那个部位,却只割断某些静脉血管,一点用处都没有。静脉血管只能让你把事情办得一塌糊涂,让你永远无法切中要害。还有就是,剃须刀片不容易握住。要想握紧刀片果断地割下去——深深地、深深地往下割,一直割到要害部位,这不容易做到。但是,*她* 不想失败,而失败的那些人实际上就是一些*压根儿不想*成功的人。但是,她想割一次就达到目的。

她走到浴室的柜橱那儿,翻找刀片,但是,一片都找不到。埃德蒙的剃刀仍然在那儿放着,她的也在那儿,可是,两个剃刀上面都没有刀片,旁边包刀片的包装盒也不见了。这都是可以理解的,因为早些时候,类似这样的东西早就从房中被人拿走了。即便如此,这并不成什么问题,谁都可以买一包剃须刀片的。

她返回厨房,将挂历从墙上取下,从上面选出一个日期:9月23日,那一天是埃德蒙的生日。她还在那个日期上写上"片儿"两个字,代表"剃须刀片"的意思。她定下这个日期的那一天是9月9日,这样,她正好有两周的宽限期将自己的事情处理妥当。其间,她要做的事情很多：旧账单要偿清，新遗嘱要立下，房子需要清扫干净，比利余下四年的大学学费要处理妥当，要给孩子们、她自己父母、埃德蒙的母亲分别写信，以及诸如此类的事情。

　　这两周期间，尽管她忙得很，却发现那十四天的时间漫长而遥远，过得很慢、很慢，很是不合心意。她很想快点用上刀片，每天一大早，她就数着还剩下多少天，就像一个孩子数着天数，盼望着圣诞节的到来。不管埃德蒙死的时候去了哪里，即便是坟墓，她也迫不及待要奔他而去。

　　就在这两周中间一天早晨八点半的时候，她的朋友伊丽莎白·保莱蒂前来拜访。当时，安娜正在厨房弄咖啡，门铃一响，她吓了一跳。紧接着，门铃又是长长的一阵鸣响，她又吓了一跳。

　　利兹（伊丽莎白的昵称——译者注）穿过正门，风风火火走了进来，嘴里跟往常一样说个不停："安娜，我亲爱的，我需要你的帮助！办公室里人人都患上了感冒，你一定得来帮忙！不要跟我辩解啊！我知道你会打字，我也知道，你活在这个世界上，除了闷闷不乐、意志消沉，整天屁大点儿可做的事情都没有。赶紧抓起帽子，带上小包，我们这就出发。赶快行动，姑娘，赶快行动啊！看样子，我要迟到啦！"

　　安娜说："走开，利兹，让我一个人待着。"

　　"出租车在外面等着呢，"利兹催促道。

　　"拜托，"安娜说，"现在不要硬逼我了。我不会去的。"

　　"你一定要跟我来，"利兹说。"打起精神来，你那些令人称道的、守孝的苦日子已经结束啦。"

　　安娜还在继续推脱，但是，在利兹的软磨硬泡之下，她最终同意去一趟，只待几个小时就回来。

　　伊丽莎白·保莱蒂负责经营一家孩子领养协会，是全市最好的一家。她的员工中，有九个人患了流感。除了她之外，只剩下两个还在继续工作。"你对这项工作一无所知，"她在出租车里说道，"但是，你必须尽你所能，帮助我们……"

　　办公室里一片喧闹、混乱的场景，一个接一个的电话几乎让安娜疯掉。她不断地从一个小隔间跑到另一个小隔间，记录下一个个电话信息，而这些信息她并不明白是什么意思。有好几个女孩子在等候室里等着，个个脸色苍白，面无表情，而她的部分任务就是将她们的回答打到一张正式的表格上。

"父亲的名字呢？"

"不知道。"

"一点印象都没有？"

"父亲的名字与这事儿有什么关系？"

"我亲爱的，要是知道了父亲的名字，除了你同意之外，还要征得父亲的同意，这孩子才能让他人收养啊。"

"对于这一点，你肯定吗？"

"天啊，我刚才这样跟你说过了，难道不是吗？"

午餐时间，有人给她拿来三明治，但是她没有时间吃。那天晚上九点的时候，安娜摇摇晃晃回到了家，感到精疲力竭、饥饿难忍，同时，对于一天中自己所了解到的东西感到极为震惊。她喝下一杯烈酒，煎了几个蛋，放上点熏咸肉，吃完就上床睡觉了。

"明早八点我去接你，"利兹当时这样说道。"看在上帝的分上，你可要做好准备啊。"安娜准备好了。从那时起，她就一发而不可收了。

事情就是那么简单。

打一开始的时候起，她所需要的就是一份工作，一份辛苦的好工作，还要去解决很多的问题。当然，要去解决别人的问题，而不是她自己的问题。

这份工作十分艰巨，而且，还令精神得不到松弛，但是，安娜每时每刻都沉浸其中。大约——我们现在不得不将时间大大向前跨越一下——大约一年半以后，她又开始感觉好了起来，处于还算是开心的状态。她发现，栩栩如生地勾勒出丈夫的模样，眼前准确地浮现出丈夫跑上楼梯迎接她的情形，再现晚上吃饭时丈夫坐在她对面的景象，这样的事儿变得愈来愈难了。丈夫的声音听起来到底是什么样子，她回忆起来越来越不容易了。就连丈夫的那张脸的模样，要是不事先看一下照片的话,在她的头脑中,也不像当初那样记忆犹新、醒目突出了。她仍然不断地想他,可是,她发现,现在就算是想的话,也不是那样潸然泪下了。回头看一看自己不长时间以前的表现,她感到稍微有点尴尬。她开始稍微在意自己的穿着打扮和头发样式,又开始使用唇膏,也开始将腿上的毛刮掉了,就连食物吃起来也津津有味了。有人冲她微笑,她也冲对方微笑,而且是实实在在的微笑。换句话说,她又一次融入了社会,并为自己活了下来而感到开心。

就在这一时刻,安娜必须得为办公室出一趟公差,到德克萨斯州的达拉斯去一趟。

通常情况下,利兹的办公室业务就局限在本州范围内,但是,这次跨州出差是因为一对夫妇。这对夫妇通过利兹这家机构收养了一个婴儿,随后从纽约州搬走,移居到德克萨斯州。现在,他们搬走有五个月时间了,这家的妻子写信说,她不想再抚养这个孩子了,因为她的丈夫——她在信中这样表示——在他们搬到德克萨斯州之后没有多久,就突然死于心脏病,而她本人几乎立刻就改嫁了,但是,她的新任丈夫"觉得不可能去接受一个收养的孩子……"

现在,这种情况很严重。撇开孩子本身的福利不说,这里涉及法律义务方方面面的问题。

安娜从纽约乘很早一班飞机去达拉斯,早饭前到达了目的地。办理完宾馆入住手续后,接下来她用了八个小时的时间跟这个事件的有关人员接触。那天做完了所有该做的之后,大约是下午四点半,她也感到疲乏不堪。于是,她打出租车回到了宾馆,上楼进了自己的房间,给利兹打了个电话,通报了当天的情况。然后,她就脱衣洗浴,在浴缸里暖暖地泡了很长时间。洗完后,她用浴巾将自己裹起来,躺到床上,吸着香烟。

她代表孩子一方所做出的种种努力,毫无结果。对方出场的,一直是那两名律师,而且一直用蔑视的态度对待她。她厌恶这两个家伙。她憎恶他们两个傲慢的姿态,憎恶他们两个话语里那种软中带硬的暗示;任凭她怎么去做,都不会给他们的当事人产生丝毫的影响。其中的一个家伙在整个讨论过程中,始终将双脚搭在桌子上。

第一章 不堪回首 第二节 《最后之举》The Last Act

两个家伙的肚子部位都长了一圈圈的肥肉,肥肉就像液体一般溢出,然后被衬衫兜住,打起一道道大大的皱褶悬挂在裤子的顶部,而裤子的顶部则被裤带勒住。

安娜一生中已经有很多次去过德克萨斯州了,但是,到目前为止,从未独自一人去过。以前每一次都是跟埃德蒙一起去的,埃德蒙因公事出差,她就陪伴着他。每次一到德克萨斯,他就跟她讲一般的德克萨斯州人的情况,说如何、如何难以喜欢他们。来到这里的人大可不必理会他们的粗劣和低俗,实际上,他们并非如此。但是,德克萨斯人中,似乎仍然留存一种冷酷无情的品质。他们身上具有某种野蛮、残酷的东西,凡事无动于衷,令人不可能加以原谅。他们没有肚量去同情、去怜悯、去关爱,他们唯一拥有的,就是所谓的美德,即职业性仁慈。他们一遇到陌生人,就将这种美德卖弄式地炫耀一番,而且没完没了地炫耀。他们周身都涂满了这种美德,他们的声音里、笑容里都富含这种美德,犹如沾满了糖浆一般。可是,这种美德却让安娜感到了寒冷,让她的内心感到相当的寒冷,冷得不得了。

"他们为什么那么喜欢粗暴行事呢?"她那时经常问这样的问题。

"因为他们还没长大,"埃德蒙会这样回答。"他们是一群危险的孩子,尽量模仿自己的祖辈闯来闯去。他们的祖辈曾经都是些开拓先驱,而他们却不是。"

看起来,当今这些德克萨斯人似乎生活在某种自高自大的意志力之中——不是去推挤人,就是被人推挤。人人都在推挤他人,同时,人人又被他人推挤。夹在他们中间的陌生人,最为万全的做法就是,向身旁跨出一步,坚定地宣布:"我不会推挤任何人,也不受任何人推挤。"但是,那样做是办不到的,特别是在达拉斯这样的城市,那样做是办不到的。在德克萨斯州的所有城市当中,达拉斯总是一个最令安娜烦乱不安的城市。她寻思着,这是一座荒蛮的城市,简直到了让人贪婪成性、欲罢不能、冷酷无情的地步。在这里,金钱至上,人们为钱而奔走,任何表面的假象、虚假的文明以及蜜如糖浆般的谈论都无法掩盖这样的事实:这只金色的大果子内部已经腐烂。

安娜身上裹着浴巾躺在床上。这一次,她只身一人来到了达拉斯。目前,没有埃德蒙坚实有力的臂膀将她围拢,也没有埃德蒙浓情甜美的爱意将她融化。或许正是由于这一点,她才突然之间感觉有点心神不宁。于是,她又点燃一支香烟,试图驱走这阵突如其来的不安的心绪,但是,没有效果,心绪反而变得更加不安。一小块硬硬的恐惧的绳结开始在她的心头盘起,没有松开的迹象,却随着时间一分一秒地消逝而愈盘愈大。这种感觉令人很是不快,就像一个人夜晚独自待在房中——听到,或者认为自己听到,隔壁房间传来的一个脚步声。

在这里,传来的是一百万个脚步声,而且,她一个没有遗漏,都听到了。

她下床走到窗前,身上仍裹着浴巾。她住的房间在二十二楼,房间窗户开着。这座大城市沐浴在傍晚的阳光里,灰白之中带着乳黄的色调。下方的街道密密麻麻布满了汽车,人行道上人来人往。结束了一天的工作,大家推推搡搡,匆匆忙忙地赶着回家。她感觉,自己需要一位朋友,很渴望此时此刻有一个人跟自己聊天。她多想走进一户人家,这家有丈夫、妻子、孩子,还有一屋子、一屋子的玩具。这家的丈夫和妻子会到正门口迎接她,伸开双臂迎接她,大声喊道:"安娜啊!见到你真是不可思议啊!能待多长时间?一周?一个月?还是一年?"

突然之间,就像在类似的情形下经常发生的情况一样,她的大脑里"咔嗒"一下,她想起了什么,大声说道:"康拉德·克罗伊格!老天在上啊!*他这个人*就住在达拉斯……起码,他以前住在……"

在纽约上高中时,她跟康拉德是同学。自那之后,他们再也没有见过面。当时,他俩都是十七岁左右,而且,康拉德狂热追求她,是她的爱人,是她的所有。一年多的时间里,他们形影不离,相互发誓忠于对方、永不分离,还承诺不久的将来就结婚。接下来,就在突然之间,埃德蒙·库珀闪亮登场,闯入了她的生活。当然,她跟康拉德之间的爱恋就此结束,但是,康拉德似乎并没有把这次戛然而止的爱恋太当回事儿。当然,这事儿并没有将他*击垮*,因为多说两个月过后,他就开始跟同班的另一个女孩子打得火热。

第一章 不堪回首 第二节 《最后之举》The Last Act

现在想想,那个女孩子叫什么名字来着?
她是一个大女孩儿,端庄健美,乳房发达,火红色的头发。她的名字很不同寻常,是一个很古旧的名字。叫什么来着?阿拉贝拉?不,不叫阿拉贝拉。尽管不叫阿拉贝拉,但应该叫阿拉什么的。阿拉明蒂?对啦!就叫阿拉明蒂!更有甚者,一年左右的时间内,康拉德·克罗伊格就娶了阿拉明蒂,带着她回到了达拉斯——他的出生地。

安娜走到床头桌那儿,拿起了电话簿。

康拉德·P·克罗伊格医生。

那准是康拉德无疑,他那时总说自己要当一名医生。电话簿里提供了他的办公号码和住宅号码。

她应不应该打电话给他?
为什么不呢?
她瞥了一眼手表,时间是五点二十分。她拿起听筒,让接线员接通了他办公室的电话。

"克罗伊格医生的外科诊所,"一名女孩子的声音传了过来。
"你好,"安娜说。"克罗伊格医生在吗?"
"医生现在没空。我可以问,是谁打来的电话吗?"
"麻烦你告诉他,是安娜·格林伍德给他打的电话。"
"谁?"
"安娜·格林伍德。"
"好的,格林伍德小姐。你希望预约一下吗?"
"不了,谢谢你。"
"有什么可以为你效劳的吗?"
安娜告诉对方自己所住宾馆的名字,让对方转给克罗伊格医生。
"我很乐意转达,"这位秘书说道。"再见,格林伍德小姐。"
"再见,"安娜说。她想知道的是,这么多年以后,康拉德·P·克罗伊格医生是否还会记得她的名字。她相信,他会记得的。她又回到床上躺下,脑海里尽量去回忆康拉德以前的模样:他是相当的英俊潇洒——高高的个子……清瘦……宽肩膀……几乎纯黑的头发……那张脸,妙不可言……那张结实的脸,如雕刻一般,像希腊众英雄中的一位——珀尔修斯,抑或尤利西斯。尽管如此,但首先,他是个很温柔的男孩子——庄重、体面、安静,不是经常地吻她,只是在晚上道别时,才吻她。就算是吻她,也从来都没有像其他男孩子那样,急不可耐地激情拥吻。星期六晚上看完电影,送她回家时,他常常把他那辆老别克车停在她家房子外面,跟她并排坐在车里,只是交谈,谈未来——谈完他的未来,再谈她的未来,还谈到,他要回达拉斯做个名医。他没有对她急不可耐地激情拥吻,也没有做出与之相关的所有愚蠢的行为,这些都令她印象深刻。那个时候,她常说,他尊重我、爱我。她说的或许没错。不管怎么说,他是个不错的男子,是一个优秀的人。要不是因为埃德蒙·库珀超级不错、超级优秀的话,她敢肯定,自己就会嫁给康拉德·克罗伊格的。

电话响起,安娜随即拿起听筒。"喂,"她说。"你好。"

"安娜·格林伍德吗?"

"康拉德·克罗伊格!"

"我亲爱的安娜啊!真令人吃惊,太棒了!我的老天啊,这么多年过去了。"

"漫长的时间,的确不假。"

"简直就是毕生的时间。你的声音一点没变啊。"

"你的也是啊。"

"是什么风把你吹到了我们这座锦城的?要待很长的时间吗?"

"不,明天就回去。打电话给你,希望你不要介意。"

"真见鬼,不,安娜,你打电话来,我很开心。你还好吗?"

"是的,我很好。我现在很好。埃德蒙死后,短时间内,我很受煎熬。"

"什么!?"

"两年半以前,他出车祸身亡。"

"哦,可惜啊。安娜,我*真的*很难过。多么糟糕的事情啊。我……我不知道该说什么来……"

"什么都不用说。"

"你现在还好吧?"

"我很好,奴隶一般工作着。"

"这样的女孩子,才是……"

"你那……你那阿拉明蒂怎么样了?"

"噢,她很好。"

"有孩子吗?"

"有一个,"他回答。"是个男孩儿。你呢?"

"有三个,两个女孩儿,一个男孩儿。"

"哇,哇,真想不到啊!现在听着,安娜……"

"我听着呢。"

"我为什么不赶到宾馆,请你喝一杯呢?我很愿意过去见见你,我敢肯定,你一丝一毫都没变化。"

"康拉德,我看起来老了。"

"你说谎啊。"

"我也感觉自己老了。"

"你需要良医吗?"

"是的。我的意思是,不需要。当然,我不需要。我不再需要医生啦。我所需要的是……怎么说呢……"

"是什么?"

"康拉德,这个地方令我不安。我想呢,我需要一个朋友,这就是我所需要的。"

"你已经得到一位朋友啦。我还有一位病人需要治疗,然后,就没事儿了。我在你楼下一个酒吧见你,叫什么屋来着,我忘记那个酒吧的名字啦。六点钟见,还有大约半个小时的时间。你方便吗?"

"方便,"她回答。"当然可以啦。那么……谢谢你,康拉德。"她放下听筒,起床,开始穿衣服。

她感觉有点紧张、慌乱,因为自从埃德蒙死后,她从未跟一个男人单独出去喝过什么东西。回去后,要是她将这件事告诉雅各布斯医生,他一定会很高兴的。他不会对她大张旗鼓地表示祝贺,但是,他一定会很高兴的。他会说,这只是一个开端,朝正确的方向迈出了一步。她仍然定期去他那里看病,而现在,她的情况有所好转,于是,他转弯抹角的提示就显得不那么转弯抹角了。他曾经不止一次对她说,除非她实际上用另一个男人在身体方面"替代"埃德蒙,否则,她的抑郁症状和自杀倾向永远都不会完全消失。

"可是,对于一个自己爱得发狂的人,是不可能替代的。"他最后一次提起这个话题的时候,安娜就是这样对他说的。"苍天在上,医生,上个月克拉姆琳-布朗太太的长尾小鹦鹉死去时——给你提个醒,是她的*长尾小鹦鹉*,不是她的丈夫,她大受打击,发誓永远都不再养鸟了啊!"

"库珀太太,"雅各布斯医生说,"一般来说,人是不跟长尾小鹦鹉发生性关系的。"

"哦……那倒是……"

"鹦鹉不用替代,那就是原因所在。但是,丈夫去世后,活下来的妻子仍然具有活力,还是一个健康的女人。要是可能的话,三年之内,她不可避免地要找到一个替代品。妻子死后,丈夫也是一样的。"

又是性事。那类医生头脑中想的,始终只有这样一件事情。他的大脑里,除了性事,没有别的。

安娜穿好衣服,乘电梯下楼的时候,已经是六点十分了。她一走进楼下的酒吧,一名男子就从那里其中一张桌子的旁边站了起来,此人正是康拉德。他一定是一刻不停地盯着门口看,只见他走过地板出来迎接她,脸上露出紧张兮兮的笑容。安娜也冲着他微笑着。这种场合,人总是会微笑的。

"哇,哇,"他说。"哇,哇,哇。"由于期望他会常规性的轻轻吻一下她的面颊,她就在他面前仰起了脸,仍然面带微笑,可是,她却忘记了康拉德是多么正式的一个人。他只是拉起她的手,放在自己的手上,握了握手——只握了一次。"真是没有想到啊,"他说。"来,坐下来。"

这间屋子跟别的宾馆里的酒吧没有什么不同之处:光线幽暗,摆满了一张张小桌子,每张桌子上都放了一碟花生,墙壁的四周安装了一体式皮革长座椅。男侍者一律穿着白色的夹克衫、褐紫色的短裤。

康拉德带她来到角落处一张桌子前,面对面坐下来。一名侍者马上俯身近前。

"你喝点什么?"康拉德问。

"我可以来杯马提尼吗?"

"当然可以。伏特加要吗?"

"不要。请来点杜松子酒吧。""一杯杜松子酒加马提尼,"他对侍者吩咐道。"不,来两杯。安娜,你或许记得,我喝酒很不在行,但是,我想,今天这个场合需要好好庆祝一下。"

侍者走开了。康拉德坐在椅子上将身体向后一靠,仔细打量着她。"你看起来相当不错啊,"他说。

"康拉德,你自己看起来也相当不错的,"她对他说。实际上,他的确相当不错。二十五年的时间过去了,他竟然没怎么显老,真是令人吃惊不小。他还是跟以前一样的清瘦、帅气,而事实上,是更加的清瘦、帅气。他那一头黑发依然是黑色的,眼睛清澈明亮,看起来完完全全像一名至多三十岁的男子。

"你*年纪*比我大,对吗?"他说。

"你这问的算是什么问题呢?"她笑着说道。"是的,康拉德,我正好大你一岁,我今年四十二。"

"我想曾经是这样的。"他还在用特别关切的目光打量着她,双眼在她整张脸上、脖子上、双肩上扫了个遍,弄得安娜感到自己的脸都变得绯红。

"你这个做医生的,是不是获得了巨大的成功?"她问道。"你是城里最好的医生吗?"

他将头偏向一侧,偏得很厉害,其中一只耳朵几乎触到了肩膀的顶部。这种大幅度的举止,安娜以前总是最喜欢的。"成功?"他问。"现如今,在大城市里,只要是医生,都能获得成功——我的意思是说,金钱方面的成功。可是,至于我在工作方面是不是绝对一流的,则是另一回事了。我只能希望并祈祷我术业有成。"

酒送来了,康拉德举起杯子说:"欢迎你来到达拉斯,安娜。你给我打了电话,我十分开心。再次见到你,真是很好。"

"康拉德,见到了你,也真是很好。"她这样说,而且说的是真心话。

她喝下了一大口酒。他看了看她的杯子,发现杯子里的酒喝下去了一半。"你喜欢杜松子酒胜过伏特加吗?"他问。

"确实,"她回答,"是的。"

"你应该完全变换一下。"

"为什么?"

"杜松子酒对女性不好。"

"不好?"

"对女性来说,杜松子酒糟糕得很。"

"我敢肯定,对男性来说,杜松子酒也糟糕得很,"她说。

"事实上,不是这样的。对男性来说,它的糟糕程度几乎没有对女性那样厉害。"

"为什么它对女性糟糕得很呢?"

"事实如此,"他说。"是因为女子的体格构造吧。安娜,你从事的是什么类型的工作?是什么风把你吹到了达拉斯来的?跟我讲讲吧。"

"对女性来说,为什么杜松子酒糟糕得很呢?"她冲着他笑着问道。

他回应一笑,摇了摇头,但没有回答。

"继续说啊,"她说。

"不啦,不说这个话题了。"

"你不能就像这样把我吊到半空中,"她说。"那样做不公平。"

停顿一会儿之后,他说:"好吧,如果你真的想知道,我告诉你,杜松子酒里含有一定量的油脂,是用杜松浆果压榨出来的,用来调味。"

"这种油脂有什么影响吗?"

"影响很多。"

"是啊,但是,那又会怎么样?"

"令人恐惧的事情啊。"

"康拉德,别羞羞答答的啦,我现在已经是一个大女孩了。"

她寻思着,他仍然是过去那个老样子的康拉德,仍然一如既往地缩头缩脚、谨小慎微、羞羞答答。那时,正是由于这一点,她很喜欢他。"如果这种酒真的会令我恐惧的话,"她说。"那么,你不告诉我恐惧的地方在哪里,就是你不够友善了。"

他用右手的大拇指和食指轻轻地、柔柔地掐捏着自己左耳的耳垂,然后说道:"好吧,安娜,事情的实质是,杜松浆果的油脂会影响子宫,使子宫出现炎症。"

"现在,继续讲。"

"我没有说笑。"

"这种酒也叫'母亲的灾难',"安娜说。"已经是老掉牙的故事啦。"

"我想不是的。"

"可是,你讲的跟女子怀孕有关啊。"

"安娜,我不是在谈所有的女子,"现在,他已经不再微笑,而是一脸严肃的表情,似乎在为她的健康担忧。

"你专攻哪方面?"她问他。"医学哪一个领域的?你还没有告诉过我呢。"

"妇科学和产科学。"

"啊哈!"

"杜松子酒你已经喝了很多年了吗?"他问。

"哦,大约二十年了吧,"安娜回答。

"喝得很厉害吗?"

"看在老天的分上,康拉德,别再为我的内部器官担心啦。请再给我来杯杜松子酒吧。"

"当然。"

他招呼一下侍者,说道:"一杯伏特加加马提尼。"

"不,"安娜纠正道,"杜松子酒加马提尼。"

他叹了口气,摇了摇头,说:"这年月,没有谁会听自己医生的话了。"

"你不是我的医生啊。"

"是的,"他说。"但我是你的朋友。"

"说说你的妻子吧,"安娜说道。"她还是那么漂亮吗?"

他停顿了一会,然后说道:"实际上,我们离婚了。"

"哦,不会吧!"

"我们两个人的婚姻总共才持续了两年的时间,就算这两年,维持起来也艰难得很。"

不知是为什么,这话令安娜感到极度震惊。"可是,她是一个那么漂亮的女孩啊,"她说。"发生什么事情了?"

"没有一件事情没有发生过,你所能想到的一切糟糕的事情都发生了。"

"那,孩子呢?"

"儿子她领走了,做母亲的总是这样的。"他的话听起来很是尖酸刻薄。"他带着儿子回纽约了,儿子一年回来看我一次,是夏天的时候。现在,他二十岁了,在普林斯顿。"

"是一个很优秀的男孩吧?"

"一个很出色的男孩,"康拉德说。"但是,我几乎不了解他,就算了解,也没什么意思。"

"那么,你从未再婚吗?"

"没,从未。可是,我的事儿就这样吧,谈谈你的事儿啊。"

他慢悠悠地、一点点地引导她,将话题集中到她自己的健康上面,以及埃德蒙死后她所经历的那些糟糕时光。她发觉,跟他谈起自己的这些事情,一点顾忌都没有,因此,她几乎把自己的事情和盘托出。

"可是,是什么使你的医生认为,你还没有完全康复呢?"他问道。"在我看来,你似乎没有那种自杀的倾向。"

"我也认为,我没有这个倾向。除非有的时候,不过,不是很经常,你注意一下,只是偶尔有的时候我感到抑郁、沉闷,我就有这样一种感觉:只需轻轻那么一推,我就被送到了危险的边缘。"

"在哪方面呢?"

"我就是有点焦虑不安,会慢慢走向浴室的柜橱。"

第一章 不堪回首 第二节 《最后之举》The Last Act

"浴室的柜橱里有什么东西呢?"

"没有太多的东西,只是放了个普通的设备,就是女孩子用来刮腿毛的那种东西。"

"我明白了。"康拉德打量着她的脸,打量了好一阵儿,然后说道:"就在刚才你给我打电话的时候,你是那种感觉吗?"

"没有太多的那种感觉,但是,我一直想着埃德蒙,那就有点儿危险了。"

"你打来电话,我很高兴。"

"我也很高兴,"她说。

安娜的第二杯马提尼快要喝完了,于是,康拉德转移了话题,开始谈起他自己的行医实践。与其说安娜是在听他说话,不如说是在盯着他看。她将一支香烟放到嘴上,用双唇夹住,然后将烟盒递给了康拉德。

"不,谢谢,"他说。"我不抽烟。"他从桌子上拿起火柴,为她点燃了香烟,然后吹灭火柴,问道:"你抽的烟是用薄荷醇处理过的吗?"

"是的,没错。"

她深深吸入一口,接着,慢慢地将烟向空中吐了出来。"现在,接着说,告诉我,这些含薄荷醇的香烟会将我的整个生殖系统熏枯,"她说。

他笑了笑,摇了摇头。

"那么,为什么要问呢?"

"就是好奇,仅此而已。"

"你说谎啊,这一点,我可以从你的脸上看出来。你要告诉我,重度吸烟者的肺癌发生率的数字是多少吧。"

"安娜,肺癌与薄荷醇一点儿关系都没有。"说完这话,他微微一笑,抿了一小口他自己杯中的原汁原味的马提尼酒,而到目前为止,杯中的酒他几乎一口都没动。他将杯子小心地放回到桌子上。"你还没有告诉我,你做的是什么样的工作呢,"他继续说,"而且,你来达拉斯的原因也没说呢。"

"先给我说说薄荷醇吧。就算它的糟糕程度是杜松浆果汁的一半,我想,我也应该立马知道。"

他笑了笑,摇了摇头。

"拜托!"

"不,夫人。"

"康拉德,你就是不应该如此这般挑起话题,然后再一下子放下不提。短短五分钟时间里,这已经是第二次啦。"

"我不想总谈医科话题,让人厌烦。"他说。

"你没有令人厌烦呐。这样的话题令人着迷。快啊!告诉我!别那么小气!"

她坐在那儿,喝下了两大杯马提尼,感觉晕晕乎乎的,却又十分清醒,这种状态令她身心愉悦,更何况,眼前这位男子举止优雅、温和安静,跟他说话流畅轻松,令人舒心。他也没有含糊其辞,躲躲闪闪,只不过表现出了他自己的正常状态——谨小慎微。

"说出来会令人头晕目眩吗?"她问。

"不,你不能那样说。"

"那就继续说吧。"

他拿起放在她面前的那盒香烟,仔细看了看上面的标签。"问题的关键是这样的,"他说道。"要是你吸入了薄荷醇,薄荷醇就会溶进你的血液。安娜,那就没有什么好处了,会对你产生一些作用,肯定会对中枢神经系统产生特定的影响。医生开药方的时候,偶尔会用到它。"

"这我知道,"她说,"像滴鼻剂和吸入剂之类的药。"

"那只是其中一个低级的用处。你知道其他方面的用处吗?"

"伤风时,可以用它擦拭胸部。"

"要是你愿意的话,可以那么用,但是不会有什么效果。"

"将其放入药膏,会治愈龟裂的嘴唇。"

"那是樟脑的作用。"

"的确啊。"

他等着她再猜出一样。

"快啊,告诉我吧,"她说。

"告诉你,答案会让你略微意想不到的。"
"我已经为这种意想不到做好了准备。"
"薄荷醇,"康拉德说,"是一种有名的抗催欲剂。"
"一种抗什么?"
"它会抑制性欲。"
"康拉德,你在捏造事实。"
"我向你发誓,我没有。"
"谁在用它呢?"
"当今,没有几个人用它啦。它的味道太冲,而硝酸钾就好多了。"
"哦,是的。我知道硝酸钾这种东西。"
"你知道硝酸钾什么?"
"他们给囚犯用,"安娜说。"他们每天早晨将其喷洒到玉米花上,好让囚犯吃了后保持安静。"
"他们也在香烟里使用它,"康拉德说。
"你的意思是说,用在囚犯抽的香烟里?"
"我的意思是说,用在所有的香烟里。"
"那是无稽之谈。"
"是吗?"
"当然是的。"
"你为什么那样说?"
"没有谁会忍受得了它,"她说。
"癌症大家都能忍受得了。"
"那可大不一样了,康拉德。你怎么会知道,他们将硝酸钾放进香烟里?"
"香烟放进烟灰缸里的时候,"他说,"你从未想过是什么东西使香烟继续燃烧吗?烟草是不会自动燃烧起来的,凡是抽过烟斗的人都知道这一点。"
"他们使用的是特殊的化学品,"她说。
"正是。他们采用的是硝酸钾。"

"硝酸钾会燃烧吗?"

"当然会。旧式火药的主要成分之一就是硝酸钾,导火索用的也是硝酸钾。你抽的香烟就是一条上等的慢燃式导火索,难道不是吗?"

安娜看了看自己的香烟,发现尽管自己两三分钟没有吸上一口,但是,香烟依然慢慢地燃烧着,一缕细细的蓝灰色烟雾从香烟的前端盘旋上升。

"那么说,这里面含有薄荷醇和硝酸钾?"她问。

"绝对含有。"

"而且,它们都是抗催欲剂?"

"是的。你摄入的是双份的剂量。"

"荒谬可笑啊,康拉德。我吸入的剂量太少了,不会产生什么影响的。"

他微微一笑,但并没有回应。

"那里面含有的剂量,不足以抑制蟑螂的活性,"她说。

"那只是你的想法啊,安娜。你一天抽多少支烟?"

"大约三十支吧。"

"哇,"他说,"我猜想,这不关我的事啊。"他暂停一会儿,然后补充道:"但是,我和你今天就会好得多——要是那样的话。"

"要是哪样的话?"

"要是由我负责的话。"

"康拉德,你到底什么意思啊?"

"我只是想说,曾经那么一段时间,如果你不是突然之间决定撇下我的话,这一切的悲惨境遇都不会发生在你我身上。我们会结婚,依然是幸福的一对儿。"

他的脸突然之间变得尖锐起来,很是异常。

"撇下你?"

"对我是一个相当大的打击啊,安娜。"

"哦,天呐,"她说,"可是,在那个年龄段,你撇下我,我撇下你,是常有的事儿,难道不是吗?"

"我怎么会知道,"康拉德说。

"为了那件事儿,你不会还在生我的气吧?"

"生气!"他说。"老天啊,安娜!生气是小孩子丢失玩具时候的情绪啊!而我丢失了一个妻子啊!"

她盯着他,说不出话来。

"告诉我,"他继续说,"难道你一点也想不到我当时的感受吗?"

"可是,康拉德,我们当时太*年轻*,不懂事啊。"

"那件事毁了我,安娜。那件事就差让我彻底毁掉了。"

"可是,怎么会……"

"什么怎么会?"

"要是那件事儿意义如此重大,你怎么会转身就走,几周后又跟另外一个女孩订婚了呢?"

"你从未听说过心灰意懒这个词儿吗?"他问道。

她点着头,眼睛沮丧地凝视着他。

"安娜,我当时疯狂地爱着你。"

她没有回答。

"很抱歉,"他说。"刚才犯傻,一通发泄,请原谅。"

长时间的沉默。

康拉德在椅子上将身体向后靠去,从远处打量着她,只见她从烟盒里又拿出一支香烟,随后点燃。然后,她熄灭火柴,将火柴杆小心地放进烟灰缸。她再次抬起头时,他仍然看着她。他那遥远的眼神中透射出一种热切的神情。

"你在想什么呢?"她问。

他没有回答。

"康拉德,"她说,"对我过去的所为,你还恨我吗?"

"恨你?"

"对,恨我。我有一种异样的感觉,认为你恨我。我敢肯定,你恨我,尽管这么多年已经过去。"

"安娜,"他说。

"嗯,什么事儿,康拉德?"

他猛地将椅子往桌子跟前拉了一下,身体前倾。"你的心里是否曾经想过……?"

他没往下说。

她等待着。

突然之间,他庄重地看着她,眼神是那么的热切,引得她向前靠了靠。

"我的心里曾经想过什么?"她问。

"想过这样一个事实:我和你……我们两个人……有点未尽事宜。"

她盯着他看。

他的两只眼睛如星星般闪亮,也看向她。"拜托,"他说,"别那么大惊小怪。"

"大惊小怪?"

"看你那样,就好像我刚才要求你跟我一起从窗户跳出去似的。"

现在,屋子里聚满了人,变得吵闹不堪,如同参加鸡尾酒会一般,只有大声喊叫,对方才能听得见。

康拉德两只眼睛落在她的脸上,等待着她的回答,充满了急切、渴望的神情。

"我想再来一杯马提尼,"她说。

"必须喝吗?"

"是的,"她说,"必须喝。"

她一生中,只跟一个男人做过爱,那就是她的丈夫埃德蒙。

那种感觉总是美不可言。

做过三千次爱?

她想,不止三千次,或许要多得多。谁会去数数有多少次呢?

尽管没人去数,但是,为了深入这个话题,可以假设一下(因为实际上一定会有一个准确的数字),这个准确次数的数字是三千六百八十……

……而且,每次行房都是在同样一个女人和同样一个男人之间进行的,每次做爱都是一种不掺杂质的、激情四溢的、真情实感的行

第一章 不堪回首 第二节 《最后之举》The Last Act

为……

……接下来,在第三千六百八十一次的时候,一个全新的人、一个自己不爱的陌生人突然之间闯了进来,甚至是在半推半就的情况下闯了进来,这究竟该如何是好?

他这就叫擅自闯入。

以前所有的记忆都会喷涌而出。就算是轻松躺着,这些记忆也会令她窒息身亡。

回想几个月前,在跟雅各布斯医生的一次会面中,她就这一点向医生提出了疑问,老雅各布斯医生当时说:"我亲爱的库珀太太,浮现以前的记忆是荒谬愚蠢的举动。我希望你忘掉那些记忆,现在可以存在的只有目前的东西。"

"可问题是,我如何才能到达那个地步?"她当时说。"我如何才能一下子鼓足勇气上楼,走进卧室,身体里流淌着的是冰冷的血,当着一个新人、一个陌生人的面,宽衣解带……?"

"冰冷的血!"他大叫起来。"老天啊,我说女士,那是热血沸腾啊!"后来,医生对她说:"不管在什么情况下,库珀太太,你一定得相信我的话。我对你说啊,不管是哪名女子经过了二十多年的房事磨炼后,被剥夺了性爱的权利——如果我理解正确的话,对于你而言,你被剥夺了异乎寻常频繁的性爱的权利——这名女子就会持续不断地遭受严重的心理性紊乱之苦,直到以前的常规重新建立起来为止。你现在感觉好多了,这点我知道,但是,我有责任告诉你,你绝没有恢复正常的……"

面对着康拉德,安娜说道:"这个提议不会碰巧是一个治疗学方面的方法吧,对不对?"

"一个什么?"

"一个治疗学方面的方法。"

"你到底想说什么呢?"

"这听起来,简直就像我的医生雅各布斯策划出来的一个情节啊。"

"听着,"他说。现在,他越过桌子向前倚去,一个手指尖触碰到她的左手。"以前与你相识的时候,我过于年轻、过于紧张,那样的提议未能说出口,尽管我很想说。当时,不管怎么说,我认为凡事不用操之过急,那样做没有任何的必要。我当时寻思着,我们前方还有整个一辈子的时间呢。可谁曾想,你会撇下我呢。"

安娜要的马提尼酒送过来了,她随即端起酒,快速喝了起来。她清清楚楚地知道,酒会对她产生什么样的影响——会令她飘飘欲仙,而第三杯马提尼总是会达到这样的效果。给她喝下三杯马提尼酒,用不了几秒钟的时间,她的身体就会处于完全失重的状态,她就会像一缕氢气满屋子飘浮。

她坐在那儿,双手握着酒杯,那酒杯就好似一件圣物。接着,她又喝下一大口,杯子里现在没有剩下多少酒了。通过杯子的边沿看出去,她看到康拉德正看着她喝酒,一边看,一边却表现出不以为然的神态。她冲着他微笑,笑得光彩照人。

"做手术的时候,你不反对使用麻醉剂,对不?"她问道。

"安娜,拜托你,不要那样说话。"

"我开始飘浮起来了,"她说。

"这我看出来了,"他回应道。"你为什么不就此打住?"

"你说什么呢?"

"我是说,为什么不停止喝酒?"

"你想让我告诉你原因吗?"

"不想,"他回答。他的双手轻轻向前移动一下,好像要从她手中将杯子拿走似的。于是,她快速将杯子靠到嘴唇上,高高地倾斜酒杯,就这样持续了好几秒,好让最后一滴酒流入嘴中。再次抬起头看着康拉德的时候,她发现他将一张十美元的钞票放到侍者的托盘上,听见侍者说:"谢谢您,先生。真的谢谢您。"接下来,她知道的是,她飘浮着走出了酒吧,穿过宾馆的前厅。康拉德的一只手托着她的一只胳膊肘的下方,引导着她走向电梯。接着,他俩飘上了二十二楼,沿着走廊走向她住的卧室门口。她从自己的小钱袋里摸出钥匙,打开房门,漂移进屋。康拉德跟在她身后,随手带上了门。接着,突然之间,他一下子抓住了她,将她揽入自己巨大的臂弯里,如饥似渴地对她狂吻起来。

她任由他狂吻。

他将她的嘴、面颊、脖子吻了个遍,一边狂吻,一边喘着粗气。她没有闭眼,以一种怪异的、超然的方式看着他。用这种方式看到的景象,让她模模糊糊地想起一名牙医脸部模糊的特写镜头:牙医正在研究她口腔上部的一颗后牙。

接下来,突然之间,康拉德将舌头伸入她的一只耳朵,这对她产生的是触电般的效果,就如同一只通上了二百伏特电压**的插头被推进空插座一般——所有的灯一下子都亮了起来。此时此刻,她的骨头开始融化,溶化后炎热的汁液流淌进她的四肢。于是,她春心荡漾,一下子爆发出来,进入一种极度兴奋的癫狂状态——妙不可言、无所畏惧、熊熊燃烧,而这种状态在过去逝去的时光里,埃德蒙只要在她的手部的这儿或那儿触摸一下,就会经常性地被激发出来。她的双臂紧紧搂住康拉德的脖子,开始以热吻回应他,而且吻得比他所有的吻更加如饥似渴。他想,她刚一开始吻的时候,看起来好像要将他活吞下去。但是很快,他就掌控了局面,恢复到方才的状态。

他们站在那儿如此激烈地拥吻着,拥吻了多长时间,安娜丝毫的概念都没有,但是,时间一定是相当的长。安娜感到如此的幸福,如此的……如此的*信心*十足。最终,她再一次变得信心十足——突然之间信心喷涌而出,势不可挡,她甚至想扯开衣服,在屋子中间为康拉德疯狂地跳一支舞。但是,她最终还是没有做出这样的愚蠢之举。正好相反,她却飘走了,飘到了床边,坐了下来,急促地呼吸起来,而康拉德则快速坐到她身边。她将头倚靠在他的胸部,容光焕发地坐在那儿,他则轻轻地抚摸着她的头发。接着,她解开他衬衫上的一个扣子,将手滑了进去,贴到他的胸部。抚摸着他的肋骨,她感觉到了他的心跳。

"在这儿,我看到了什么呢?"康拉德说。

"在哪儿,你看到了什么呢,我亲爱的?"

"在你的头皮上。你得看看这儿,安娜。"

"你替我看看吧,我最亲爱的。"

"说正经的，"他说，"你知道这看起来像什么吗？这看起来有一点点雄激素性脱发的迹象。"

"很好。"

"不，不是很好。实际上，这是毛囊出现了炎症，会导致秃顶，这在上了年纪的女性身上相当常见。"

"哦，闭嘴，康拉德，"她边说，边亲吻他脖子的一侧。"我的一头秀发棒极了。"

她端坐在床边，将他的夹克衫拽下，接着，她解下他的领带，撇到屋子的另一头。

"我衣服后面有一个小小的搭钩，"她说。"拜托把这个搭钩解开。"

康拉德解开了搭钩，拉开了拉链，帮她脱下了衣服。她穿的是一件漂亮的、淡蓝色的宽松衬裙，康拉德穿的是一件普通的白色衬衫，做医生的经常穿这样的衬衫。可是现在，康拉德的衬衫领口敞开着，这跟他很相配，因为他的脖子两侧各有一条小小的凸起肌腱垂直向上伸展，而且，他一转头，皮肤里的肌腱就随之移动。在安娜眼里，这是世界上最美的脖子。

"我们俩慢慢、慢慢地进行，"她说。"再慢慢达到我们期盼的痴狂的状态啊。"

他的眼睛在她的脸上停留了一会，然后下移，将她的身体自上而下看了个遍。同时，她发现他微笑起来。

"康拉德，我们要一瓶香槟，多些情调，放纵一下，可以吗？我可以叫房间服务。香槟拿进来的时候，你可以藏到浴室里。"

"不行，"他说。"你已经喝得够多了。请站起来。"

他说话的语调使她一下子就站了起来。

"到这儿来，"他说。

她靠近了他，他依然坐在床上。现在，他用不着起身，只是向前一伸手，就开始脱她身上剩下的衣服——不慌不忙、从容不迫。突然之间，他的脸变得有几分灰白。

"哦，亲爱的，"她说，"多么妙不可言啊！你身上出现那种传说中有名的东西啦！你两只耳朵的每一侧都出现了一团厚实的毛发啊！你知道那意味着什么，是吧？那绝对是好的迹象，表明你有巨大的阳刚之气啊！"她弯下身，亲吻他的一只耳朵，他则继续脱她身上的衣物——胸罩、鞋、紧身褡、短裤，最后脱的是长筒袜，然后，他将脱下来的衣物扔到地板上，堆成了一堆。就在他将她最后一只长筒袜剥离下来、扔到地板上的同时，他转过身去——身体急转过去，就好像她根本不存在似的。现在，他开始脱自己的衣服。

她身上除了皮肤，已经是一丝不挂。她就这样站在那儿，离他如此的近，而他甚至连看也没再看她一眼，这种感觉相当怪异。或许，男人就是这样行事的，但是，埃德蒙也许是个例外。具体如何，她又怎么会知道？康拉德先将自己的白衬衫脱掉，仔仔细细地叠好，然后站起身，拿起衬衫走到一把椅子那儿，将衬衫在椅子的一只把手上放好。紧接着，他脱衬衣，也如法炮制。然后，他又坐到床边，开始脱鞋。安娜一动不动地待在那儿，眼睛看着他。他情绪的突然转变，以及他的沉默不语，还有令人奇怪的专注，使她感到有一点儿害怕，但同时，也使她兴奋。他的行为中有种不为人知的因素，几乎含有一种危险的成分，感觉他就好像是某种大型动物，正轻柔地迈步，走向猎物。对，一只花斑豹。

她看着他，犹如被催眠一般着了迷。她看着他的手指——外科医生的手指，只见那些手指解开了左脚上那只鞋的鞋带，将鞋带松了松，轻轻把鞋从脚上移下来，然后整齐地将鞋放入床底下——鞋的一半伸进床底，另一半则露了出来。接着，开始脱另一只鞋，也是一样的脱法。然后，他开始脱袜子，先脱左脚的，后脱右脚的，两只袜子叠放到一起，分毫不差地横放在两只鞋的足尖部位。最后，这些手指向上移动，移动到裤子的顶部，解开裤子上的一颗纽扣，接着开始对拉链操作起来。裤子脱下后，他将其沿着裤线折叠好，然后拿到椅子那儿，在椅子上放好。随后，脱内裤，也如法炮制。

现在，康拉德赤身裸体，走回床边，坐了下来。最终，他转过头，注意到了她的存在。她站在那儿，等待着……浑身发抖。他看着她，慢慢地上下打量起来。接着，他冷不防"嗖"的一下伸出一只手，抓住了她的手腕,猛地一拉,她就四肢朝上横躺到床上了。

这种放松感是巨大的。安娜甩开双臂搂住了他,将他紧紧地拉向自己,哇,拉得太紧啦,唯恐他脱身而走。她怕得要死,生怕他脱身而走、不再回来。他们俩就这样躺在那儿:她紧紧将他搂住,就好像他是这个世界上剩下的、她唯一可以抓住的东西,而他则表现得出奇的安静,警惕地这儿看看、那儿看看,表情热切、专注,慢悠悠地从她的缠绕中解脱出来。现在,他开始用他的那些手指——外科医生娴熟的手指——在她身上一系列不同的部位触摸起来,弄得她再一次陷入极度兴奋的癫狂状态。

接下来的短暂时间里,他做出的动作既令人震惊,又妙不可言。她清楚,他只是要让她准备好,让她进入状态。或者,像医院里的人说的那样,让她做好准备,以便做手术。噢,天呐,可是,就连眼前这样微乎其微的准备活动,她一丁点儿都不了解,或者说,从未经历过。一切都来得非常之快,因为在她看来不过是几秒钟的时间里,她就到达了令她无法忍受的那一点,到了那一点她再也无法返回了。此时此刻,整个房间仿佛被压缩成一粒炫目的微小光斑,这粒光斑只要轻轻再去碰一下,就会爆炸,将人撕成碎片。就在这个节骨眼儿上,康拉德迅速向上一翻,身体划出一个抛物线的轨迹,一下子翻到了她的身体上面,要贪婪地做出最后之举。

至此,安娜感觉,自己的激情正从身体内被抽取出来,就像一根长长的带电神经——犹如一根长长的带电细线——正被人从身体里往外抽。抽的同时,她冲着康拉德大喊,继续、继续,不要停手。她就这样大喊着,喊到一半的时候,她听到从她自己上方某个部位传来另一个声音。这个声音不是她自己发出的,可变得越来越大、越来越大,而且,越来越连续,连续不断,经久不衰,非要让人听到不可:

"我是说,你藏了什么东西没有?"说话的人想知道答案。

"哦,亲爱的,你说的是什么东西呢?"

"我一直在问你,你藏了什么东西没有?"

"谁?我吗?"

"这个地方有点阻碍感。你一定是戴了避孕帽,或者类似的器具。"

"当然没有啦,亲爱的。一切都美不可言。哦,别再出声啦。"

"*哪有那么妙不可言啊,安娜*。"

整个房间就像银幕上的一幅图片,又变得清晰起来。图片的前景是康拉德的脸,从裸露的肩膀上伸出来,悬吊在她的上方。他那双眼睛笔直看着她的眼睛,嘴却依然说个不停。

"要是你使用装置的话,那么,看在老天的分上,要学会采用正确的方式。没有什么能比粗心大意的放置更令人恼火的啦。避孕帽一定要靠后放置,靠到子宫颈上。"

"可是,我什么都没有戴呀!"

"没有吗?那么,怎么还有阻碍的感觉啊。"

现在,不仅仅是整个房间,就连整个世界也似乎开始从她的身底下慢慢地滑走了。

"我感到恶心,"她说。

"你什么?"

"我感到恶心。"

"安娜,别像孩子那么幼稚。"

"康拉德,我想请你走开,现在就走吧。"

"你到底在说什么呢?"

"从我这儿走开,康拉德!"

"岂有此理,安娜。好吧,我刚刚说话了,很抱歉。就这样吧。"

"*走开!*"安娜大喊,"*走开!走开!走开!*"

她尽力将他推开,但是,他块头很大,人很强壮,令她无法动弹。

"你冷静一下,"他说。"放松。你不能像这样突然间说翻脸就翻脸,这一切才进行到一半啊。看在老天的分上,不要哭了。"

"让我一个人待着,康拉德,我求你了。"

他似乎用到了身体上所有部位才将她抓紧——胳膊、胳膊肘、手、手指、大腿、膝盖、脚、脚踝等都用上了。他将她贴得牢牢的,那架势简直太像一只癞蛤蟆——大个头的、紧紧攀附着的癞蛤蟆,抓紧、抓牢,不让她挣脱。有一次,她看见过一只癞蛤蟆,跟他现在所作所为一模一样。当时,它正跟一只青蛙在一条小溪边的一块石头上交尾,只见它蹲坐在那儿,一动不动的,一只眼睛里闪着不怀好意的黄色微光,用两只强有力的前爪紧紧攀附着青蛙,不让其脱身,看着就令人反感……

"现在,安娜,不要奋力挣脱了,你的行为就像一个歇斯底里的小孩子。看在老天的分上,女人,你有什么可担心的呢?"

"你把我弄疼了!"她叫道。

"把你弄疼了?"

"弄得我疼得厉害啊!"

她跟他说这话,仅仅是想让他放开手。

"你知道为什么会疼吗?"他问道。

"拜托,康拉德!"

"安娜,现在等一分钟,允许我解释……"

"不,"她奋力挣扎,意欲脱身,但是,他仍然紧紧贴住,令她无法动弹。

"疼痛的原因是,"他继续说,"你没有分泌出任何的液体。实际上,黏膜干燥得……"

"住嘴!"

"实际的名称是老年萎缩性阴道炎。安娜,这种病是随着年龄的增加而产生的,称其为老年阴道炎,原因就在于此。对此,人是无能为力地去……"

就在那时,她开始尖声喊叫。喊叫声不是很大,但她的确是在喊叫——是一种极其可怕的、痛苦不堪的、难以忍受的喊叫。听了几秒钟这样的喊叫之后,康拉德以一个优雅的动作,一下子从她身上翻滚下来,双手将她推向一边。由于用力过猛,一下子将她推倒在地板上。

她慢慢地爬了起来,摇摇晃晃地走进浴室,边走边喊:"埃德蒙!……埃德蒙!……埃德蒙!……"声音很怪异,似乎是在乞求。浴室的门随即关上。

康拉德静静地躺在那儿,听着门后边传出来的声音。起先,他听

第一章 不堪回首　第二节 《最后之举》*The Last Act*

到的仅仅是这位女子啜泣的声音,但是几秒钟过后,他听见柜橱被打开时金属物发出的咔嗒声。转瞬之间,他坐起身,用手一撑,从床上一跃而下,开始以极快的速度穿衣服。他的那些衣服早已平平整整地叠好、放在那儿,穿起来很方便,因此呢,不出两三分钟的工夫,他就穿上了衣服。穿好后,他穿过屋子走到镜子前,用手绢将脸上的口红印记擦去。然后,他从自己的衣兜里掏起一把梳子,梳理一下他那头细细的黑发。然后,又一次绕着床走了一圈,看看有没有落下什么东西。接着,就像是一个人蹑手蹑脚离开孩子正在里面睡觉的房间,他小心谨慎地跨出门,轻轻地将门随手带上,来到了走廊。

第二章 冤冤相报

在中国的影视及文学作品中,特别是武侠类作品中,常常会听到或看到这样一句话:"冤冤相报何时了,得饶人处且饶人。"剖析开来,若做不到"得饶人处且饶人"的话,那结果只能是"冤冤相报何时了"了。具体来说,凡事不要做得太绝,要留有一定的余地,因为理解和误解都是相互的。理解可以形成良性循环,而误解则如同瘟疫,会迅速蔓延,造成可怕的连锁反应。按照中国的传统思想,我们要以德报怨,以直报怨,或者以德报德,万万不可冤冤相报而深陷"怪圈"。

"冤冤相报"应为佛家用语,按照目前的解释,至少有两层意思,一个意思是指冤仇终会有报应,另一个意思是指仇人互相报复,但后一个意思用的较多。宋代洪迈在《夷坚丙志·安氏冤》中写道:"汝既有冤,吾不汝治,但曩事岁月已久,冤冤相报,宁有穷期"(商务印书馆辞书研究中心,2002:925);元末凌濛初在其编著的拟话本小说集《初刻拍案惊奇》中写道:"至于佛家果报说六道众生,尽是眷属冤冤相报,杀杀相寻,就说他几年也说不了";清代小说家曹雪芹在《红楼梦》第五回中写道:"冤冤相报自非轻,分离聚合皆前定。"这真是迎合了那句老话"冤冤相报何时了"啊。

在英国作家罗尔德·达尔笔下,不管从哪层意思来看,都可寻到"冤冤相报"的踪迹。在《最后颂歌》中,主人公莱昂内尔偶然间从格拉迪斯·庞森比女士那里听到了自己的女朋友珍妮特·德佩拉贾对自己的一些"负面"的看法,令他窘迫难当,于是,他决定采用一种方式报复一下自己的女朋友,而受到报复后的女朋友则不动声色,采用另一种方式反过来给了主人公莱昂内尔来了个"致命"的回击性报复;在《复仇公司》中,那些实施人身攻击的专栏作家遭到了报复,报复他们的貌似主人公组建的"复仇公司",实质是那些受尽侮辱的当事人,但是,谁又能知道"复仇公司"组建者的命运最终会怎样呢?

还是让我们走进罗尔德·达尔的世界,去体会那冤冤相报的结局吧。

第一节 《最后颂歌》Nunc Dimittis

罗尔德·达尔的《最后颂歌》(Nunc Dimittis)首次发表在《科利尔周刊》(Collier's Weekly,也有人译作《柯里尔》《科里尔》或《柯莱尔斯》)1953年9月4日出版的那一期上,当时的题目叫《阴险的单身汉》(The Devious Bachelor)。后来,这篇小说以《最后颂歌》(Nunc Dimittis)这个标题被收录到《罗尔德·达尔短篇故事集锦》(The Collected Short Stories of Roald Dahl)、《如你之人》(Someone like You)、《五部畅销书集》(5 Bestsellers)、《出乎意料的故事集》(Tales of the Unexpected)、《完全出人意料故事集》(Completely Unexpected Tales)、《罗尔德·达尔选集》(The Roald Dahl Omnibus)以及《罗尔德·达尔二十九篇成人故事集》(Twenty Nine Kisses from Roald Dahl)等书中。此外,这部小说还被改编成电视系列剧——1980年5月3日播映的《出乎意料的故事集》(Tales of the Unexpected)第二部中的第10集(Episode 2.10),可见其影响力之大。

也许是出于作品所发表的不同媒体的考虑吧,罗尔德·达尔具有给自己几乎相同内容的作品冠以不同标题的倾向,例如,这部小说发表在《艾勒里·昆恩悬疑小说杂志》(Ellery Queen's Mystery Magazine)135期上时,标题是《行家的复仇》(A Connoisseur's Revenge);《南方来客》(*Man from the South*)①发表在《科利尔周刊》时,标题叫《收藏品》(*Collector's Item*);《创世新灾》(*Genesis and Catastrophe*)②发表在《花花公子》(*Playboy*)杂志时,标题为《优秀之子》(*A Fine Son*);还有就是,达尔的两部带有寓言性质的短篇小说,内容和情节几乎相同,但结局似乎有所不同,标题却迥然不同,分别为《熏制奶酪》(*Smoked Cheese*)和《倒立之鼠》(*The Upsidedown Mice*)③,可见达尔驾驭自己作品的不凡功力和随机应变的灵活性。

一、原作导读

这篇小说情节较为曲折,可谓一波三折,跌宕起伏。读者心中所有的悬疑,到了故事结尾处,才得以释放,顿生豁然开朗的感觉。

这篇小说是以第一人称"我"(名叫"莱昂内尔·兰普森")的视角展开的,但跟罗尔德·达尔其他很多作品中的"我"不同的是,本篇的叙述者"我"不是"隐身"的,而是具有举足轻重的地位,其作用不仅仅是"纽带"或者"桥梁",而是整部小说的主体。

莱昂内尔·兰普森是个"钻石王老五"级别的人物,喜欢精美的艺术品,也喜欢跟上层社会的人为伍。一天晚上在阿申登家赴宴完毕,他开车送格拉迪斯·庞森比女士回家。在他的眼里,格拉迪斯丑陋不堪、个头矮小……反正,他对她没有什么好印象。当时,格拉迪斯小姐已经有了几分醉意,但还要挽留莱昂内尔,要他"临回家前喝最后一杯"(one for the road)。万般无奈,他只好答应。其间,格拉迪斯向莱昂内尔炫耀自己花大价钱让名声大噪的男画家约翰·罗伊登为她本人画一幅全身肖像画,并道出这位画家画所有女性肖像画的

---

① 关于这篇小说,感兴趣的读者可参阅本研究所成系列书的第1卷第一章第一节。
② 关于这篇小说,感兴趣的读者可参阅本研究所成系列书的第3卷第四章第一节。
③ 关于这两部作品,感兴趣的读者可参阅本书第三章的第一节和第二节。

秘密:先画女子躶体的画像,再画穿内衣的,最后画正常穿衣服的,后画的叠加到先前的画面上。这个"秘密"虽然让莱昂内尔震惊,却令他一下子明白一个问题:为什么全城有钱的女性都争先恐后要请约翰·罗伊登给自己画像?紧接着,格拉迪斯话题一转,带有挑拨之意谈起了莱昂内尔和珍妮特·德佩拉贾之间关系,并将自己当天下午从珍妮特本人那里听到的话跟他讲了一遍。当然,珍妮特那些话都是一些不中听的、责备莱昂内尔行为的话语,诸如"令人厌倦透顶的老家伙"(crashing old bore)之类话语,令莱昂内尔颜面扫地,无地自容,当场昏厥过去。

那个可怕的晚上剩下时间里所发生的事情,我几乎什么都记不起来了,就有一点除外:我模模糊糊记得,却又颇感不安地猜疑,感觉当时好像任由格拉迪斯·庞森比以各种不同的方式对我加以安慰。后来,我相信我走出了那所房子,坐上车回到了家。可是,我对周围的一切几乎没有任何意识,直到第二天早晨从床上醒来,意识才得以恢复。

I can remember practically nothing of the rest of that terrible night except for a vague and disturbing suspicion that when I regained consciousness I broke down completely and permitted Gladys Ponsonby to comfort me in a variety of different ways. Later, I believe I walked out of the house and was driven home, but I remained more or less unconscious of everything around me until I woke up in my bed the next morning.

意识恢复之后的莱昂内尔想到了约翰·罗伊登奇特的绘画技法,发誓要借此报复一下珍妮特。他不惜重金请约翰给珍妮特画像,但告诉约翰说,画像的事儿出于某种原因不想让珍妮特知道。然后,他出国度假,目的是等待画作的完成。四个月后,莱昂内尔返回,珍妮特的肖像画如期完成,参加展出,好评如潮。展出完毕,约翰将画如约递送给莱昂内尔。身为绘画清理和复原方面专家的莱昂内尔则迫不及待地开始了马不停蹄的清理工作……最后,画布上只剩下真人大小的珍妮特,赤裸着身体站在他的面前。

莱昂内尔邀请珍妮特和社会所有名流到自己家共进晚宴。席间,他玩起了"烛光晚餐"的游戏,有意不点灯,让餐厅处于昏暗之中。宴会行将结束之际,他让女仆"啪"地点亮了电灯,让珍妮特的躶体肖像画暴露于众目睽睽之下……随即,莱昂内尔溜出了房间。就在离开房间那一刻,他看到了令他终身难忘的一幕。

这一幕是关于珍妮特的,只见她双手举到空中停住,犹如冻僵一般直挺挺的。这之前,她正向桌子对面的某个人打招呼呢。她的嘴向下张开,超过五厘米宽。僵住之际,就带着这副表情——吃惊不已、懵懂不解,恰似一秒钟之前,她被一枪毙命,子弹正穿心脏。

It was Janet, with both hands in mid-air, stopped, frozen rigid, caught in the act of gesticulating towards someone across the table. Her mouth had dropped open two inches and she wore the surprised, not-quite-understanding look of a person who precisely one second before has been shot dead, right through the heart.

这一行为给莱昂内尔带来的快乐情绪还没有持续多久,就被两天后一个早晨的电话给浇灭了。电话是珍妮特打来的,电话里说,他所有的朋友都不搭理他,不再跟他交往了,但是,除她之外。接下来,他收到一个邮包,里面附带一封信,是珍妮特寄来的道歉信,她在信中表示原谅了他的行为,永远爱他,认为那是他无心开的一个玩笑,还寄给他一罐鱼子酱——那可是他最喜欢吃的、无论如何都无法抗拒的美味佳肴啊。于是,莱昂内尔转"喜"为"忧",情绪由最高点一下子跌落到最低点。但是,莱昂内尔却没有因此而忘记吃些鱼子酱来安慰一下对自己对珍妮特的愧疚。他一连吃下好几勺珍妮特寄来的美味鱼子酱。

甚至有可能吃下的有点儿太多了,因为在刚刚过去的约一小时之内,我一直感觉不太精神。或许,我应该立即上楼取些小苏打服用一下。等身体状况好转,我可以轻轻松松回来,将剩下的吃完。

It is even possible that I took a shade too much, because I haven't been feeling any too chipper this last hour or so. Perhaps I ought to go up right away and get myself some bicarbonate of soda. I can easily come back and finish this later, when I'm in better trim.

二、原作释读

虽然没有过多的生僻词,这篇小说阅读起来还是具有一定的难度。其中,理解好小说起始部分的铺垫至关重要,还要将开始部分与结尾参照起来,才能更好地理解故事最终的走向。其中英国英语的一些非正式的表达以及一些古旧的用词,恐怕是理解本篇小说的障碍。

Nunc Dimittis[①]

It is nearly midnight, and I can see that if I don't make a start with writing this story now, I never shall. All evening I have been sitting here trying to force myself to begin, but the more I have thought about it, the

---

① 本部小说原文出自"DAHL, R. *The Collected Short Stories of Roald Dahl*. London: Penguin Books Ltd., 1992"。

Nunc Dimittis: the Song of Simeon(Luke 2:29-32)used as a canticle in Christian liturgy, especially at compline and evensong 西缅祷词(见《路加福音》第 2 章 29-32 节,尤在晚祷或夜歌时用作基督教礼拜仪式中的赞美诗)

其英文版的第一句是这样的:
Now Thou dost dismiss Thy servant, O Lord, according to Thy word in peace.
主啊,如今可以照你的话释放仆人安然去世。

more appalled① and ashamed and distressed I have become by the whole thing.

    My idea—and I believe it was a good one—was to try, by a process of confession and analysis, to discover a reason or at any rate some justification② for my outrageous③ behaviour towards Janet de Pelagia. I wanted, essentially, to address myself to an imaginary and sympathetic listener, a kind of mythical④ *you*, someone gentle and understanding to whom I might tell unashamedly every detail of this unfortunate episode. I can only hope that I am not too upset to make a go of it.

    If I am to be quite honest with myself, I suppose I shall have to admit that what is disturbing me most is not so much the sense of my own shame, or even the hurt that I have inflicted upon poor Janet; it is the knowledge that I have made a monstrous fool of myself and that all my friends—if I can still call them that—all those warm and lovable people who used to come so often to my house, must now be regarding me as nothing but a vicious, vengeful⑤ old man. Yes, that surely hurts. When I say to you that my friends were my whole life—everything, absolutely

---

    ①   appal or appall: *Verb* [with obj.] (often as "be appalled") greatly dismay or horrify 使惊骇;使恐惧(e. g. Bankers are appalled at the economic incompetence of some ministers. 银行家因一些部长在经济问题上的无能而感到震惊。)

    ②   justification: *Noun* reasonable grounds for complaint, defence, etc 正当的理由;辩解的理由(e. g. There's no justification for dividing the company into smaller units. 没有理由把公司划分成小单位。)

    ③   outrageous: *Adjective* shockingly bad or excessive 丑恶的;肆无忌惮的;毫无节制的;难以容忍的(e. g. an outrageous act of bribery 肆无忌惮的贿赂行为。)

    ④   mythical: *Adjective* fictitious 杜撰的;虚构的(e. g. a mythical customer whose name appears in brochures 小手册里有名有姓、实际却是子虚乌有的顾客)

    ⑤   vengeful: *Adjective* seeking to harm someone in return for a perceived injury 图谋报复的(e. g. a vengeful ex-con 图谋报复的前罪犯)

everything in it—then perhaps you will begin to understand.

  Will you? I doubt it unless I digress① for a minute to tell you roughly the sort of person I am.

  Well—let me see. Now that I come to think of it, I suppose I am, after all, a type; a rare one, mark you②, but nevertheless a quite definite type—the wealthy, leisurely, middle-aged man of culture, adored (I choose the word carefully) by his many friends for his charm, his money, his air of scholarship, his generosity, and I sincerely hope for himself also. You will find him (this type) only in the big capitals—London, Paris, New York; of that I am certain. The money he has was earned by his dead father whose memory he is inclined to despise③. This is not his fault, for there is something in his make-up④ that compels him secretly to look down upon all people who never had the wit to learn the

---

  ① digress: *Verb* [no obj.] leave the main subject temporarily in speech or writing(演讲或写作)离题(e. g. I have digressed a little from my original plan. 我有点偏离我原先的计划了。)

  ② mark you: (chiefly Brit.) used to emphasize or draw attention to a statement(主要为英国英语用法)注意;听着(e. g. I was persuaded, against my better judgement, mark you, to vote for him. 我被说服投了他的票,请注意,这不符合我的理智判断。)

  ③ despise: *Verb* [with obj.] feel contempt or a deep repugnance for 鄙视;厌恶(e. g. He despised himself for being selfish. 他厌恶自己的自私。)

  ④ make-up: *Noun* the combination of qualities that form a person's temperament 性格;气质(e. g. a curiously unexpected timidity in his make-up 他性格中让人难以预料的令人奇怪稍微胆怯)

difference between Rockingham and Spode①, Waterford② and Venetian, Sheraton and Chippendale, Monet③ and Manet④, or even Pommard⑤ and Montrachet⑥.

---

① Spode: *Noun* [mass noun] (trademark) fine pottery or porcelain made at the factories of the English potter Josiah Spode (1755—1827) or his successors, characteristically consisting of ornately decorated and gilded services and large vases. (商标)斯波德陶瓷(英国陶瓷工匠乔赛亚·斯波德[1755—1827]及后继者制造的装饰华丽的镀金陶瓷餐具和大花瓶。)

② Waterford: *Noun* a county in the south-east of the Republic of Ireland, in the province of Munster; main administrative centre, Dungarvan 沃特福德郡(位于爱尔兰共和国东南部芒斯特省,主要行政中心邓加文。)

③ Claude Monet (1840—1926), French painter. A founder member of the Impressionists, his fascination with the play of light on objects led him to produce series of paintings of single subjects painted at different times of day and under different weather conditions, such as the Water-lilies sequence (1899—1906; 1916 onwards) 克洛德·莫奈(1840—1926,法国画家;印象派创始人之一,对光对物像的影响着迷使他创作描绘一天中不同时间或不同天气中单主题的系列画,如《睡莲》系列[1899—1906;1916 年以后]。)

④ édouard Manet (1832—1883), French painter. He adopted a realist approach which greatly influenced the Impressionists, using pure colour to give a direct unsentimental effect. Notable works: Déjeuner sur l' herbe (1863), Olympia (1865), and A Bar at the Folies-Bergère (1882) 艾杜瓦·马奈(1832—1883,法国画家,他采用的现实主义手法对印象派画家有极大影响,使用纯色来达到直观而冷静的效果。著名作品包括《草地上的午餐》[1863],《奥林匹亚》[1865]和《福里-白热尔的酒吧间》[1882]。)

⑤ Pommard: *Noun* Pommard produces purely red wine—no whites 波马特酒(法国波马特地区只出产红葡萄酒,不出产白葡萄酒。)

⑥ Montrachet: *Noun* [mass noun] a white wine produced in the Montrachet region of France 蒙特拉谢白葡萄酒(产于法国蒙特拉谢地区)

He is, therefore, a connoisseur①, possessing above all things an exquisite taste. His Constables②, Boningtons③, Lautrecs④, Redons⑤, Vuillards⑥, Matthew Smiths⑦ are as fine as anything in the Tate; and be-

---

① connoisseur: Noun an expert judge in matters of taste 鉴赏家;鉴定家;行家(e.g. a connoisseur of music 音乐鉴赏家)

② John Constable (1776—1837), English painter. Among his best-known works are early paintings like Flatford Mill (1817) and The Hay Wain (1821), inspired by the landscape of his native Suffolk. 约翰·康斯特布尔(1776—1837,英国画家;著名作品有从其家乡萨克福郡的风景中获得灵感的早期画作《弗拉特福特磨坊》[1817]和《干草车》[1821]。)

③ Richard Parkes Bonington (1802—1828): British painter 理查德·帕克斯·伯宁顿(1802—1828,英国画家。)

④ Henri Toulouse-Lautrec (1864—1901), French painter and lithographer. His reputation is based on his colour lithographs from the 1890s, depicting actors, music-hall singers, prostitutes, and waitresses in Montmartre; particularly well known is the Moulin Rouge series (1894) 亨利·土鲁兹-罗特列克(1864—1901,法国画家,石版画家;19世纪90年代,他因描绘蒙马特尔地区演员、音乐厅歌手、妓女及女侍者的彩色石版画而出名,尤以《红磨坊》系列[1894]著称。)

⑤ Odilon Redon (1840—1916), French painter and graphic artist. He was a leading exponent of symbolism and forerunner of surrealism, especially in his early charcoal drawings of fantastic or nightmarish subjects. 奥迪隆·雷东(1840—1916,法国画家、版画艺术家,象征主义派主要代表,超现实主义派先驱,早年木炭画中的幻想或噩梦题材集中表现了他的艺术思想。)

⑥ Jean édouard Vuillard (1868-1940), French painter and graphic artist. A member of the Nabi Group, he produced decorative panels, murals, paintings, and lithographs, particularly of domestic interiors and portraits. 让·爱德华·维亚尔(1868—1940,法国画家、平面造型艺术家;作为纳比派画家,他创作了装饰性版画、壁画、油画、平版画,尤其是室内装饰画及肖像画。)

⑦ Matthew Smith (1879—1959): British painter 马修·史密斯(1879—1959,英国画家。)

cause they are so fabulous and beautiful they create an atmosphere of suspense around him in the home, something tantalizing, breathtaking, faintly frightening—frightening to think that he has the power and the right, if he feels inclined, to slash, tear, plunge his fist through a superb Dedham Vale①, a Mont Saint-Victoire, an Aries cornfield, a Tahiti maiden, a portrait of Madame Cezanne. And from the walls on which these wonders hang there issues a little golden glow of splendour, a subtle emanation② of grandeur in which he lives and moves and entertains with a sly nonchalance③ that is not entirely unpractised.

He is invariably a bachelor, yet he never appears to get entangled with the women who surround him, who love him so dearly. It is just possible—and this you may or may not have noticed—that there is a frustration, a discontent, a regret somewhere inside him. Even a slight aberration④.

I don't think I need say any more. I have been very frank. You should know me well enough by now to judge me fairly—and dare I hope it? —to sympathize with me when you hear my story. You may even de-

---

① 这里的"Dedham Vale"是康斯特布尔的画作,下文的"Mont Saint-Victoire""Aries cornfield""Tahiti maiden""Madame Cezanne"分别是塞尚、凡·高、高更、洛埃·立辰斯坦(Roy Lichtenstein,1923—1997)的画作。

② emanation: *Noun* [mass noun] the action or process of issuing from a source 发出;散发(e. g. the risk of radon gas emanation 氡气散发的危险)

③ nonchalance: *Noun* the quality or state of being nonchalant; indifference 漠不关心;无动于衷;冷淡(e. g. He conceals his worries behind a mask of nonchalance. 他装作若无其事,借以掩饰内心的不安。)

④ aberration: *Noun* a departure from what is normal, usual, or expected, typically one that is unwelcome(对正常、一般或预期情况的)偏离;偏差(e. g. They described the outbreak of violence in the area as an aberration. 他们将这一地区出现的暴力行为描述为异常现象。)

cide that much of the blame for what has happened should be placed, not upon me, but upon a lady called Gladys Ponsonby. After all, she was the one who started it. Had I not escorted Gladys Ponsonby back to her house that night nearly six months ago, and had she not spoken so freely to me about certain people, and certain things, then this tragic business could never have taken place.

It was last December, if I remember rightly, and I had been dining with the Ashendens in that lovely house of theirs that overlooks the southern fringe of Regent's park. There were a fair number of people there, but Gladys Ponsonby was the only one beside myself who had come alone. So when it was time for us to leave, I naturally offered to see her safely back to her house. She accepted and we left together in my car; but unfortunately, when we arrived at her place she insisted that I come in and have "one for the road①", as she put it. I didn't wish to seem stuffy②, so I told the chauffeur to wait and followed her in.

Gladys Ponsonby is an unusually short woman, certainly not more than four feet nine or ten, maybe even less than that—one of those tiny persons who gives me, when I am beside her, the comical, rather wobbly③ feeling that I am standing on a chair. She is a widow, a few years younger than me—maybe fifty-three or four, and it is possible that thir-

---

① one for the road: (informal) a final drink, especially an alcoholic one, before leaving for home(非正式)临回家之前喝的最后一杯饮料(尤指酒)

② stuffy: *Adjective* (of a person) not receptive to new or unusual ideas and behaviour; conventional and narrow-minded(人)故步自封的;古板的;保守的;心胸狭窄的

③ wobbly: *Adjective* (of a person or their legs) weak and unsteady from illness, tiredness, or anxiety(人或脚因病、劳累、焦虑等)摇摇晃晃的;晃晃悠悠的

ty years ago she was quite a fetching① little thing. But now the face is loose and puckered② with nothing distinctive about it whatsoever. The individual features, the eyes, the nose, the mouth, the chin, are buried in the folds of fat around the puckered little face and one does not notice them. Except perhaps the mouth, which reminds me—I cannot help it—of a salmon.

In the living-room, as she gave me my brandy, I noticed that her hand was a trifle unsteady. The lady is tired, I told myself, so I mustn't stay long. We sat down together on the sofa and for a while discussed the Ashendens' party and the people who were there. Finally I got up to go.

"Sit down, Lionel," she said. "Have another brandy."

"No, really, I must go."

"Sit down and don't be so stuffy. *I'm* having another one, and the least you can do is keep me company while I drink it."

I watched her as she walked over to the sideboard, this tiny woman, faintly swaying, holding her glass out in front of her with both hands as though it were an offering③; and the sight of her walking like that, so incredibly short and squat and stiff, suddenly gave me the ludicrous④ no-

---

① fetching：*Adjective* attractive 迷人的；有魅力的（e.g. a fetching little garment of pink satin 一件迷人的粉红色缎子小衣服）

② pucker：*Verb* [no obj.]（especially of a person's face or a facial feature）tightly gather or contract into wrinkles or small folds（尤指某人脸部或面貌）起皱；起褶（e.g. The child's face puckered, ready to cry. 孩子皱起脸，就要哭了。）

③ offering：*Noun* a thing offered, especially as a gift or contribution 赠品；捐赠物品（e.g. Everyone transported their offerings to the bring-and-buy stall. 大家都把各自要捐赠的东西送到了慈善义卖市场。）

④ ludicrous：*Adjective* so foolish, unreasonable, or out of place as to be amusing 滑稽有趣的；荒唐可笑的（e.g. It's ludicrous that I have been fined. 太荒唐了，我被罚了款。）

tion that she had no legs at all above the knees.

"Lionel, what are you chuckling about?" She half turned to look at me as she poured the drink, and some of it slopped over the side of the glass.

"Nothing, my dear. Nothing at all."

"Well, stop it, and tell me what you think of my new portrait." She indicated a large canvas hanging over the fireplace that I had been trying to avoid with my eye ever since I entered the room. It was a hideous thing, painted, as I well knew, by a man who was now all the rage① in London, a very mediocre painter called John Royden. It was a full-length portrait of Gladys, Lady Ponsonby, painted with a certain technical cunning② that made her out to be a tall and quite alluring creature.

"Charming," I said.

"Isn't it, though! I'm so glad you like it."

"Quite charming."

"I think John Royden is a genius. Don't you think he's a genius, Lionel?"

"Well—that might be going a bit far."

"You mean it's a little early to say for sure?"

"Exactly."

"But listen, Lionel and I think this will surprise you. John Royden is so sought after now that he won't even *consider* painting anyone for less than a thousand guineas!"

"Really?"

---

① rage: *Noun* (the rage) a widespread temporary enthusiasm or fashion 流行;盛行(e.g. Video and computer games are all the rage. 录像和电脑游戏风靡一时。)

② cunning: *Noun* ingenuity 灵巧;熟练(e.g. What resources of energy and cunning it took just to survive. 需要有怎样的精力和灵巧才能够生存呀。)

"Oh, yes! And everyone's queueing up, simply *queueing up* to get themselves done."

"Most interesting."

"Now take your Mr. Cezanne or whatever his name is. I'll bet *he* never got that sort of money in *his* lifetime."

"Never."

"And you say *he* was a genius?"

"Sort of—yes."

"Then so is Royden," she said, settling herself again on the sofa. "The money proves it."

She sat silent for a while, sipping her brandy, and I couldn't help noticing how the unsteadiness of her hand was causing the rim of the glass to jog① against her lower lip. She knew I was watching her, and without turning her head she swivelled② her eyes and glanced at me cautiously out of the corners of them. "A penny for your thoughts③?"

Now, if there is one phrase in the world I cannot abide④, it is this. It gives me an actual physical pain in the chest and I begin to cough.

"Come on, Lionel. A penny for them."

---

① jog：Verb［with obj.］nudge or knock slightly（用肘）轻推；轻敲；轻碰（e. g. A hand jogged his elbow. 一只手轻轻地碰了碰他的肘部。）

② swivel：Verb［often with adverbial］turn around a point or axis or on a swivel（在转体上，或绕着一点或轴）旋转（e. g. She swivelled her eyes round. 她的眼睛转来转去。）

③ a penny for your thoughts：used in spoken English to ask someone what they are thinking about（用于英语口语）你呆呆地在想什么啦！

④ abide：Verb［with obj.］（can/could not abide）（informal）be unable to tolerate（someone or something）（非正式）无法忍受（某人或某事）（e. g. If there is one thing I cannot abide it is a lack of discipline. 若有什么我不能容忍的事，那就是缺乏纪律。）

I shook my head, quite unable to answer. She turned away abruptly and placed the brandy glass on a small table to her left; and the manner in which she did this seemed to suggest—I don't know why—that she felt rebuffed① and was now clearing the decks② for action. I waited, rather uncomfortable in the silence that followed, and because I had no conversation left in me, I made a great play about smoking my cigar, studying the ash intently and blowing the smoke up slowly towards the ceiling. But she made no move. There was beginning to be something about this lady I did not much like, a mischievous③ brooding④ air that made me want to get up quickly and go away. When she looked around again, she was smiling at me slyly with those little buried eyes of hers, but the mouth—oh, just like a salmon's—was absolutely rigid.

"Lionel, I think I'll tell you a secret."

"Really, Gladys, I simply must get home."

"Don't be frightened, Lionel. I won't embarrass you. You look so frightened all of a sudden."

"I'm not very good at secrets."

"I've been thinking," she said, "you're such a great expert on pictures, this ought to interest you." She sat quite still except for her fingers which were moving all the time. She kept them perpetually twisting and

---

① rebuff: *Verb* [with obj.] reject (someone or something) in an abrupt or ungracious manner 断然拒绝; 回绝; 冷落 (e.g. I asked her to be my wife, and was rebuffed in no uncertain terms. 我要求她做我的妻子，但遭到断然拒绝。)

② clear the decks: prepare for a particular event or goal by dealing with anything beforehand that might hinder progress 为（某活动或某目的）做好准备

③ mischievous: *Adjective* (of an action or thing) causing or intended to cause harm or trouble (行为或事情) 有害的; 恶意中伤的 (e.g. a mischievous allegation for which there is not a shred of evidence 毫无证据的恶意指控)

④ brooding: *Adjective* appearing darkly menacing 阴鸷的; 阴森的

twisting around each other, and they were like a bunch of small white snakes wriggling in her lap.

"Don't you want to hear my secret, Lionel?"

"It isn't that, you know. It's just that it's so awfully late..."

"This is probably the best-kept secret in London. A woman's secret. I suppose it's known to about—let me see—about thirty or forty women altogether. And not a single man. Except him, of course—John Royden."

I didn't wish to encourage her, so I said nothing.

"But first of all, promise—*promise* you won't tell a soul?"

"Dear me!"

"You *promise*, Lionel?"

"Yes, Gladys, all right, I promise."

"Good! Now listen." She reached for the brandy glass and settled back comfortably in the far corner of the sofa. "I suppose you know John Royden paints only women?"

"I didn't."

"And they're always full-length portraits, either standing or sitting—like mine there. Now take a good look at it, Lionel. Do you see how beautifully the dress is painted?"

"Well..."

"Go over and look carefully, please."

I got up reluctantly and went over and examined the painting. To my surprise I noticed that the paint of the dress was laid on so heavily it was actually raised out from the rest of the picture. It was a trick, quite effective in its way, but neither difficult to do nor entirely original.

"You see?" she said. "It's thick, isn't it, where the dress is?"

"Yes."

"But there's a bit more to it than that, you know, Lionel. I think the best way is to describe what happened the very first time I went along for a sitting①." Oh, what a bore this woman is, I thought, and how can I get away?

"That was about a year ago, and I remember how excited I was to be going into the studio of the great painter. I dressed myself up in a wonderful new thing I'd just got from Norman Hartnell②, and a special little red hat, and off I went. Mr. Royden met me at the door, and of course I was fascinated by him at once. He had a small pointed beard and thrilling blue eyes, and he wore a black velvet③ jacket. The studio was huge, with red velvet sofas and velvet chairs—he loves velvet—and velvet curtains and even a velvet carpet on the floor. He sat me down, gave me a drink and came straight to the point. He told me about how he painted quite differently from other artists. In his opinion, he said, there was only one method of attaining perfection when painting a woman's body and I mustn't be shocked when I heard what it was.'

"'I don't think I'll be shocked, Mr. Royden,' I told him."

"'I'm sure you won't either,' he said. He had the most marvellous white teeth and they sort of shone through his beard when he smiled. 'You see, it's like this,' he went on. 'You examine any painting you like of a woman—I don't care who it's by—and you'll see that although the dress may be well painted, there is an effect of artificiality, of flat-

---

① sitting: *Noun* a period of time spent as a model for an artist or photographer 被画像(或照相)的一段时间

② Norman Hartnell (1901—1979), a British fashion designer 诺曼·哈特内尔(1901—1979,英国时装设计师。)

③ velvet: *Noun* [mass noun] a closely woven fabric of silk, cotton, or nylon, that has a thick short pile on one side 丝绒;立绒;天鹅绒(丝、棉或尼龙制)

ness about the whole thing, as though the dress were draped① over a log of wood. And you know why?'"

"'No, Mr. Royden, I don't.'"

"'Because the painters themselves didn't really know what was underneath!'"

Gladys Ponsonby paused to take a few more sips of brandy. "Don't look so startled, Lionel," she said to me. "There's nothing wrong about this. Keep quiet and let me finish. So then Mr. Royden said, 'That's why I insist on painting my subjects first of all in the nude.'"

"'Good Heavens, Mr. Royden!' I exclaimed."

"'If you object to that, I don't mind making a slight concession, Lady Ponsonby,' he said. 'But I prefer it the other way.'"

"'Really, Mr. Royden, I don't know.'"

"'And when I've done you like that,' he went on, 'we'll have to wait a few weeks for the paint to dry. Then you come back and I paint on your underclothing. And when that's dry, I paint on the dress. You see, it's quite simple.'"

"The man's an absolute bounder②!" I cried.

"No, Lionel, no! You're quite wrong. If only you could have heard him, so charming about it all, so genuine and sincere. Anyone could see he really *felt* what he was saying."

"I tell you, Gladys, the man's a bounder!"

"Don't be so silly, Lionel. And anyway, let me finish. The first

---

① drape: Verb [with obj. and adverbial] arrange (cloth or clothing) loosely or casually on or round something 将(布)随便地披在……上；松松围在……上 (e.g. She draped a shawl around her shoulders. 她随便裹了条披肩。)

② bounder: Noun (informal, dated, chiefly Brit.) a dishonourable man(主要为英国英语非正式的古旧用法)不道德的人(e.g. He is nothing but a fortune-seeking bounder. 他只不过是个不讲道德的投机者。)

thing I told him was that my husband (who was alive then) would never agree.'

"'Your husband need never know,' he answered. 'Why trouble him. No one knows my secret except the women I've painted.'"

"And when I protested a bit more, I remember he said, 'My dear Lady Ponsonby, there's nothing immoral about this. Art is only immoral when practised by amateurs. It's the same with medicine. You wouldn't refuse to undress before your doctor, would you?'"

"I told him I would if I'd gone to him for ear-ache. That made him laugh. But he kept on at① me about it and I must say he was very convincing, so after a while I gave in and that was that. So now, Lionel, my sweet, you know the secret." She got up and went over to fetch herself some more brandy.

"Gladys, is this really true?"

"Of course it's true."

"You mean to say that's the way he paints all his subjects?"

"Yes. And the joke is the husbands never know anything about it. All they see is a nice fully clothed portrait of their wives. Of course, there's nothing wrong with being painted in the nude; artists do it all the time. But our silly husbands have a way of objecting to that sort of thing."

"By gad②, the fellow's got a nerve③!"

---

① keep on at: annoy (someone) by making frequent requests 对……纠缠不休(e.g. He'd kept on at her, wanting her to go out with him. 他对她纠缠不休,要她跟他出去。)

② by gad or gad: *Exclamation* (archaic) an expression of surprise or emphatic assertion(古旧用法)哎哟;天呐(用于表示吃惊或加强语气)

③ nerve: (informal) impudence or audacity(非正式)厚脸皮;大胆(e.g. He had the nerve to insult my cooking. 他还有脸对我的烹饪说三道四。)

"I think he's a genius."

"I'll bet he got the idea from Goya①."

"Nonsense, Lionel."

"Of course he did. But listen, Gladys, I want you to tell me something. Did you by any chance know about this... this peculiar technique of Royden's before you went to him?"

When I asked the question she was in the act of pouring the brandy, and she hesitated and turned her head to look at me, a little silky② smile moving the corners of her mouth. "Damn you, Lionel," she said. "You're far too clever. You never let me get away with a single thing."

"So you knew?"

"Of course. Hermione Girdlestone told me."

"Exactly as I thought!"

"There's still nothing wrong."

"Nothing." I said. "Absolutely nothing." I could see it all quite

---

① Goya (1746—1828), Spanish painter and etcher; full name Francisco José de Goya y Lucientes. He is famous for his works treating the French occupation of Spain (1808—1814), including The Shootings of May 3rd 1808 (painting, 1814) and The Disasters of War (etchings, 1810—1814), depicting the cruelty and horror of war. 戈雅(1746—1828,西班牙画家和蚀刻画制作者,全名弗朗西斯科·何塞·德·戈雅-卢西恩特斯,其成名作品描述了1808—1814年法国对西班牙的占领,其中包括绘画《1808年5月3日:枪杀马德里保卫者》[1814]和版画《战争的灾难》[1810—1814],这些作品反映了战争的残酷和恐怖。

② silky: Adjective (of a person or their speech or manner) suave and smooth, especially in a way intended to be persuasive(人及其谈吐或举止)轻柔的;圆滑的;讨好的(e.g. a silky, seductive voice 轻柔且极具魅力的声音)

clearly now. This Royden was indeed a bounder, practising as neat① a piece of psychological trickery as ever I'd seen. The man knew only too well that there was a whole set of wealthy indolent② women in the city who got up at noon and spent the rest of the day trying to relieve their boredom with bridge and canasta③ and shopping until the cocktail hour came along. All they craved was a little excitement, something out of the ordinary, and the more expensive the better. Why the news of an entertainment like this would spread through their ranks like smallpox. I could just see the great plump Hermione Girdlestone leaning over the canasta table and telling them about it... "But my dear, it's *simply* fascinating... I can't *tell* you how intriguing it is... *much* more fun than going to your doctor..."

"You won't tell anyone, Lionel, will you? You promised."

"No, of course not. But now I must go, Gladys, I really must."

"Don't be so silly. I'm just beginning to enjoy myself. Stay till I've finished this drink, anyway."

I sat patiently on the sofa while she went on with her interminable④

---

① neat: *Adjective* (informal, chiefly N. Amer.) very good or pleasant; excellent(主要为北美的非正式用法)顶呱呱的;了不起的;极好的(e.g. I've been taking lessons in tracking from this really neat Indian guide. 我向这位顶呱呱的印第安人向导学习跟踪。)

② indolent: *Adjective* wanting to avoid activity or exertion; lazy 不积极的;懒惰的;懒散的

③ canasta: *Noun* [mass noun] a card game resembling rummy, using two packs. It is usually played by two pairs of partners, and the aim is to collect sets (or melds) of cards 凯纳斯特纸牌戏

④ interminable: *Adjective* endless (often used hyperbolically)(常有夸张之意)无休止的;没完没了的;冗长不堪的(e.g. We got bogged down in interminable discussions. 我们陷在没完没了的讨论中。)

brandy sipping. The little buried eyes were still watching me out of their corners in that mischievous, canny① way, and I had a strong feeling that the woman was now hatching out some further unpleasantness or scandal. There was the look of serpents in those eyes and a queer curl around the mouth; and in the air—although maybe I only imagined it—the faint smell of danger.

Then suddenly, so suddenly that I jumped, she said, "Lionel, what's this I hear about you and Janet de Pelagia?"

"Now. Gladys, please...."

"Lionel, you're blushing!"

"Nonsense."

"Don't tell me the old bachelor has really taken a tumble at last?"

"Gladys, this is too absurd." I began making movements to go, but she put a hand on my knee and stopped me.

"Don't you know by now, Lionel, that there *are* no secrets?"

"Janet is a fine girl."

"You can hardly call her a *girl*." Gladys Ponsonby paused, staring down into the large brandy glass that she held cupped in both hands. "But of course, I agree with you, Lionel, she's a wonderful person in every way. Except," and now she spoke very slowly, "except that she *does* say some rather peculiar things occasionally."

"What sort of things?"

"Just things, you know—things about people. About you."

"What did she say about me?"

"Nothing at all, Lionel. It wouldn't interest you."

"What did she say about me?"

---

① canny: *Adjective* very clever and able to make intelligent decisions 精明的;狡猾的(e.g. Johnson was plainly a canny individual. 约翰逊显然是个狡猾的人物。)

"It's not even worth repeating, honestly it isn't. It's only that it struck me as being rather odd at the time."

"Gladys—what did she say?" While I waited for her to answer, I could feel the sweat breaking out all over my body.

"Well now, let me see. Of course, she was only joking or I couldn't dream of telling you, but I suppose she *did* say how it was all a wee[①] bit of a bore."

"What was?"

"Sort of going out to dinner with you nearly every night—that kind of thing."

"She said it was a bore?"

"Yes." Gladys Ponsonby drained the brandy glass with one last big gulp, and sat up straight. "If you really want to know, she said it was a crashing[②] bore. And then..."

"What did she say then?"

"Now look, Lionel—there's no need to get excited. I'm only telling you this for your own good."

"Then please hurry up and tell it."

"It's just that I happened to be playing canasta with Janet this afternoon and I asked her if she was free to dine with me tomorrow. She said no, she wasn't."

"Go on."

"Well—actually what she said was 'I'm dining with that crashing old bore Lionel Lampson.'"

"Janet said that?"

---

① wee: *Adjective* (chiefly Scottish) little(主要为苏格兰用法)很少的;微小的

② crashing: *Adjective* (informal) complete; total (used for emphasis) (非正式)(用于强调)十足的;彻头彻尾的

"Yes, Lionel dear."

"What else?"

"Now, that's enough. I don't think I should tell the rest."

"Finish it, please!"

"Why, Lionel, don't keep shouting at me like that. Of course I'll tell you if you insist. As a matter of fact, I wouldn't consider myself a true friend if I didn't. Don't you think it's the sign of true friendship when two people like us..."

"Gladys! *Please* hurry."

"Good heavens, you must give me time to *think*." Let me see now—so far as I can remember, what she *actually* said was this...—and Gladys Ponsonby, sitting upright on the sofa with her feet not quite touching the floor, her eyes away from me now, looking at the wall, began cleverly to mimic the deep tone of that voice I knew so well—"'Such a bore, my dear, because with Lionel one can *always* tell exactly what will happen *right* from beginning to end. For dinner we'll go to the Savoy Grill—it's *always* the Savoy Grill—and for two hours I'll have to listen to the pompous old... I mean I'll have to listen to him droning① away about pictures and porcelain—*always* pictures and porcelain. Then in the taxi going home he'll reach out for my hand, and he'll lean closer, and I'll get a whiff of stale② cigar smoke and brandy, and he'll start burbling③ about

---

① drone: Verb speak tediously in a dull monotonous tone 低沉单调地说(e. g. He reached for another beer while Jim droned on. 吉姆还在唠唠叨叨时,他伸手又拿了一瓶啤酒。)

② stale: Adjective (of food) no longer fresh and pleasant to eat; hard, musty, or dry(食物)不新鲜的;走味的;变硬的;发霉的;干的

③ burble: Verb speak in an unintelligible or silly way, especially at unnecessary length 嘟嘟囔囔地说;絮絮不休(e. g. He burbled on about annuities. 为养老金的事,他不停地嘟囔。)

how he wished—oh, how he wished he was just twenty years younger. And I will say, 'Could you open a window, do you mind?' And when we arrive at my house I'll tell him to keep① the taxi, but he'll pretend he hasn't heard and pay it off quickly. And then at the front door, while I fish for my key, he'll stand beside me with a sort of silly spaniel② look in his eyes, and I'll slowly put the key in the lock, and slowly turn it, and then—very quickly, before he has time to move—I'll say good night and skip inside and shut the door behind me...' Why, Lionel! What's the matter, dear? You look positively ill..."

At that point, mercifully③, I must have swooned④ clear away. I can remember practically nothing of the rest of that terrible night except for a vague and disturbing suspicion that when I regained consciousness I broke down completely and permitted Gladys Ponsonby to comfort me in a variety of different ways. Later, I believe I walked out of the house and was driven home, but I remained more or less unconscious of everything around me until I woke up in my bed the next morning.

I awoke feeling weak and shaken. I lay still with my eyes closed,

---

① keep: *Verb* retain one's place in or on (a seat or saddle, the ground, etc.) against opposition or difficulty(在座位、鞍子或地面上等克服障碍或困难)坐稳；站稳(e.g. Can you keep your saddle, or shall I carry you on a pillion? 你能在马鞍上坐稳吗，或者我用后鞍带你?)

② spaniel: *Noun* used in similes and metaphors as a symbol of devotion or obsequiousness(用于明喻或暗喻)忠诚；谄媚(e.g. I followed my uncles around as faithfully as any spaniel. 我一直像一条忠实的猎一样追随在我叔叔的身边。)

③ mercifully: *Adverb* to one's great relief; fortunately 令人感到宽慰地；幸运地(e.g. Mercifully, I was able to complete all I had to do within a few days. 幸运的是我能够在短短几天内完成我该做的一切。)

④ swoon: *Verb* [no obj.] faint from extreme emotion 昏倒(e.g. I don't want a nurse who swoons at the sight of blood. 我不需要一看到血就昏倒的护士。)

trying to piece together the events of the night before—Gladys Ponsonby's living-room, Gladys on the sofa sipping brandy, the little puckered face, the mouth that was like a salmon's mouth, the things she had said... What was it she had said? Ah, yes. About me. My God, yes! About Janet and me! Those outrageous, unbelievable remarks! Could Janet really have made them? Could she?

I can remember with what terrifying swiftness my hatred of Janet de Pelagia now began to grow. It all happened in a few minutes—a sudden, violent welling up of a hatred that filled me till I thought I was going to burst. I tried to dismiss it, but it was on me like a fever, and in no time at all I was hunting around, as would some filthy gangster, for a method of revenge.

A curious way to behave, you may say, for a man such as me; to which I would answer no, not really, if you consider the circumstances. To my mind, this was the sort of thing that could drive a man to murder. As a matter of fact, had it not been for a small sadistic[①] streak[②] that caused me to seek a more subtle and painful punishment for my victim, I might well have become a murderer myself. But mere killing, I decided, was too good for this woman, and far too crude for my own taste. So I began looking for a superior alternative.

I am not normally a scheming person; I consider it an odious[③] business and have had no practice in it whatsoever. But fury and hate can concentrate a man's mind to an astonishing degree, and in no time at all

---

① sadistic: *Adjective* pertaining to or characterized by sadism; deriving pleasure or sexual gratification from extreme cruelty 有(性)虐待狂的。

② streak: *Noun* usu. [with adj.] a continuous period of specified success or luck(成功或幸运的)一段时间,一阵子(e.g. The theatre is on a winning streak. 那个剧院这一阵子非常火爆。)

③ odious: *Adjective* extremely unpleasant; repulsive 可憎的;令人厌恶的

a plot was forming and unfolding in my head—a plot so superior and exciting that I began to be quite carried away at the idea of it. By the time I had filled in the details and overcome one or two minor objections, my brooding vengeful mood had changed to one of extreme elation①, and I remember how I started bouncing up and down absurdly on my bed and clapping my hands. The next thing I knew I had the telephone directory on my lap and was searching eagerly for a name. I found it, picked up the phone, and dialled the number.

"Hello," I said. "Mr. Royden? Mr. John Royden?"

"Speaking."

Well—it wasn't difficult to persuade the man to call around and see me for a moment. I had never met him, but of course he knew my name, both as an important collector of paintings and as a person of some consequence② in society. I was a big fish for him to catch.

"Let me see now, Mr. Lampson," he said, "I think I ought to be free in about a couple of hours. Will that be all right?"

I told him it would be fine, gave my address, and rang off.

I jumped out of bed. It was really remarkable how exhilarated I felt all of a sudden. One moment I had been in an agony of despair, contemplating murder and suicide and I don't know what, the next, I was whis-

---

① elation：*Noun* [mass noun] great happiness and exhilaration 兴高采烈；欢欣鼓舞(e.g. Richard's elation at regaining his health was short-lived. 理查德身体康复后的喜悦没维持多久。)

② consequence：*Noun* (dated) social distinction(古旧用法)显赫；显要(e.g. a woman of consequence 名女人)

tling an aria① from Puccini② in my bath. Every now and again I caught myself rubbing my hands together in a devilish③ fashion, and once, during my exercises, when I overbalanced doing a double-knee-bend, I sat on the floor and giggled like a schoolboy.

At the appointed time Mr. John Royden was shown in to my library and I got up to meet him. He was a small neat man with a slightly ginger goatee④ beard. He wore a black velvet jacket, a rust-brown tie, a red pullover, and black suede⑤ shoes. I shook his small neat hand.

"Good of you to come along so quickly, Mr. Royden."

"Not at all, sir." The man's lips—like the lips of nearly all bearded men—looked wet and naked, a trifle indecent⑥, shining pink in among all that hair. After telling him again how much I admired his work, I got straight down to business.

---

① aria: *Noun* (Music) a long accompanied song for a solo voice, typically one in an opera or oratorio(音乐)(多指歌剧或清唱剧中的)咏叹调

② Giacomo Puccini (1858—1924), Italian composer. Puccini's sense of the dramatic, gift for melody, and skilful use of the orchestra have contributed to his enduring popularity. Notable operas: La Bohème (1896), Tosca (1900), and Madama Butterfly (1904). 贾科莫·普契尼(1858—1924,意大利作曲家,普契尼对戏剧感悟力和旋律方面的天赋以及管弦乐的熟练运用使他拥有持久盛名;主要作品有:《艺术家的生涯》[1896],《托斯卡》[1900]和《蝴蝶夫人》[1904]。

③ devilish: *Adjective* of, like, or appropriate to a devil in evil and cruelty 恶魔般的;邪恶的;残忍的(e. g. devilish tortures 残酷的折磨)

④ goatee or goatee beard: *Noun* a small pointed beard like that of a goat 山羊胡子

⑤ suede: *Noun* [mass noun] leather, especially kidskin, with the flesh side rubbed to make a velvety nap 绒面革;起毛革(尤指小山羊皮)

⑥ indecent: *Adjective* not conforming with generally accepted standards of behaviour or propriety; obscene 下流的;猥亵的(e. g. The film was grossly indecent. 这部电影下流不堪。)

"Mr. Royden," I said. "I have a rather unusual request to make of you, something quite personal in its way."

"Yes, Mr. Lampson?" He was sitting in the chair opposite me and he cocked his head over to one side, quick and perky① like a bird.

"Of course, I know I can trust you to be discreet② about anything I say."

"Absolutely, Mr. Lampson."

"All right. Now my proposition is this: there is a certain lady in town here whose portrait I would like you to paint. I very much want to possess a fine painting of her. But there are certain complications. For example, I have my own reasons for not wishing her to know that it is I who am commissioning③ the portrait."

"You mean..."

"Exactly, Mr. Royden. That is exactly what I mean. As a man of the world I'm sure you will understand."

He smiled, a crooked④ little smile that only just came through his

---

① perky: *Adjective* cheerful and lively 活跃的;生龙活虎的(e.g. She certainly looked less than her usual perky self. 她看起来确实不如往常那样生龙活虎。)

② discreet: *Adjective* careful and circumspect in one's speech or actions, especially in order to avoid causing offence or to gain an advantage(言行)谨慎的;慎重的;周到的(e.g. We made some discreet inquiries. 我们做了些周详的询问。)

③ commission: *Verb* [with obj. and infinitive] give (an artist) an order for a piece of work 委托(艺术家)创作作品(e.g. He was commissioned to do a series of drawings. 他受委托作一系列画。)

④ crooked: *Adjective* (of a smile or grin) with the mouth sloping down on one side; lopsided(笑容)嘴歪向一边的

beard, and he nodded his head knowingly① up and down.

"Is it not possible," I said, "that a man might be—how shall I put it? —extremely fond of a lady and at the same time have his own good reasons for not wishing her to know about it yet?"

"More than possible, Mr. Lampson."

"Sometimes a man has to stalk② his quarry③ with great caution, waiting patiently for the right moment to reveal himself."

"Precisely, Mr. Lampson."

"There are better ways of catching a bird than by chasing it through the woods."

"Yes, indeed, Mr. Lampson."

"Putting salt on its tail, for instance."

"Ha-ha?"

"All right, Mr. Royden, I think you understand. Now—do you happen by any chance to know a lady called Janet de Pelagia?"

"Janet de Pelagia? Let me see now—yes. At least, what I mean is I've heard of her. I couldn't exactly say I know her."

"That's a pity. It makes it a little more difficult. Do you think you could get to meet her—perhaps at a cocktail party or something like that?"

---

① knowing: *Adjective* showing or suggesting that one has knowledge or awareness that is secret or known to only a few people 会意的;心照不宣的(e.g. a knowing smile 会意的微笑)

② stalk: *Verb* [with obj.] pursue or approach stealthily 悄悄地追踪(或靠近)(e.g. a cat stalking a bird 悄悄靠近鸟儿的猫)

③ quarry: *Noun* an animal pursued by a hunter, hound, predatory mammal, or bird of prey 猎物

"Shouldn't be too tricky①, Mr. Lampson."

"Good, because what I suggest is this: that you go up to her and tell her she's the sort of model you've been searching for for years—just the right face, the right figure, the right coloured eyes. You know the sort of thing. Then ask her if she'd mind sitting for you free of charge. Say you'd like to do a picture of her for next year's Academy. I feel sure she'd be delighted to help you, and honoured too, if I may say so. Then you will paint her and exhibit the picture and deliver it to me after the show is over. No one but you need know that I have bought it."

The small round eyes of Mr. Royden were watching me shrewdly, I thought, and the head was again cocked over to one side. He was sitting on the edge of his chair, and in this position, with the pullover making a flash of red down his front, he reminded me of a robin② on a twig listening for a suspicious noise.

"There's really nothing wrong about it at all," I said. "Just call it—if you like—a harmless little conspiracy being perpetrated③ by a... well... by a rather romantic old man."

"I know, Mr. Lampson, I know..." He still seemed to be hesitating, so I said quickly, "I'll be glad to pay you double your usual fee."

That did it. The man actually licked his lips. "Well, Mr. Lamp-

---

① tricky: Adjective (of a task, problem, or situation) requiring care and skill because difficult or awkward(任务、问题或情况)需细心和技巧的;难对付的(e.g. Applying eyeliner can be a tricky business. 画眼线是件需要细心和技巧的事情。)

② robin: Noun [usu. with adj. or noun modifier] any of a number of other birds that resemble the European robin, especially in having a red breast 红襟鸟(外形似欧洲知更鸟,尤其是有红胸的鸟类)

③ perpetrate: Verb [with obj.] carry out or commit (a harmful, illegal, or immoral action) 实施(有害或不道德的行动);犯(罪)(e.g. A crime has been perpetrated against a sovereign state. 对一个主权国家犯下了罪行。)

son, I must say this sort of thing's not really in my line, you know. But all the same, it'd be a very heartless man who refused such a—shall I say such a romantic assignment?"

"I should like a full-length portrait, Mr. Royden, please. A large canvas—let me see about twice the size of that Manet on the wall there."

"About sixty by thirty-six?"

"Yes. And I should like her to be standing. That to my mind, is her most graceful attitude."

"I quite understand, Mr. Lampson. And it'll be a pleasure to paint such a lovely lady."

I expect it will, I told myself. The way you go about it, my boy, I'm quite sure it will. But I said, "All right, Mr. Royden, then I'll leave it all to you. And don't forget, please—this is a little secret between ourselves."

When he had gone I forced myself to sit still and take twenty-five deep breaths. Nothing else would have restrained me from jumping up and shouting for joy like an idiot. I have never in my life felt so exhilarated. My plan was working! The most difficult part was already accomplished. There would be a wait now, a long wait. The way this man painted, it would take him several months to finish the picture. Well, I would just have to be patient, that's all.

I now decided, on the spur of the moment, that it would be best if I were to go abroad in the interim; and the very next morning, after sending a message to Janet (with whom, you will remember, I was due to dine that night) telling her I had been called away, I left for Italy.

There, as always, I had a delightful time, marred[①] only by a con-

---

① mar: Verb impair the quality of; spoil 损害;扰乱(e.g. Violence marred a number of New Year celebrations. 暴力扰乱了许多新年庆祝活动。)

stant nervous excitement caused by the thought of returning to the scene of action.

　　I eventually arrived back, four months later, in July, on the day after the opening of the Royal Academy, and I found to my relief that everything had gone according to plan during my absence. The picture of Janet de Pelagia had been painted and hung in the Exhibition, and it was already the subject of much favourable comment both by the critics and the public. I myself refrained from going to see it, but Royden told me on the telephone that there had been several inquiries by persons who wished to buy it, all of whom had been informed that it was not for sale. When the show was over, Royden delivered the picture to my house and received his money.

　　I immediately had it carried up to my workroom, and with mounting excitement I began to examine it closely. The man had painted her standing up in a black evening dress and there was a red-plush① sofa in the background. Her left hand was resting on the back of a heavy chair, also of red-plush, and there was a huge crystal chandelier② hanging from the ceiling.

　　My God, I thought, what a hideous thing! The portrait itself wasn't so bad. He had caught the woman's expression—the forward drop of the head, the wide blue eyes, the large, ugly-beautiful mouth with the trace of a smile in one corner. He had flattered her, of course. There wasn't a wrinkle on her face or the slightest suggestion of fat under her chin. I bent forward to examine the painting of the dress. Yes—here the paint was thicker, much thicker. At this point, unable to wait another mo-

---

　　① plush: *Noun* [mass noun] a rich fabric of silk, cotton, wool, or a combination of these, with a long, soft nap 长毛绒

　　② chandelier: *Noun* a large, decorative hanging light with branches for several light bulbs or candles 枝形吊灯

ment, I threw off my coat and prepared to go to work.

　　I should mention here that I am myself an expert cleaner and restorer of paintings. The cleaning, particularly, is a comparatively simple process provided one has patience and a gentle touch, and those professionals who make such a secret of their trade and charge such shocking prices get no business from me. Where my own pictures are concerned I always do the job myself.

　　I poured out the turpentine① and added a few drops of alcohol. I dipped a small wad of cotton wool② in the mixture, squeezed it out, and then gently, so very gently, with a circular motion, I began to work upon the black paint of the dress. I could only hope that Royden had allowed each layer to dry thoroughly before applying the next, otherwise the two would merge and the process I had in mind would be impossible. Soon I would know. I was working on one square inch of black dress somewhere around the lady's stomach and I took plenty of time, cautiously testing and teasing③ the paint, adding a drop or two more of alcohol to my mixture, testing again, adding another drop until finally it was just strong enough to loosen the pigment④.

　　For perhaps a whole hour I worked away on this little square of

---

　　① turpentine: *Noun* (also as "oil of turpentine") [mass noun] a volatile pungent oil distilled from gum turpentine or pine wood, used in mixing paints and varnishes and in liniment 松节油；松木油

　　② cotton wool: [mass noun] (Brit.) fluffy wadding of a kind originally made from raw cotton, used especially for cleaning the skin or bathing wounds(英国英语)药棉；脱脂棉

　　③ tease: to separate sth. carefully from sth. else 仔细地将……(从……)分离出(e.g. birds teasing out ripe seeds from plants 小心地啄出成熟草籽的鸟)

　　④ pigment: *Noun* the natural colouring matter of animal or plant tissue 色素；颜料

第二章 冤冤相报 第一节 《最后颂歌》Nunc Dimittis

black, proceeding more and more gently as I came closer to the layer below. Then, a tiny pink spot appeared, and gradually it spread and spread until the whole of my square inch was a clear shining patch of pink. Quickly I neutralized with pure turps①.

So far so good. I knew now that the black paint could be removed without disturbing what was underneath. So long as I was patient and industrious I would easily be able to take it all off. Also, I had discovered the right mixture to use and just how hard I could safely rub, so things should go much quicker now.

I must say it was rather an amusing business. I worked first from the middle of her body downward, and as the lower half of her dress came away bit by bit on to my little wads of cotton, a queer pink undergarment② began to reveal itself. I didn't for the life of me know what the thing was called, but it was a formidable apparatus constructed of what appeared to be a strong thick elastic material, and its purpose was apparently to contain and to compress the woman's bulging figure into a neat streamlined shape, giving a quite false impression of slimness. As I travelled lower and lower down, I came upon a striking arrangement of suspenders③, also pink, which were attached to this elastic armour and hung downwards four or five inches to grip the tops of the stockings.

Quite fantastic the whole thing seemed to me as I stepped back a pace to survey it. It gave me a strong sense of having somehow been

---

① turps = turpentine: *Noun* [mass noun] (informal) turpentine(非正式)松节油

② undergarment: *Noun* an article of underclothing 内衣;衬衣

③ suspenders: *Plural Noun* a pair of straps that pass over the shoulders and fasten to the waistband of a pair of trousers or a skirt at the front and back to hold it up(复数名词)吊裤带;吊袜带

cheated; for had I not, during all these past months, been admiring the sylph①-like figure of this lady? She was a faker. No question about it. But do many other females practise this sort of deception, I wondered. I knew, of course, that in the days of stays② and corsets③ it was usual for ladies to strap themselves up; yet for some reason I was under the impression that nowadays all they had to do was diet.

When the whole of the lower half of the dress had come away, I immediately turned my attention to the upper portion, working my way slowly upward from the lady's middle. Here, around the midriff④, there was an area of naked flesh; then higher up upon the bosom itself and actually containing it, I came upon a contrivance⑤ made of some heavy black material edged with frilly⑥ lace. This, I knew very well, was the brassiere⑦—another formidable appliance upheld by an arrangement of black

---

① sylph: *Noun* an imaginary spirit of the air 气精;气仙;空气精灵 *Noun* a slender woman or girl 身材苗条的女人

② stays: *Noun* (historical) a corset made of two pieces laced together and stiffened by strips of whalebone(历史上的用法)胸衣;紧身褡;紧身背心

③ corset: *Noun* a woman's tightly fitting undergarment extending from below the chest to the hips, worn to shape the figure(妇女束腰肚以调整身材的)紧身内衣

④ midriff: *Noun* the region of the front of the body between the chest and the waist 上腹部

⑤ contrivance: *Noun* [count noun] a device, especially in literary or artistic composition, which gives a sense of artificiality(尤指文学或艺术作品中的)雕琢;渲染;人为修饰

⑥ frilly: *Adjective* decorated with frills or similar ornamentation 用褶边(或类似褶边的东西)装饰的(e.g. a frilly apron 有褶边的围裙)

⑦ brassiere: *Noun* full form of bra(乳罩)的完全拼写形式

straps as skilfully and scientifically rigged① as the supporting cables of a suspension bridge.

　　Dear me, I thought. One lives and learns.

　　But now at last the job was finished, and I stepped back again to take a final look at the picture. It was truly an astonishing sight! This woman, Janet de Pelagia, almost life size, standing there in her underwear—in a sort of drawing-room, I suppose it was—with a great chandelier above her head and a red-plush chair by her side; and she herself—this was the most disturbing part of all—looking so completely unconcerned, with the wide placid blue eyes, the faintly smiling, ugly-beautiful mouth. Also I noticed, with something of a shock, that she was exceedingly bow-legged, like a jockey②. I tell you frankly, the whole thing embarrassed me. I felt as though I had no right to be in the room, certainly no right to stare. So after a while I went out and shut the door behind me. It seemed like the only decent thing to do.

　　Now, for the next and final step! And do not imagine simply because I have not mentioned it lately that my thirst for revenge had in any way diminished during the last few months. On the contrary, it had if anything③ increased; and with the last act about to be performed, I can tell you I found it hard to contain myself. That night, for example, I didn't even go to bed.

---

　　① rig: *Verb* assemble and adjust (the equipment of a sailing boat, aircraft, etc.) to make it ready for operation 装配并调整(帆船、飞机等的设备)

　　② jockey: *Noun* a person who rides in horse races, especially as a profession (尤指职业的)赛马骑师

　　③ if anything: used to express an opinion about sth, or after a negative statement to suggest that the opposite is true(用于表达看法,或用在否定句之后表示恰恰相反)真要说起来;依我看(e.g. I'd say he was more like his father, if anything. 依我看,如果一定要说他像谁的话,他比较像他的父亲。)

You see, I couldn't wait to get the invitations out. I sat up all night preparing them and addressing the envelopes. There were twenty-two of them in all, and I wanted each to be a personal note. "I'm having a little dinner on Friday night, the twenty-second, at eight. I do hope you can come along... I'm so looking forward to seeing you again..."

The first, the most carefully phrased, was to Janet de Pelagia. In it I regretted not having seen her for so long... I had been abroad... It was time we got together again, etc., etc. The next was to Gladys Ponsonby. Then one to Lady Hermione Girdlestone, another to Princess Bicheno[①], Mrs. Cudbird, Sir Hubert Kaul, Mrs. Galbally, Peter Euan-Thomas, James Pisker, Sir Eustace Piegrome, Peter van Santen, Elizabeth Moynihan, Lord Mulherrin, Bertram Sturt, Philip Cornelius, Jack Hill, Lady Akeman, Mrs. Icely, Humphrey King-Howard, Johnny O'Coffey, Mrs. Uvary, and the Dowager Countess of Waxworth.

It was a carefully selected list, containing as it did the most distinguished men, the most brilliant and influential women in the top crust of our society.

I was well aware that dinner at my house was regarded as quite an occasion; everybody liked to come. And now, as I watched the point of my pen moving swiftly over the paper, I could almost see the ladies in their pleasure picking up their bedside telephones the morning the invitations arrived, shrill voices calling to shriller voices over the wires... "Lionel's giving a party... he's asked you too? My dear, how nice... his food is always *so* good... and *such* a lovely man, isn't he though, yes..."

---

① 这里的"Bicheno"以及本段余下的人名都应该是当时社会上有一定知名度的人物——就像下一段中作者所说的那样——"包括上层社会最为显赫的男子,以及最杰出和最有影响力的女子"(containing as it did the most distinguished men, the most brilliant and influential women in the top crust of our society)。

Is that really what they would say? It suddenly occurred to me that it might not be like that at all. More like this perhaps: "I agree, my dear, yes, not a bad old man... but a bit of a bore, don't you think?... What did you say?... dull? But desperately, my dear. You've hit the nail on the head... did you ever hear what Janet de Pelagia once said about him?... Ah yes, I thought you'd heard that one... screamingly① funny, don't you think?... poor Janet... how she stood it as long as she did I don't know..."

Anyway, I got the invitations off, and within a couple of days everybody with the exception of Mrs. Cudbird and Sir Hubert Kaul, who were away, had accepted with pleasure.

At eight-thirty on the evening of the twenty-second, my large drawing-room was filled with people. They stood about the room, admiring the pictures, drinking their Martinis, talking with loud voices. The women smelled strongly of scent, the men were pink-faced and carefully buttoned up in their dinner-jackets②. Janet de Pelagia was wearing the same black dress she had used for the portrait, and every time I caught sight of her, a kind of huge bubble-vision—as in those absurd cartoons—would float up above my head, and in it I would see Janet in her underclothes, the black brassiere, the pink elastic belt, the suspenders, the jockey's legs.

I moved from group to group, chatting amiably with them all, listening to their talk. Behind me I could hear Mrs. Galbally telling Sir Eustace Piegrome and James Pisker how the man at the next table to hers at

---

① screamingly: *Adverb* [as sub-modifier] to a very great extent; extremely 非常; 极其(e.g. a screamingly dull daily routine 极端枯燥的例行公事)

② dinner-jacket or dinner jacket: *Noun* a man's short jacket without tails, typically a black one, worn with a bow tie for formal occasions in the evening(多指黑色配蝴蝶结领结用于晚间正式场合的男士)无尾礼服

Claridges the night before had had red lipstick on his white moustache. "Simply *plastered*① with it," she kept on saying, "and the old boy was ninety if he was a day②..." On the other side, Lady Girdlestone was telling somebody where one could get truffles③ cooked in brandy, and I could see Mrs. Icely whispering something to Lord Mulherrin while his Lordship kept shaking his head slowly from side to side like an old and dispirited metronome④.

Dinner was announced, and we all moved out.

"My goodness!" they cried as they entered the dining-room. "How dark and sinister!"

"I can hardly see a thing!"

"What divine little candles!"

"But Lionel, how romantic!"

There were six very thin candles set about two feet apart from each other down the centre of the long table. Their small flames made a little glow of light around the table itself, but left the rest of the room in darkness. It was an amusing arrangement and apart from the fact that it suited

---

① plaster: *Verb* (plaster something with/in) coat or cover something with (a substance), especially to an extent considered excessive(尤指过度地)涂满;盖满(e.g. a face plastered in heavy make-up 一张涂了厚厚一层化妆品的脸)

② if he/she is a day: at least (appended to a statement about a person's age) 至少(加在关于某人年龄的话语之后)(e.g. He must be seventy if he's a day. 他肯定至少有70岁了。)

③ truffle: *Noun* a strong-smelling underground fungus that resembles an irregular, rough-skinned potato, growing chiefly in broad-leaved woodland on calcareous soils. It is considered a culinary delicacy and found, especially in France, with the aid of trained dogs or pigs 块菌;块菰;松露

④ metronome: *Noun* a device used by musicians that marks time at a selected rate by giving a regular tick 节拍器

my purpose well, it made a pleasant change. The guests soon settled themselves in their right places and the meal began.

They all seemed to enjoy the candlelight and things went famously, though for some reason the darkness caused them to speak much louder than usual. Janet de Pelagia's voice struck me as being particularly strident①. She was sitting next to Lord Mulherrin, and I could hear her telling him about the boring time she had had at Cap Ferrat② the week before. "Nothing but Frenchmen," she kept saying. "Nothing but Frenchmen in the whole place..."

For my part, I was watching the candles. They were so thin that I knew it would not be long before they burned down to their bases. Also I was mighty nervous—I will admit that—but at the same time intensely exhilarated, almost to the point of drunkenness. Every time I heard Janet's voice or caught sight of her face shadowed in the light of the candles, a little ball of excitement exploded inside me and I felt the fire of it running under my skin.

They were eating their strawberries when at last I decided the time had come. I took a deep breath and in a loud voice I said, "I'm afraid we'll have to have the lights on now. The candles are nearly finished. Mary," I called. "Oh, Mary, switch on the lights, will you please,"

There was a moment of silence after my announcement. I heard the maid walking over to the door, then the gentle click of the switch and the room was flooded with a blaze of light. They all screwed up their eyes,

---

① strident：*Adjective* loud and harsh; grating 大声的；刺耳的(e. g. His voice had become increasingly sharp, almost strident. 他的声音越来越尖厉,几乎到了刺耳的程度。)

② Cap Ferrat：Cap Ferrat (English：Cape Ferrat) is situated in Alpes-Maritimes in southeastern France. It is located in the commune of Saint-Jean-Cap-Ferrat. 费拉角(位于法国东南部的滨海阿尔卑斯省,属圣让卡普费拉管辖范围)。

opened them again, gazed about them.

At that point I got up from my chair and slid quietly from the room, but as I went I saw a sight that I shall never forget as long as I live. It was Janet, with both hands in mid-air, stopped, frozen rigid, caught in the act of gesticulating① towards someone across the table. Her mouth had dropped open two inches and she wore the surprised, not-quite-understanding look of a person who precisely one second before has been shot dead, right through the heart.

In the hall outside I paused and listened to the beginning of the uproar, the shrill cries of the ladies and the outraged unbelieving exclamations of the men; and soon there was a great hum of noise with everybody talking or shouting at the same time. Then—and this was the sweetest moment of all—I heard Lord Mulherrin's voice, roaring above the rest, "Here! Someone! Hurry! Give her some water quick!"

Out in the street the chauffeur helped me into my car, and soon we were away from London and bowling② merrily along the Great North Road towards this, my other house, which is only ninety-five miles from Town anyway.

---

① gesticulate: *Verb* [no obj.] use gestures, especially dramatic ones, instead of speaking or to emphasize one's words 做手势(尤指夸张的手势);用手势(或动作)加重语气;用手势表达(e.g. They were shouting and gesticulating frantically at drivers who did not slow down. 他们向没有减速行驶的驾车人呼喊并拼命打手势。)

② bowl: *Verb* [no obj., with adverbial of direction] move rapidly and smoothly in a specified direction(沿着特定方向)急速移动(e.g. They bowled along the country roads. 他们在乡间大道上急速前进。)

第二章 冤冤相报 第一节 《最后颂歌》Nunc Dimittis

The next two days I spent in gloating①. I mooned② around in a dream of ecstasy, half drowned in my own complacency and filled with a sense of pleasure so great that it constantly gave me pins and needles all along the lower parts of my legs. It wasn't until this morning when Gladys Ponsonby called me on the phone that I suddenly came to my senses and realized I was not a hero at all but an outcast③. She informed me—with what I thought was just a trace of relish that everybody was up in arms, that all of them, all my old and loving friends were saying the most terrible things about me and had sworn never never to speak to me again. Except her, she kept saying. Everybody except her. And didn't I think it would be rather cosy, she asked, if she were to come down and stay with me a few days to cheer me up?

I'm afraid I was too upset by that time even to answer her politely. I put the phone down and went away to weep.

Then at noon today came the final crushing blow. The post arrived, and with it—I can hardly bring myself to write about it, I am so ashamed—came a letter, the sweetest, most tender little note imaginable from none other than Janet de Pelagia herself. She forgave me completely, she wrote, for everything I had done. She knew it was only a joke and I must not listen to the horrid things other people were saying about me. She loved me as she always had and always would to her dying day.

---

① gloat: Verb [no obj.] contemplate or dwell on one's own success or another's misfortune with smugness or malignant pleasure 沾沾自喜;幸灾乐祸(e. g. His enemies gloated over his death. 敌人对他的死幸灾乐祸。)

② moon: Verb [no obj., with adverbial] behave or move in a listless and aimless manner 懒散度日;浪荡(e. g. I don't want her mooning about in the morning. 我不想让她浪荡一上午。)

③ outcast: Noun a person who has been rejected by their society or social group 社会弃儿

Oh, what a cad①, what a brute I felt when I read this! The more so when I found that she had actually sent me by the same post a small present as an added sign of her affection—a half-pound jar of my favourite food of all, fresh caviare②.

I can never under any circumstances resist good caviare. It is perhaps my greatest weakness. So although I naturally had no appetite whatsoever for food at dinner-time this evening, I must confess I took a few spoonfuls of the stuff in an effort to console myself in my misery. It is even possible that I took a shade③ too much, because I haven't been feeling any too chipper④ this last hour or so. Perhaps I ought to go up right away and get myself some bicarbonate⑤ of soda. I can easily come back and finish this later, when I'm in better trim.

You know—now I come to think of it, I really do feel rather ill all of a sudden.

三、翻译探索

本篇小说的翻译中,需要突破的是作者提到的一些艺术家及其作品的翻译,还要处理好小说各个部分的衔接。同时,还要处理好作者对于所厌烦之人所采用的"深恶痛绝"的口吻和笔调。

---

① cad: Noun (dated or humorous) a man who behaves dishonourably, especially towards a woman(古旧或幽默的用法)行为不端的男人(尤指对待妇女方面)(e.g. her adulterous cad of a husband 她那与人通奸的无耻丈夫)

② caviare or caviar: Noun [mass noun] the pickled roe of sturgeon or other large fish, eaten as a delicacy 鱼子酱

③ a shade: a little 有点;略微

④ chipper: Adjective (informal) cheerful and lively(非正式)活泼的;兴高采烈的

⑤ bicarbonate: Noun (also as "bicarbonate of soda") [mass noun] sodium bicarbonate 小苏打;碳酸氢钠

最后颂歌

将近午夜时分。我明白,到了这个时候,要是不开始动笔写本篇故事,我就永远都动不了笔了。整个晚上,我就一直坐在这儿,尽量强迫自己动笔开写。可问题是,整个这件事情,我越想,越感到惊骇、羞愧和沮丧。

我的想法——我相信我的想法很不错——就是通过坦白认错、解释分析这一过程,为我对珍妮特·德佩拉贾的令人无法容忍的所作所为找到一个理由,或者,无论如何,找到某种合情合理的说辞。从本质上来说,我想对着一个假想中的、对我抱以同情心的对象诉说,而这个对象类似于一个虚构的你,也就是某位温和的、善解人意之人。对这样一个人,我或许会和盘托出这个令人遗憾的插曲而毫无羞愧之感。我只是希望,我不会心烦意乱到了这样的地步,甚至连尝试都不敢去尝试一下。

我要是能够做到对自己开诚布公的话,我想我必须承认,最令我烦躁不安的不是我自身的愧疚感,甚至也不是我强加到可怜的珍妮特身心上的伤害,而是得知我自己就是一个丑陋、可恶的蠢货。这样说来,我所有的朋友——要是我还能有资格称他们为朋友的话,也就是所有那些热心肠的可爱之人,现在一定把我看成一个邪恶的、报复心很强的老男人了,而那些朋友以前甚至踏破了我家的门槛。没错,出现那种情况,肯定令人伤心的。要是我对你说,我的朋友就是我人生的全部,我人生的所有,我人生的一切,那么,你或许就会开始有所理解了。

你会理解吗?对此,我表示怀疑,除非我将这个话题岔开一会儿,跟你大致讲讲我是一个什么样的人。

噢——容我想想。细细想来,我认为,不管怎样,我算是一类人,一类稀有之人。但是,请注意,不管怎么说,我是这样一个中年人,其特点毋庸置疑——手头宽绰、优哉从容、颇具涵养,而且受人敬重(这个词的选用,我是很谨慎的)——很多朋友敬重其魅力、金钱、学识、慷慨,我也衷心希望他名副其实。只有在大都市——伦敦、巴黎、纽约,你才会找到他这个人(或者符合这一类型特点的人)。对此,我很肯定。他拥有的钱财是他已故的父亲挣来的,但是,他对父亲的钱财却持有鄙视的态度。这样做,不是他的错,因为在他的气质构成中,有某种东西暗自迫使他去低看一类人,而他看低的这类人都缺乏才智,说不出罗金厄姆跟斯波德、沃特福德郡跟威尼斯人、谢拉顿家具跟齐彭代尔家具、莫奈跟马奈之间的差别,甚至不具备才智来区分波马特葡萄酒跟蒙特拉谢葡萄酒之间的差别。

因此呢,他就是一位鉴赏方面的行家里手,而且最重要的一点是,他拥有高雅的品味。他收藏的名家画作,有康斯特布尔的、有伯宁顿的、有罗特列克的、有雷东的、有维亚尔的、还有马修·史密斯的。这些名家的画作跟泰特画廊的任何一件藏品比起来,都毫不逊色。由于他收藏的这些画作如此非同凡响、如此美妙绝伦,以至于在他的家中,这些画作为他营造出一种悬念般的氛围,这种氛围令人感到遥不可及、动人心魄,又稍微带点恐惧的气息,而这种气息会令人恐惧地想到:要是他真有这方面意愿的话,他就有能力,也有权利挥舞拳头砸穿这些名画家笔下的壮美的戴德姆山谷、圣维克多尔山、阿尔勒的玉米地,还有优雅的塔希提岛少女和塞尚夫人肖像,从而将他们捅破、撕毁。更有甚者,从这些奇迹般画作悬挂的墙壁上,一股微弱的、华贵的金光流淌而出,还散发出一种微妙的、尊贵的气息。他就在这种氛围下生活着,走来走去、自娱自乐,脸上露出一种漠然的表情,这种表情也不能完全说不是他刻意训练的结果。

自始至终,他都是一位单身汉,然而,看起来他从未与任何一名围绕左右的女子纠缠不清,即便那名女子深深爱着他。极有可能的是,不管你注意到,还是没有注意到,他内心深处的某个地方会感到沮丧、不满,会留下遗憾,甚至整个人会稍微有点失常。

我想,我没有必要再多说什么了,我已经很坦诚了。到现在为止,你应该对我有了足够的了解,足以公正地判断出我是一个什么样的人了。那么,我是否可以斗胆抱有这样一个希望——希望你听了我的故事会对我寄予同情呢?进而,你会做出决定,认为对于已经发生的事情不应该过多地指责我,而应该指责一位名叫格拉迪斯·庞森比的女士。说来说去,她才是挑起事端的始作俑者。将近六个月前的那个夜晚,要是我没有护送格拉迪斯·庞森比回家的话,要是她当时没有随口说出某些人、某些事的话,那么,这种悲惨的事情从来就没有可能会发生。

如果我没有记错的话,当时是去年的十二月份,我一直跟阿申登一家人在他们家漂亮的房子里吃饭,从他们家的房子可以俯瞰到摄政公园的南段。当时有很多人赴宴,但是来宾中独来独往的、还坐在我身边的唯有格拉迪斯·庞森比。所以嘛,告辞的时候,自然而然地,我就主动提出将她安全送回家。她没有拒绝,于是,我们一起乘我的车离开。但不幸的是,到了地方后,她坚持要我到她的家里,要我"临回家前喝最后一杯",那是她当时的原话。我不希望自己看起来有一副架子十足的样子,所以我就告诉我的专职司机等我,然后随她进了门。

格拉迪斯·庞森比这个女子,个头特别矮小,肯定不超过一米四六或者四七,或许更矮。像她这样的微型人给我的感觉是:站在她的旁边时,有一种滑稽好笑的感觉,甚至有一种晃晃悠悠的感觉,感觉自己站在一把椅子上。她是个寡妇,比我小几岁——年纪或许有五十三四的样子。极有可能的是,三十年前,她是一个相当娇媚的小可人。可是现在,她脸部松弛,满是皱纹,无论什么样的典型特征都找不到了。眼睛、鼻子、嘴、下巴的个体特征也找不到了,被她那张布满皱纹的小脸上肥肉的皱褶淹没掉了,谁都不会注意到它们的存在。例外的或许是那张嘴,禁不住让我想起——大马哈鱼的嘴。

客厅里,她给我拿白兰地的时候,我注意到她的手有点儿抖。我对自己说,这个女士累了,我一定不要待太长时间。我们俩一起在沙发上坐了一会儿,谈论着阿申登家的晚宴以及当时参加晚宴的那些人。最后,我起身要离开。

"坐下,莱昂内尔,"她说。"再来一杯白兰地。"

"不啦,真的,我必须得走了。"

"坐下,不要一副架子十足的样子。*我自己*要再喝一杯。我喝酒,你起码要陪我待一会儿。"

她一边往餐具柜那边走,我一边看着她——这个微型女子,只见她轻微地左摇右晃,双手握住杯子举到身前,就好像那只杯子是别人馈赠的礼品似的。看到她那样的步态,看到她如此矮小、粗胖、僵直,我突然之间产生一个滑稽荒唐的意念,感觉她膝盖以上根本就没有长出大腿来。

"莱昂内尔,你在暗自笑什么?"她倒酒的时候,身体转过一半,眼睛看着我,一些酒从杯子里溢了出来。

"没什么,我亲爱的。根本没有笑什么。"

"哦,别笑了。告诉我,你对我的这幅新肖像画是怎么看的吧。"她指了指挂在壁炉上方的一大幅帆布画,而那幅画,自从我进屋那一刻起,双眼就唯恐避之不及呢。那幅画令人生厌,就我所知,是一个名叫约翰·罗伊登的男画家画的。在伦敦,他现在可是风光得很,却是一个很平庸的画家。那是格拉迪斯——庞森比女士——的一幅全身肖像画,是用某种灵巧的技法画上去的,令她成为一个很是高挑的、相当迷人的人物。

"有魅力,"我回答。

"的确如此!你喜欢,我很高兴。"

"相当有魅力。"

"我认为,约翰·罗伊登是个天才。难道你不是这样认为的吗,莱昂内尔?"

"噢——那或许有点扯远了。"

"你的意思是说,这样肯定地说,有点太早?"

"正是。"

"可你听着,莱昂内尔——我认为你听后会大吃一惊的。现在,约翰·罗伊登可是炙手可热啊,给他的钱要是不到一千几尼的话,他甚至不予*理睬*啊!"

"真的吗?"

"哦,真的!谁想画像,谁就要排队,*排队等候*轮到自己才能画上。"

"真是有趣儿啊。"

"现在,拿你喜欢的塞尚先生来说吧——不管他是否叫这个名字。我敢打赌,他一生中从未挣过那么多钱。"

"从未。"

"那么,你说,他曾经是个天才吗?"

"应该——是的。"

"那么,罗伊登也是,"她说,然后又坐到沙发上。"钱证明了这一点。"

她安静地坐了一会儿,小口喝着白兰地。我忍不住看过去,看她那只手的抖动程度,手抖动得厉害,以致玻璃杯的边沿不断碰触她的下嘴唇。她知道我在看她,所以,她并没有转头,而是转动眼睛,从眼角处谨慎地斜视着我。"你呆呆地想什么呢?"

现在,要是这个世界上有一句话令我无法忍受,那就是这句话。这句话令我的胸口着实一痛,开始咳嗽起来。

"快点,莱昂内尔,说说你呆呆地在想什么。"

我摇了摇头,根本没有能力做出回答。她突然间转过身,将白兰地杯子放到左侧一张小桌子上。她这一行为方式似乎表明,她感到自己遭到了冷遇,现在做好了准备要采取行动。我也不知道,自己为什么会这么想。我等待着。在随后的静谧中,我感到相当不自在。由于无话可说,我就一个劲儿抽雪茄烟,一边专心盯着烟灰看,一边慢慢地将烟雾喷向天花板。可是,她并未动弹。这个女子身上开始滋生出某种我不太喜欢的东西——某种带有恶意的阴森森的神情,这种神情令我很想立刻起身离开。转回头看我之际,她狡黠地冲我微笑着,笑容只是从她那双埋进皱褶里的小眼睛里发出的,不是从那张嘴里发出的。噢,那张嘴——大马哈鱼一般的嘴,很是僵硬,毫无表情。

"莱昂内尔,我想,我要告诉你一个秘密。"

"格拉迪斯,说真的,我必须得回家了。"

"你怕什么呀,莱昂内尔,我不会让你难堪的。看看你,突然之间恐惧不已。"

"我不太擅长听别人的秘密。"

"我一直在想,"她说,"你对绘画如此擅长,这秘密应该能引起你的兴趣。"她一动不动地坐着,只有手指总是在动来动去。她一刻不停地将手指彼此绕来绕去,弯来弯去,手指弯得就像一团小白蛇在她的大腿上蠕动。

"莱昂内尔,难道你不想听听我的秘密吗?"

"不是听不听的事儿,你知道的,只是时间真的是太晚了……"

"我这或许是在整个伦敦保守得最好的秘密,而且是女人的秘密。我想呢,知道这个秘密的,大约有——容我想想啊——总共约有三四十名女子,而且,没有一个男人知道这个秘密,除了他之外。当然,他就是约翰·罗伊登。"

我不愿意给她鼓劲儿、让她继续说下去,于是,我什么话都不说了。

"可是首先,你要答应——答应不会告诉任何人吗?"

"哎呀!"

"你答应吗,莱昂内尔?"

"嗯,格拉迪斯,好吧,我答应。"

"不错!现在听着啊。"她伸手够来白兰地杯子,舒舒服服坐回到沙发中,坐到沙发远端那个角上。"我想,你知道约翰·罗伊登只为女子画像这件事儿吧?"

"我不知道。"

"而且,画的都是全身像——或者是站着的,或者是坐着的,就像那儿挂着的、我的那幅肖像一样。莱昂内尔,现在好好看看那幅肖像。看到衣服画得多么漂亮了吗?"

"噢……"

"拜托你走过去,仔仔细细看一看。"

我不情愿地站起身,走了过去,仔细观察起来。令我吃惊的是,我注意到,衣服部分的颜料涂敷得很厚重,实际上从画面的其他部分凸显出来。这种技法在表现方式上相当有效,但问题是,这种技法不难做到,也完全不是当初绘画时的原貌。

"看到了吗?"她说。"衣服部分颜料很厚,是不是呢?"

"是的。"

"但是,要知道,莱昂内尔,这里面的门道远非那个。我想,最好描述一下我第一次去画像时所发生的事情。"

噢,我当时想,这个女子多么令人厌烦,可是,我又怎么能脱身呢?

"那是一年前的事情了。我记得,走进这位伟大画家的工作室之前,我是多么的激动啊。我一番打扮,穿上从时装大师诺曼·哈特内尔那儿新买的衣服,戴上一顶特制的小红帽,就出发了。罗伊登先生到门口迎接我,当然,我一下子就被他吸引住了。他留着一小块儿尖尖的胡须,蓝色的眼睛摄人心魄,身穿一件黑色的天鹅绒夹克衫。画室很大,里面摆着红色的天鹅绒沙发、天鹅绒椅子,挂着天鹅绒窗帘,地面上甚至铺着天鹅绒地毯——看得出来,他很喜欢天鹅绒。他招呼我坐下,给了我一杯喝的,就直奔主题。他对我说了他跟其他艺术家在绘画方面大不相同之处。他还说,以他看来,画女性身体,只有一种方法可以获得完美。得知是何种方法后,你一定不要感到震惊。"

"'我想,我不会感到震惊的,罗伊登先生,'我对他说。"

"'我也敢肯定,你不会的,'他说。他长了一口绝美的白牙齿,微笑时,似乎透过胡须闪闪发光。'你看,事情是这样的,'他继续说。'你仔细查看任何一幅你喜欢的女子画像——是谁画的,我不管——你就会发现,尽管衣服或许会画得很好,却有一种不自然的矫揉造作的效果,整幅作品有种沉闷感、平淡感,那衣服就好像是随随便便披到一段木头上似的。你知道是什么原因吗?'"

"'不,罗伊登先生,我不知道。'"

"'因为衣服下面有什么,绘画者本人真的不知道啊!'"

格拉迪斯·庞森比暂停了一下,又喝下几口白兰地。"莱昂内尔,不要看起来如此惊愕,"她对我说。"这事儿没有什么不妥之处。保持安静,让我把话说完。接着,罗伊登说:'对于我所画的对象,我首先坚持要画其裸体,那就是原因所在。'"

"'老天啊,罗伊登先生!'我大声说。"

"'如果你表示反对,庞森比女士,我不介意做一个小小的让步,'他说。'可是,我更喜欢刚开始提出的绘画方式。'"

"'罗伊登先生,我真的不知道。'"

"'那样画完之后,'他继续说,'我们必须得等上几个星期,让颜料变干。然后,你回来,我接着往上画你穿的贴身衣裤。变干后,我再画上外衣。你看,就这么简单。'"

"这家伙绝对没有道德可言!"我叫道。

"不,莱昂内尔,不!你大错特错了。要是你听到了他的话——极其富有魅力,极其真诚,真心实意,那就好了。谁都看得出,他所说的,是他内心的*真情实感*。"

"我告诉你,格拉迪斯,这家伙就是没有道德可言!"

"不要如此顽固不化,莱昂内尔。不管怎样,容我把话说完。我首先跟他说的是,我的丈夫(当时还在世)永远不会同意的。"

"'你丈夫永远不需要知道的,'他回答。'没有道理惊动他。我的秘密,除了我画的女子,没人知道。'"

"接下来,我又稍微表达了一下我的反对意见,我记得他说:'我亲爱的庞森比女士,这件事儿根本没有什么道义、不道义的。只有非职业人员绘画时,艺术才是不道义的,这跟医学是一样的。在你的医生面前,脱下衣服接受检查,你不会拒绝的,对不对?'"

"我对他说,如果我耳朵疼去看医生,我就不会脱衣服,听得他大笑起来。可是,他还是继续动员我,我必须说的是,他的话很具说服力。因此,过了一会儿,我让步了,过程就是那样。所以嘛,现在,莱昂内尔,我亲爱的,你知道了这个秘密。"她站起身,走过去又为自己倒了些白兰地。

"格拉迪斯,事情真的是这样的吗?"

"当然是真的。"

"你的意思是说,所有的对象,他都那样去画吗?"

"没错。有意思的是,对这一切,做丈夫的全然不知。他们所看到的无非是各自妻子穿着整齐的肖像画。当然啦,画裸体肖像也没有什么不妥的,艺术家无时无刻不在画裸体画,可问题是,愚蠢的丈

第二章 冤冤相报 第一节 《最后颂歌》Nunc Dimittis

夫就是对此类事情持反对态度。"

"天呐,这家伙胆子可够大的啦!"

"我想,他是位天才。"

"我敢打赌,他的这一想法来自戈雅大师。"

"胡说八道,莱昂内尔。"

"当然没错的,但是,听着,格拉迪斯,我想要你告诉我一点事儿。去画肖像之前,你是否也许知道……知道罗伊登这种奇特的画法?"

问这个问题的时候,她正往杯子里倒酒呢,只见她迟疑了一会儿,转过头来看看我,嘴角两边动了动,露出一丝轻柔的微笑。"莱昂内尔,你这个混蛋,"她说。"你太过聪明,我没有一件事情能逃过你的眼睛。"

"那么说,你知道?"

"当然。埃尔米奥娜·格德尔斯通告诉我的。"

"跟我所想的一模一样!"

"这仍然没有什么不妥的呀。"

"没什么,"我说。"绝对没什么。"现在,这一切我看得清清楚楚了。这个叫罗伊登的,的确没有道德可言。他所实施的这一心理伎俩,其干净利索的程度,不亚于我所见过的任何一个。这个城市里有一大批富有的懒散女子,这些女子睡到大中午才起床,然后打桥牌、玩凯纳斯特纸牌、逛街购物,以缓解无聊情绪,从而打发一天中剩余的时光,一直熬到鸡尾酒会开始为止。对于这一点,这个人再也清楚不过了。她们所渴望的,就是一点点的兴奋——某种异乎寻常的东西,而且,越昂贵,越好。哇——难怪,这样消遣性的消息,如同天花一般,在她们圈子里很快就一传十、十传百了。我眼前仿佛浮现出这样的情景:又圆又胖的大块头埃尔米奥娜·格德尔斯通俯身凯纳斯特纸牌桌上方,告诉大家伙儿……"可是,我亲爱的,这事儿*简直——是迷人啊……这事儿多么令人着迷,我无法说出来呀……比看医生的乐趣多得多啦……*"

"莱昂内尔,你不会对任何人讲,对吗?你答应过的。"

"是的,当然不会,可是现在,我必须得走了,格拉迪斯,我真的必须走了。"

"不要如此犯傻。我才刚刚开始有点儿享受的感觉。不管怎样,再待一会儿,等我把这杯喝完。"

我耐着性子坐到沙发上,而她则继续没完没了地一小口、一小口喝着白兰地。她那双埋入皱褶之中的小眼睛仍然从眼角处瞥向我,还是那种带有恶意的、狡黠的神情。我有一种强烈的感觉,认为这个女人现在正进一步盘算着要说出什么令人不快的事,或者某种流言飞语。那双眼睛里含有巨蛇的狡诈目光,还撇着嘴,撇嘴的样子很是古怪。空气中——尽管或许只是我的想象——飘荡着某种微弱的危险气息。

接着,突然之间——突如其来地,令我惊跳起来,她说:"莱昂内尔,有关你和珍妮特·德佩拉贾之间的事情,我听到的是怎么回事儿呢?"

"现在,格拉迪斯,拜托……"

"莱昂内尔,你脸红啦!"

"胡扯。"

"难道你要告诉我,老单身汉最终动真心了吗?"

"格拉迪斯,这也太荒谬了。"我开始动身要走,但是,她一只手放到我的膝盖上,没让我起身。

"到现在为止,莱昂内尔,难道你不知道世上本无秘密可言吗?"

"珍妮特是个好女孩。"

"你几乎无法称她为女孩。"格拉迪斯·庞森比暂停下来,低头盯着大大的白兰地杯子的里面,那只杯子她是用两只手捧着的。"可是,莱昂内尔,我当然同意你的观点,各个方面来说,她都是一个令人愉快的人。除了,"现在,她说话速度慢了下来,"除了偶尔有些时候,她确实*说出*一些异乎寻常的事情来。"

"什么样的事情?"

"就那些事情,你知道的——关于人的那些事情。关于你的事情。"

"关于我,她说了什么?"

"没什么,莱昂内尔。你不会感兴趣的。"

"关于我,她说了什么?"

"她说你的,甚至不值得去重复。实话实说,不值得重复。只是当时听的时候,我有一种怪怪的感觉。"

"格拉迪斯——她说了什么?"等待她回答的当儿,我感觉到身体里呼呼往外冒汗。

"噢,现在,容我想想啊。当然,她只是说笑,否则,我也不会想到要告诉你呀。但是我想,她的确说过,这一切略微有点令人厌倦乏味。"

"一切什么?"

"几乎每晚都跟你出去吃饭之类的事情吧——那种事儿罢了。"

"她说过,那事儿令人厌倦乏味?"

"是的。"格拉迪斯·庞森比最后一大口将白兰地杯喝空,然后笔直坐起。"要是你真想知道,她当时说,这一切令人厌倦乏味透顶。然后,还说……"

"她还说什么了?"

"莱昂内尔。现在听着——没有必要激动,我只是为你好才跟你讲。"

"今天下午,我只是赶巧跟珍妮特玩起了凯纳斯特纸牌,就问她明天是否有空跟我一起吃晚饭。她说没空,不去了。"

"接着讲。"

"哦——当时她的原话是'我要跟那个令人厌倦透顶的老家伙莱昂内尔·兰普森共进晚餐。'"

"珍妮特是那样说的?"

"是的,莱昂内尔,亲爱的。"

"还说了什么?"

"现在,说得够多了。我想,我不应该和盘托出的。"

"拜托,讲完!"

"嗨,莱昂内尔,不要如此那般冲我大呼小叫。当然,你要是坚持要听,我会跟你讲的。事实上,要是不和盘托出,我想我还不算是真朋友呢。难道你不认为,这是真正友谊的见证,当像我们俩这样的人……"

"格拉迪斯!*拜托* 不要磨磨蹭蹭。"

"老天呐,你得给我时间*想想* 啊。现在,容我想想——就我记得的来说,她实际说的是这样的……"此时,格拉迪斯·庞森比在沙发上挺直身体坐起,双脚并没有踏踏实实地接触地面,眼睛现在也不看向我了,而是看着墙壁,嘴里开始熟练地模仿起那种低沉的语调——我再也熟悉不过的语调:"如此令人厌倦乏味,我亲爱的。一个人要是从*最开始* 到最后,跟莱昂内尔待在一起,*总是* 能够一字不差地说出下一步会出现什么情况。就晚饭来说,我们俩会去那家萨瓦烧烤馆———成不变的萨瓦烧烤馆。在那儿,长达两个小时的时间里,我不得不听着夸夸其谈的老……我的意思是说,我不得不听着他'嗡嗡嗡'单调地讲个不停,尽讲些绘画啦,瓷器啦———成不变的绘画和瓷器。然后,打出租车回家。在出租车里,他会拉起我的手,将身体靠得更近些。每每此时,我就会闻到一股发霉的雪茄烟气味,还夹杂着白兰地的味道,于是,他就开始嘟嘟囔囔说起来,说他多么希望——哦,多么希望年轻二十岁。我就说:'你能否打开一扇车窗,介意吗?'到我家时,我会告诉他,待在车里别下来,但是,他却假装没听见,飞速付完车钱。走到正门时,我往兜子里摸钥匙,他就站在我身边,眼睛里带着点儿傻乎乎的、谄媚的神情。我慢慢地将钥匙插入锁孔,慢慢地转动,然后——"倏"的一下,趁他来不及动弹的当儿,我说声'晚安',闪进屋内,随手关上了门……'嘿,莱昂内尔!怎么啦,亲爱的?毋庸置疑,你看起来生病了……'"

令人感到宽慰的是,就在那一刻,我当时一定是当场一下子昏厥过去了。那个可怕的晚上剩下时间里所发生的事情,我几乎什么都记不起来了,就有一点除外:我模模糊糊记得,却又颇感不安地猜疑,感觉当时好像任由格拉迪斯·庞森比以各种不同的方式对我加以安慰。后来,我相信我走出了那所房子,坐上车回到了家。可是,我对周围的一切几乎没有任何意识,直到第二天早晨从床上醒来,意识才得以恢复。

第二章 冤冤相报 第一节 《最后颂歌》Nunc Dimittis

醒来时,我感到虚弱,浑身就像散了架,闭着眼睛一动不动地躺着,脑子里尽量去拼凑刚刚过去那个夜晚所发生的一件又一件事情——有格拉迪斯·庞森比家的客厅,有格拉迪斯坐在沙发上小口喝着白兰地的情景,有那张满是皱褶的小脸,有类似大马哈鱼嘴的那张嘴,还有她说的话……她说了什么来着?噢,是的,关于我的一些话。我的天啊,想起来了!是关于我和珍妮特的一些话!那些肆无忌惮的、难以置信的话语!珍妮特真的能说出那些话吗?她能说出来吗?

我记得,当时我对珍妮特·德佩拉贾的憎恨开始滋生,而且滋生的速度之快令人恐惧。只不过是几分钟的时间而已——猛烈的憎恨之感突然之间就膨胀起来,将我的身体胀得鼓鼓的,感觉就要爆炸。我尽量要将这种憎恨感驱散,但这种感觉就像发烧患病一般挥之不去。于是,我不容耽搁,四处搜寻,就像某些卑劣的恶棍所做的那样,要搜寻出一个报复的方法。

你或许会说,像我这样的男人,那样行事有些不可思议。对于你的说法,我的回应是:错——要是你想想当时的情形的话,并非不可思议。在我看来,这种事儿能够逼迫一个男人去谋杀。实际上,我差点就成为一个谋杀犯了,多亏当时眼前闪现出一阵带点儿性虐待狂内容的场景,这种场景令我搜寻到一种更加隐秘的、令对方更加痛苦的惩罚方式。可话说回来了,只是要她的命,我认为那对这个女人过于仁慈,而对于我的品味而言,那又太过粗鲁。因此,我开始找寻一种高级的替代方式。

正常来说,我不是一个图谋不轨的人。我认为图谋不轨是一个令人作呕的行径,从不染指任何形式的图谋不轨行为。但是,勃然大怒和憎恨之感能够以令人惊讶的程度攫住一个男人的心。于是,顷刻之间,一个不可告人的计划立即成形,在我的头脑中展现——如此高级的一个计划,令我兴奋不已,以至于对此我达到了相当忘乎所以的地步。排除掉一两个小小的不利因素,将这个计划想到羽翼丰满的时候,我那沉思已久的报复心理已经发生了转变,变得心花怒放。我记得,当时我开始在床上荒唐地上蹿下跳,还拍打着双手。我知道,下一步所做的就是将电话簿拿来放到大腿上,开始急不可耐地查找一个人的名字。找到了,于是,我拿起话筒,拨通了号码。

"你好,"我说。"罗伊登先生吗? 约翰·罗伊登先生?"

"是我。"

噢——说服这位男子过来一下,跟我见上一面,不是什么难事。我从没见过他,当然,他知道我的名字——我既是一个绘画作品的收藏名家,又是一位在社会上有一定影响力的人物。对他来说,我可是一条可以逮住的大鱼。

"现在让我看看啊,兰普森先生,"他说,"我想,两三个小时过后,我应该有时间。你看可以吗?"

我对他说,可以,然后告诉他我的地址,就挂断了电话。

我从床上跳下来。这事儿真是太棒了,突然之间,我愉悦不已。刚才那会儿,我还悲观绝望、痛苦不堪,打算谋杀和自杀,我自己也不知道是怎么了。这会儿,躺在浴缸里吹起了口哨,吹奏的是普契尼的一段咏叹调。时不时地,我竟恶魔般地将双手放到一起摩擦起来。而在做一个双膝弯曲的动作时,由于失衡而歪倒,整个人一屁股坐到地板上,竟然像一个小学生一般咯咯笑了起来。

约翰·罗伊登按照约定的时间到来,被人领到我的图书室,我起身迎接。他个子不高,很是整洁,留着山羊胡子,胡子稍微带点姜黄色。他身穿一件黑色的天鹅绒夹克衫,系着一条赭棕色的领带,外面披上一件红色的套衫,脚穿黑色的绒面鞋子。我握了握他那只整洁的小手。

"罗伊登先生,你这么快就来了,很感激。"

"不用客气,先生。"跟几乎所有留胡子男子的嘴唇一样,这位男子的嘴唇裸露在外,看起来很湿润,胡须之中闪着粉色的光亮,有点猥琐的样子。对他的画作又表示了一番赞许后,我就直切主题。

"罗伊登先生,"我说。"我要请求你做一件相当不一般的事情,这事儿本身颇具个人私隐性。"

"好的,兰普森先生,什么事情?"他坐在我对面的椅子上,仰起头歪向一侧,速度很快,显得很活跃,那样子很像是一只鸟儿。

"当然啦,我知道,对我说的事情,你会慎重对待的,我能够信任你。"

"绝对能够,兰普森先生。"

"好的。现在,我的提议是这样的:这座城市里有一位女士,她的肖像我想让你来画。我特想拥有一幅画有她的精美画作。但是,存在着某些难言之隐,比如说,我有个人的理由,不希望让她知道,是我委托你画的肖像。"

"你的意思是……"

"正是,罗伊登先生。那正是我的意思。你我同为男人,我敢肯定,你会明白的。"

他微笑起来——嘴歪向一边,微微一笑,笑容刚好透过胡须看得见。他会意地上下点了点头。

"一个男人或许——"我说,"该怎么说好呢——特别、特别喜欢一名女士,而同时却有些个人的正当理由,还不希望她知道这一点,这是否有可能呢?"

"岂止是可能啊,兰普森先生。"

"有的时候,一个男人要谨小慎微、悄无声息地靠近他所追逐的目标,要耐心地等到恰如其分的时刻再现身。"

"的的确确,兰普森先生。"

"要捉住一只鸟,满树林里跑,追来追去是不行的,还有更好的方法。"

"是的,确实,兰普森先生。"

"比方说,往其尾巴上撒盐。"

"哈哈,嗯?"

"好吧,罗伊登先生,我想你明白的。现在——你是否恰好有机会认识一位女士,名叫珍妮特·德佩拉贾呢?"

"珍妮特·德佩拉贾?现在容我想想啊——是的。至少,我的意思是说,听人说过她。准确地说,我不了解她。"

"那有点儿可惜,事情有些更加难办了。你认为,你能设法见到她吗?或许在一个鸡尾酒会上,或者类似的场合?"

"这事儿不应该太难办的,兰普森先生。"

"很好,因为我的提议是这样的:你接近她,对她说,她正好是你多年以来找寻的那种模特——脸蛋正好,体形正好,眼睛的颜色也正好。这类事情你是熟悉的。然后,问她是否介意当你的模特,免费为她画像,说你为了明年的皇家学院大奖,很愿意为她画一幅肖像。我很有把握地感觉,她会很乐意帮你的忙,也会感到荣耀之至——要是我可以这么说的话。接下来,你为她画像,然后展出。展出结束,将画像送给我。除了你之外,没有人知道是我将画像买下来的。"

我想,当时罗伊登那张小小的圆脸正机灵地朝我看来,脑袋又歪向了一侧。他当时坐在椅子边上。这个坐姿,再加上套衫在身前闪耀的红色光芒,让我眼前浮现出一只红襟鸟,那只鸟蹲在细枝上,疑神疑鬼地听着周围的动静。

"整桩事情真的没有什么不妥之处,"我说。"要是你愿意,就叫它无害的小计谋——策划实施的……哦……是一个相当浪漫的老男人吧。"

"我知道,兰普森先生,我知道……"他似乎仍处在迟疑之中,于是,我急忙说:"在你正常收费的基础上,我很乐意加倍支付。"

这下妥了,只见他舔了舔双唇。"好吧,兰普森先生,我必须说的是,此类事情真的不在我的职责范围之内,你是了解的。但是,不管怎么说,要是拒绝如此一个——我可否这么说——拒绝如此一个浪漫的任务,我就是一个无情无义的人了呢?"

"罗伊登先生,拜托,我想要一张全身画像,一张大大的帆布画像——让我想想啊,大约是那边墙上那幅马奈作品的两倍大小。"

"大约是一米八乘以一米一?"

"是的。我想要她站立着的画像。对我来说,她最优雅的姿态就是站立的样子。"

"我十分理解,兰普森先生。画如此可爱的一位女士,我乐意之至。"

我心里想,我料到你会乐意的。我的伙计,看你处理这件事的方式,我就十分肯定,你会乐意的。但是,我却说:"好吧,罗伊登先生,那么,这件事情我就全交给你了。拜托,不要忘记:这是你我之间的一个小秘密。"

他离开后,我强迫自己安静地坐下来,深呼吸长达二十五次。我像傻子一般跳了起来,高兴得大喊大叫——这个架势,势不可当。一生之中,我从未感到如此激动兴奋。我的计划奏效啦!其最难实施的部分大功告成。现在,只有等待——漫长的等待。看这个人的绘画方式,画作完成得几个月时间。那么,我仅仅需要耐心等待即可,别无他法。

现在,我连想也没有多想,就决定在这段过渡时期出国游逛。就在第二天早晨,给珍妮特传达了我的意思(你会记得,那天晚上我预计要跟她共进晚餐的),告诉她我被人请走,要到别的地方去一下。然后,我就离开,前往意大利。

在意大利,就像以往任何时候一样,我玩得很开心,只是一想到要返回实施行动的现场,我的心就经常会因为紧张、兴奋而感到一阵烦乱。

四个月后,我最终还是返回了。那是七月的一天,是皇家学院大奖开幕后的第二天。我发现,在我离开的这段时间里,一切都按照计划进行,这令我舒了一口气。珍妮特·德佩拉贾的画像已经完成,挂在展览大厅展出,成为批评家和大众好评如潮的对象。我强忍着没有去现场观看,但是,罗伊登打电话对我说,有好几个人前来打听,希望买下此画,却都被告知,此画非卖品。展览结束后,罗伊登将画送到我家里,拿了钱走人。

我立马将画搬进楼上的工作间,开始仔细检查起来,心情激动的程度节节攀升。那人给她画的是一幅她身穿黑色晚礼服的站立肖像,背景是一个红色长毛绒沙发,左手搭在一把重实的椅子靠背上,那把椅子也是红色长毛绒质地的。画面的天花板上垂下一盏巨大的枝形水晶吊灯。

我的天呐,我想,这是多么龌龊的一件事情啊!但,这幅肖像本身不是那么糟糕的。他抓住了这个女子的神态——头部前倾,蓝色的眼睛睁得大大的,漂亮的嘴巴很是丑陋,一只嘴角带有一丝微笑。

当然,他把她画得比本人好看,脸上没有一丝皱纹,也一点儿都看不出下巴底下堆积的脂肪。我弯腰仔细察看画上的衣服。是的——衣服处的颜料厚一些,相当厚。就在此时,我一刻也不能等下去了,脱掉外衣,扔到一旁,准备要开始工作了。

到此,我应该提一句,我本人是绘画清理和复原方面的专家。特别值得一提的是,清理工作相对来说,过程很简单。做这个工作,一个人需要的就是耐心和轻柔的触碰。那些干这一行的人严守行业机密,收费昂贵得惊人,但是,他们从我这儿揽不到什么生意的。就我收藏的那些画作而言,我总是亲自动手做清理工作。

我倒出松节油,然后加入几滴酒精,将一小团儿脱脂棉放进混合后的溶液里蘸一下,拿出来再挤一挤,接着轻轻地——很是轻柔地在衣服的黑色颜料上面擦拭,一圈一圈地擦拭。我唯一希望的就是,罗伊登在每一层彻底干透后,再画上另一层,否则的话,两层就会溶到一起,我就不可能按照预计的程序工作了。到底是不是这样的,我一会儿就能知道。我先拿这个女子腹部的一块黑色衣服区域——面积有两平方厘米半还多——试验一下,花费了好长的时间。对颜料谨慎测试、细心剥离,向混合液里多加一两滴酒精,再测试,又加进一滴酒精。最终,溶液的浓度足以将颜料化开。

在这一小块方形区域上试验,大概用去了整整一个小时的时间。其间,越来越接近下面一层的时候,我的动作也越来越轻柔。接着,下面出现一个微小的粉红点,然后这一点逐渐扩大,越来越大,直至我试验清理的这块方形区域变成一片清晰明亮的粉红色。于是,我飞快使用纯松节油来中和一下这个区域。

至此,一切顺利。现在,我知道,黑颜料可以移除,却不会弄坏下面的画面。只要我有耐心,付出一些辛苦,就能够轻易地将所有的黑色颜料剥离。况且,我已经试验出合理的溶液浓度,还有安全的擦拭力度。因此呢,现在工作会干得更快一些。

我必须要说的是,这件事儿做起来相当有意思。我先从她身体中部开始,往下擦拭。随着一小块、一小块脱脂棉将她衣服中下部的颜料一点儿、一点儿地擦拭掉,一件奇特的粉红色贴身内衣开始显露出来。就算是要了我的命,我也弄不明白这东西叫什么名字,但是可以肯定,这东西是一个令人惊叹的复杂装备,看起来像是由一种结实的、厚实的弹性材料构成,其目的很明显,就是束缚、挤压女子鼓胀的体形,将身体塑造成匀称的流线形状,给人一种很是纤细苗条的假象。随着擦拭、清理工作越来越往下进行,我看到了一些整齐排列的吊带,很引人注目,也是粉红色的,附加到这副具有弹性的保护壳上。这些吊带向下垂去,垂下约有十二厘米,跟长筒袜的顶端固定到一起。

我后退一步打量一下这幅画,在我看来,它整体上相当令人难以置信。无论怎么说,我都强烈地感觉到一种被骗的感觉。在过去的这几个月时间里,难道我不是一直很欣赏这位仙女般的窈窕淑女吗?她是个假货,这一点毫无疑问。可是,我想知道的是,许多别的女性是否也做出这种欺骗的行径。当然,我知道,在紧身背心和紧身内衣盛行的时代,女士将身体束缚起来是很平常的事情,但是,出于某种原因,我感觉当今她们这方面的做法就是节食。

整个下半部的衣服颜料都擦拭、清理掉后,我立即将注意力转向上部,从这个女子的腰部慢慢地向上擦拭。上腹部的周围有一部分肌肉裸露的区域,再往上到胸部这一区域——实际上包括胸部,我发现一块人为修饰的区域,由一些浓密的黑色材料组成,边缘是褶边蕾丝。我十分清楚,这就是胸罩——另一种令人惊叹的装备,由一组整齐的黑带子搭调起来,搭调得很精巧、很科学,就像悬索桥的支撑钢缆一样。

我的天,我想,真是活到老,学到老啊。

现在,工作最终完成了,于是我退后一步,最后看了一眼这幅画。真是一幅令人吃惊的景象啊!这个女人——珍妮特·德佩拉贾——几乎跟真人一般大小,穿着内衣,站在那儿,站的地方有点像客厅。我猜想,那地方应该是客厅——头顶悬挂着枝形吊灯,身边放了一把红色的长毛绒椅子。最令人烦恼不安的是,她本人看起来完完全全是一副漠不关心的样子——平静的蓝眼睛睁得大大的,露出微微的笑容,漂亮的嘴巴很是丑陋。我也非常吃惊地注意到,她的腿有点弯,就像是一个赛马骑手。坦率地对你讲,这一切令我尴尬不已,感觉就好像自己应该钻进鼠洞,没有权利待在屋里,也没有权利看画。因此,过了一会儿,我就走了出去,随手关上门。这样做,似乎是最体面的做法。

现在,该轮到下一步,也就是最后一步啦!不要因为近来我没有提及报复之事,就想当然地认为,在过去的几个月时间里,我对报复的渴望会在某种程度上有所减弱。正相反,要是真说起来的话,报复的渴望加强了。对于要实施的最后一个行动,我可以告诉你说,我很难抑制我的心情。就拿那天晚上来说吧,我兴奋得甚至一夜没睡。

你知道,我迫不及待地要将所有的邀请函发出去。那一晚,我一夜未眠,准备邀请函,填写信封。一共有二十二封,每一封我都要用我个人的口吻和笔调来写。"周五(二十二日)晚上八点钟,我要搞一个小小的宴请活动。我真切希望你能前来……十分盼望再次见到你……"

第一封是写给珍妮特·德佩拉贾的,措辞极其讲究。信里,我遗憾地表示这么长时间没有见到她……我一直在国外……我们再次相聚的时候到了,以及诸如此类的内容。第二封是写给格拉迪斯·庞森比的。接下来的一封写给埃尔米奥娜·格德尔斯通女士,其余的分别写给比切诺公主、卡德伯德太太休伯特·考尔爵士、加尔巴利太太、彼得·尤安托马斯、詹姆斯、皮斯克尔、尤斯塔斯、皮埃格罗梅爵士、彼得·范桑滕、伊丽莎白、莫伊尼汉、米尔赫林男爵、伯特伦·斯特尔特、菲利普·科尼利尔斯、杰克·希尔、阿克曼女士、艾斯利太太、汉弗莱·金霍华德、约翰尼、奥科菲、尤瓦瑞太太以及瓦克斯沃思的女伯爵遗孀。

这是一份精挑细选的名单,包括上层社会最为显赫的男子,以及最杰出和最有影响力的女子。

我充分意识到,大家相当看重在我家举行的晚宴,都愿意前来赴宴。现在,看着笔尖在纸面上迅速移动的情景,我眼前几乎浮现出这样的情景:邀请函到达的那天早晨,受邀的女士兴高采烈地拿起床头电话,用尖锐的声音给另一头更加尖锐的声音打起了电话:"……莱昂内尔要搞晚会啦……他也邀请你了吗？我亲爱的,太好啦……他家的东西总是*那么*好吃……多么可爱的一个男人啊,怎么说都是个好男人,是的……"

那真是她们会说出的话语吗？我突然之间想到,事情可能根本不是那个样子。或许,更像这个样子:"我同意,我亲爱的,是的,一个老男人,还不算坏……但是,有一点儿令人厌倦乏味,难道你不这样认为吗？你刚才说什么来着？……枯燥乏味？但是,极度地枯燥乏味,我亲爱的。你真的切中了要害……珍妮特·德佩拉贾有一次说他什么了,你听说过吗？……哦,是的,我想你听说过的……太有意思啦,令人忍不住要大声尖叫,难道你不这样认为吗？……可怜的珍妮特……我真不明白,她怎么能忍受他那么长时间……"

无论如何,邀请函都发了出去。两三天的时间里,除了卡德伯德太太和休伯特·考尔爵士两位外出不在之外,大家都兴高采烈地接受了邀请。

二十二日晚八点半,我家大大的客厅挤满了人,他们在屋子的各处站立着,对我家里的绘画作品赞不绝口,喝着马提尼酒,大声谈论着。女士身上散发出浓烈的香气,男子个个都是粉红面孔,将无尾礼服仔细扣好。珍妮特·德佩拉贾穿着一件黑色的礼服,跟肖像画中的那件是一样的。每次瞥见她的时候,一种大大的气泡般的幻觉就会在我的大脑里浮现,如同那些荒谬卡通里的情景。幻觉之中,我看见珍妮特穿着内衣,戴着黑色的胸罩,还有粉红色的弹性束身带、吊带以及赛马骑手的弯腿。

我在一伙、一伙的人之间穿梭,跟大家和和气气地聊着,同时也听着他们的谈话。我听见身后加尔巴利太太对尤斯塔斯·皮埃格罗梅爵士和詹姆斯·皮斯克尔两个人说,前天晚上到克拉里奇家赴宴时,坐在她邻桌的那名男子白胡子上如何、如何带有红色的唇膏的印记。"就是*涂抹过多了*,"她继续说道,"而且,那位老男人至少有九十岁……"在另一边,格德尔斯通女士正跟人讲,到哪里能买到白兰地泡的松露,我还看见艾斯利太太跟米尔赫林男爵小声嘀咕着什么,而那位男爵则慢慢地将头从一边摇晃到另一边,就像是一个有了年头儿而变得毫无生气的节拍器。

有人宣布晚宴开始,我们大家都走出客厅。

"我的老天呐!"他们进入餐厅后大喊起来。"多么糟啊,太黑啦!"

"我几乎什么都看不见啊!"

"小小蜡烛多么美妙啊!"

"哇,莱昂内尔,多浪漫的情调啊!"

沿着长长的餐桌的正中央,摆上了一趟纤细的蜡烛,一共有六支,每两支相距约六十厘米,微小的火焰在桌面上闪着微光,令房间其余的地方黑黝黝的一片。这一布置很有趣味性,除了能很好地迎合我的个人目的之外,这一不同寻常的布置也令客人愉悦。客人很快地各就各位,晚宴开始了。

他们似乎都很享受这场烛光晚宴,事情进展得相当顺利,尽管出于某种原因,暗黑的环境令大家说话声音比往常大了些。珍妮特·德佩拉贾说话的声音在我听来,格外刺耳。她紧挨着米尔赫林男爵坐着,我听见她跟他谈论着一周前在费拉角度过的枯燥时光。"除了法国人,什么都没有,"她继续说。"整个地方,什么都没有,除了法国人……"

就我个人而言,我关注的是蜡烛——很是纤细,用不了多久就会燃到根部。同时,我也是紧张得不得了,这一点我得承认,但是,紧张感也跟强烈的喜悦感同步伴随。几乎令我达到了如醉如痴的地步。每次听到珍妮特的声音,或者瞥见她的脸笼罩在烛光的阴影之中,一个装满兴奋之情的小球球就会在我的体内炸开花,感觉爆炸产生的火焰在皮肤底下流淌。

大家都在吃草莓的时候,我觉得时刻终于到了。于是,我深吸一口气,大声说道:"我想,现在,我们必须得开灯了,蜡烛几乎燃尽。玛丽,"我叫道。"噢,玛丽啊,开灯,请你打开灯。"

我的话宣布完之后,出现了片刻的沉默。我听见女仆向门走去的声音,然后听见"啪"的一声,开关被轻轻一按,整个房间一下子亮起了刺眼的光。大家都眯起了眼睛,然后再次睁开,彼此看去

第二章 冤冤相报 第一节 《最后颂歌》Nunc Dimittis

就在那一刻,我从椅子上起身,悄无声息地溜出了房间,但是,就在我离开的时候,我看到了那一幕——令我终生难忘的一幕。这一幕是关于珍妮特的,只见她双手举到空中停住,犹如冻僵一般直挺挺的。这之前,她正向桌子对面的某个人打招呼呢。她的嘴向下张开,超过五厘米宽。僵住之际,就带着这副表情——吃惊不已、懵懂不解,恰似一秒钟之前,她被一枪毙命,子弹正穿心脏。

在屋外的门厅里,我暂停了一下,听着喧嚣初起时发出的声音——女士尖锐的喊叫声,以及男士震惊之余发出的狐疑的感叹声。很快,一阵巨大的嘈杂之声响起,其间,大家你说我喊,同时进行。接下来就是最最甜蜜、最最温馨的时刻,我听到米尔赫林男爵的声音——盖过其余那些人的声音:"喂!来个人呀!赶快!快给她拿点儿水喝!"

走到外面的大街上,我的专职司机协助我上了车,很快驶离伦敦,沿着大北路疾驰而去,向着我的另一所房子,那地方距离城里有一百五十多公里。

紧接着的两天时间,我在幸灾乐祸式的沾沾自喜中度过。我四处闲荡,兴奋得狂喜,如梦游一般。近乎沉浸在自我满足情绪之中,内心充满了愉悦之情,这种愉悦之情过于强烈,以至于两条腿整个下半部总是有一种针刺般的发麻感觉。直到今天早晨接完格拉迪斯·庞森比给我打来的电话,我才一下子恢复了意识,意识到自己根本不是什么英雄,而是一只被遗弃的狗熊。她对我说——我认为她说的带有一丝享受的味道,大家都揭竿而起,而且,所有的人,不论是我的老朋友,还是我喜爱的朋友,都对我横眉冷对、冷言冷语,还发誓永远、永远都不搭理我了。但是,她一再说,除了她之外。大家都那样,她除外。她问我,要是她过来,跟我待几天,安慰安慰我,我是否会感觉温暖、舒适一些呢?

我想,我当时恐怕过于心烦意乱,甚至没有对她的话有礼貌地回应一下,就放下电话,走到别处,号啕大哭。

接下来,就在今天中午,最后一个沉重的打击到来了。寄来一个邮包,里面附带一封信函——我几乎下不了决心再往下写了,我很羞愧。那封信里有一张小小的便条，上面写的是最甜蜜、最温柔的内容，可以想象不会是别人写的，正是珍妮特·德佩拉贾本人亲自写的。她写道，她完全原谅了我，原谅了我所做的一切；她知道，这一切都是在开玩笑，他人说我的那些冷言冷语，我一定不要放在心上；她爱我，而且永远地爱我，会一直爱到她生命的终止。

读到这些言词，我感到，我简直就是一个欺负女性的无耻之徒，简直就是一个残忍的野兽！当我发现她实际上给我寄来了一份小礼物来额外表示她的爱意的时候，这种感觉就更强烈了。礼物是一个二百克容量的罐子，里面装的是我最喜欢吃的东西——新鲜的鱼子酱。

不管在什么情况下，我从来都拒绝不了美味鱼子酱的诱惑。或许，这是我最大的弱点吧。因此，尽管到了今天晚上吃饭的时候，我没有一丁点儿胃口吃任何东西——那是很自然的事情，但是，我必须得承认的是，为了极力安慰一下痛苦不堪的自我，我一连吃下好几勺鱼子酱。甚至有可能吃下的有点儿太多了，因为在刚刚过去的约一小时之内，我一直感觉不太精神。或许，我应该立即上楼取些小苏打服用一下。等身体状况好转，我可以轻轻松松回来，将剩下的吃完。

你知道——现在，仔细一想，我突然之间真的感觉自己病得不轻了。

第二节 《复仇公司》Vengeance Is Mine Inc.

罗尔德·达尔的《复仇公司》(*Vengeance Is Mine Inc.*)被收录在《罗尔德·达尔短篇故事集锦》(*The Collected Short Stories of Roald Dahl*)、《完全出人意料故事集》(*Completely Unexpected Tales*)、《更多出人意料故事集》(*More Tales of the Unexpected*)、《后续出人意料故事集》(*Further Tales of the Unexpected*)、《<伟大写手>及其他故事集》(*The Great Automatic Grammatizator and Other Stories*)以及《<卖伞男子>及其他故事集》(*The Umbrella Man and Other Stories*)等书中。此

外,这部小说还被改编成电视系列剧——1980年8月30日播映的《出乎意料的故事集》(*Tales of the Unexpected*)第三部中的第4集(Episode 3.4),可见其影响力之大。

一、原作导读

这篇故事是以第一人称"我"的视角展开的,主人公是"我"以及一个名叫"乔治"(George)的年轻男子。尽管如此,叙述者"我"几乎是"隐身"的,作用并不是很大,可以说,只是起到了"纽带"或者"桥梁"的作用,可以看成作家达尔本人的化身。

两个年轻人(叙述者"我"和乔治)一边讨论着早晨报纸上的内容,一边为他们经济上的拮据而悲叹,苦于手头太紧。报纸上说,一个名叫莱昂内尔·潘塔隆的人报道了好几位社会知名人物的花边新闻。莱昂内尔是政治栏目和社会新闻栏目伟大的专栏作家。于是,"我"萌生了一个绝妙的想法:被莱昂内尔"侮辱"过的那些人很想照着他的鼻子打上一拳,但是,他们的社会地位又不允许他们那样做。何不做这样的生意:替这些人出气,收取一些费用?两位年轻人当即讨论细节,开始实施他们的赚钱计划。他们设计出各种复仇服务项目,每个项目价码各异:

1. 拳击对方鼻子,打一次,使劲打 500 美元
2. 把对方眼睛打青 600 美元
3. 拳击对方鼻子,同时将其眼睛打青 1000 美元
4. 趁对方停车之际,将一条响尾蛇(毒液已经抽取出来)放入对方车内,放到脚踏板的附近。 1500 美元
5. 将对方诱拐到车内,脱光所有的衣服,但不脱内裤、鞋和袜子。然后,在交通高峰期,将其丢出车外,丢到第五大街上 2500 美元

1. Punch him on the nose, once, hard $500
2. Black his eye $600
3. Punch him on the nose and black his eye $1000
4. Introduce a rattlesnake (with venom extracted) into his car, on

the floor by his pedals, when he parks it　　　　　　　$1500

5. Kidnap him, take all his clothes away except his underpants, his shoes and socks, then dump him out on Fifth Ave. in the rush hour
　　　　　　　　　　　　　　　　　　　　　　　　　$2500

　　他们印制了名片,散发给那些受到莱昂内尔"羞辱"的人,还成立了"复仇公司"。两天的时间里,他们接到了好几份订单,这令他们对未来充满了幻想。"我"进一步出谋划策,提出"一次行动服务多个客户"的设想,而每个客户都会认为此次复仇服务是为自己提供的,可谓"一劳永逸""一举多得"。最后,针对拳打莱昂内尔鼻子这项服务,一共有三位客户订购,于是,他们决定从这项服务开始做起。

　　针对这项服务,他们制订了详细的计划:鉴于莱昂内尔在夜晚很晚的时候出没于企鹅俱乐部,他们到那儿把他"约"出来,乔治负责拳击他的鼻子,然后跑开,"我"则坐在租来的车里等待着……同时,通知那三位客户观看实施复仇的整个过程的时间和地点。

　　这个复仇服务实施的很成功,他们随即驾车沿着满是积雪的街道快速逃离现场。但是,他们很快意识到,他们被人跟踪了,而且怎么甩都甩不掉。无奈之下,他俩只好停车。

　　车外传来一个人的声音:"好了,伙计们,怎么这么着急?"
　　"没有着急,"我回答。"我们只是赶着回家。"
　　"是吗?"
　　"哦,是的。我们现在正在回家的路上。"
　　"我收到了你们的电报,在大街对面看到了整个过程。干得好,我给你们俩双倍报酬,值这个价。这是我看到过最有意思的事儿。再见,伙计们。当心点儿,他们现在会尾随而来。我要是你们的话,我就离开这座城镇。再见。"我们还没来得急说什么,他就消失不见了。

　　A voice from outside said, "All right boys, what's the hurry?"
　　"No hurry," I answered. "We're just going home."

"Yea?"

"Oh yes, we're just on our way home now."

"I got your wire and I watched the whole thing from across the street. You did a fine job. I'm paying you boys double. It was worth it. Funniest thing I ever seen. Goodbye boys. Watch your steps. They'll be after you now. Get out of town if I were you. Goodbye." And before we could say anything, he was gone.

原来,跟踪他们的是其中一位顾客,真是虚惊一场啊。两位年轻人淘到了第一桶金,开心无比,筹划着美好的未来。

"……我们将成为国际电影摄影场的显赫成员,影星会冲我们微笑,服务生领班会向我们鞠躬。或许,在即将到来的时间里,莱昂内尔·潘塔隆甚至或许在他的栏目里提到我们。"

"那或许会非同寻常,"我说。

"岂止是,"他高兴地说。"岂止是非同寻常。"

"... We will become prominent members of the international set and film stars will smile at us and head-waiters will bow to us and perhaps, in time to come, perhaps we might even get ourselves mentioned in Lionel Pantaloon's column."

"That would be something," I said.

"Wouldn't it just," he answered happily. "Wouldn't that just be something."

二、原作释读

本篇小说没有涉及过多的技术性很强的词汇,这给读者的阅读和理解带来了便利。因此,阅读难度不是很大,但是,某些背景方面的知识对于小说情节的理解起到一定的作用,读者在阅读中要加以辨别和领悟。

Vengeance[①] Is Mine Inc. [②]

It was snowing when I woke up.

I could tell that it was snowing because there was a kind of brightness in the room and it was quiet outside with no footstep-noises coming up from the street and no tyre-noises but only the engines of the cars. I looked up and I saw George over by the window in his green dressing-gown[③], bending over the paraffin[④]-stove, making the coffee.

"Snowing," I said.

"It's cold," George answered. "It's really cold."

I got out of bed and fetched the morning paper from outside the door. It was cold all right and I ran back quickly and jumped into bed and lay still for a while under the bedclothes, holding my hands tight between my legs for warmth.

"No letters?" George said.

"No. No letters."

"Doesn't look as if the old man's going to cough up[⑤]."

"Maybe he thinks four hundred and fifty is enough for one month,"

---

① vengeance: *Noun* [mass noun] punishment inflicted or retribution exacted for an injury or wrong 报仇;复仇;报复

② 本部小说原文出自"DAHL, R. *The Collected Short Stories of Roald Dahl*. London: Penguin Books Ltd., 1992"。

③ dressing-gown or dressing gown: *Noun* a long loose robe, typically worn after getting out of bed or bathing(起床或洗澡后穿)晨衣;浴袍

④ paraffin: *Noun* (also as "paraffin oil" or "liquid paraffin")(Brit.) a colourless, flammable, oily liquid similarly obtained and used as fuel, especially kerosene(英国英语)煤油

⑤ cough up: to surrender (money, information, etc), esp. reluctantly(特别指不情愿)交出(钱或信息等)

I said.

"He's never been to New York. He doesn't know the cost of living here."

"You shouldn't have spent it all in one week."

George stood up and looked at me. "*We* shouldn't have spent it, you mean."

"That's right," I said. "We." I began reading the paper.

The coffee was ready now and George brought the pot over and put it on the table between our beds. "A person can't live without money," he said. "The old man ought to know that." He got back into his bed without taking off his green dressing-gown. I went on reading. I finished the racing page and the football page and then I started on Lionel Pantaloon, the great political and society columnist. I always read Pantaloon—same as the other twenty or thirty million other people in the country. He's a habit with me; he's more than a habit; he's part of my morning, like three cups of coffee, or shaving.

"This fellow's got a nerve," I said.

"Who?"

"This Lionel Pantaloon."

"What's he saying now?"

"Same sort of thing he's always saying. Same sort of scandal. Always about the rich. Listen to this: '... seen at the Penguin Club... banker William S. Womberg with beauteous① starlet② Theresa Williams... three nights running... Mrs. Womberg at home with a head-

---

① beauteous: *Adjective* (poetic/literary) beautiful(诗歌或文学作品中的用法)漂亮的；美丽的

② starlet: *Noun* (informal) a young actress with aspirations to become a star (非正式)新秀女演员(e.g. a Hollywood starlet 一名好莱坞女新秀)

· 207 ·

ache... which is something anyone's wife would have if hubby was out squiring① Miss Williams of an evening...'"

"That fixes Womberg," George said.

"I think it's a shame," I said. "That sort of thing could cause a divorce. How can this Pantaloon get away with stuff like that?"

"He always does, they're all scared of him. But if I was William S. Womberg," George said, "you know what I'd do? I'd go right out and punch this Lionel Pantaloon right on the nose. Why, that's the only way to handle those guys."

"Mr. Womberg couldn't do that."

"Why not?"

"Because he's an old man," I said. "Mr. Womberg is a dignified and respectable old man. He's a very prominent banker in the town. He couldn't possibly..."

And then it happened. Suddenly, from nowhere, the idea came. It came to me in the middle of what I was saying to George and I stopped short and I could feel the idea itself kind of flowing into my brain and I kept very quiet and let it come and it kept on coming and almost before I knew what had happened I had it all, the whole plan, the whole brilliant magnificent plan worked out clearly in my head; and right then I knew it was a beauty.

I turned and I saw George staring at me with a look of wonder on his face. "What's wrong?" he said. "What's the matter?"

I kept quite calm. I reached out and got myself some more coffee before I allowed myself to speak.

"George," I said, and I still kept calm. "I have an idea. Now lis-

---

① squire: *Verb* (dated) (of a man) have a romantic relationship with (a woman)(古旧用法)(男子)与(一名女子)有一段风流韵事

ten very carefully because I have an idea which will make us both very rich. We are broke, are we not?"

"We are."

"And this William S. Womberg," I said, "would you consider that he is angry with Lionel Pantaloon this morning?"

"Angry!" George shouted. "Angry! Why, he'll be madder than hell!"

"Quite so. And do you think that he would like to see Lionel Pantaloon receive a good hard punch on the nose?"

"Damn right he would!"

"And now tell me, is it not possible that Mr. Womberg would be prepared to pay a sum of money to someone who would undertake to perform this nose-punching operation efficiently and discreetly on his behalf?"

George turned and looked at me, and gently, carefully, he put down his coffee-cup on the table. A slowly widening smile began to spread across his face. "I get you," he said. "I get the idea."

"That's just a little part of the idea. If you read Pantaloon's column here you will see that there is another person who has been insulted today." I picked up the paper. "There is a Mrs. Ella Gimple, a prominent socialite① who has perhaps a million dollars in the bank..."

"What does Pantaloon say about her?"

I looked at the paper again. "He hints," I answered, "at how she makes a stack of money out of her own friends by throwing roulette② par-

---

① socialite: *Noun* a person who is well known in fashionable society and is fond of social activities and entertainment 社交界名人

② roulette: *Noun* [mass noun] a gambling game in which a ball is dropped on to a revolving wheel with numbered compartments, the players betting on the number at which the ball comes to rest 轮盘赌

ties and acting as the bank."

"That fixes Gimple," George said. "And Womberg. Gimple and Womberg." He was sitting up straight in bed waiting for me to go on.

"Now," I said, "we have two different people both loathing Lionel Pantaloon's guts this morning, both wanting desperately to go out and punch him on the nose, and neither of them daring to do it. You understand that?"

"Absolutely."

"So much then," I said, "for Lionel Pantaloon. But don't forget that there are others like him. There are dozens of other columnists who spend their time insulting wealthy and important people. There's Harry Weyman, Claude Taylor, Jacob Swinski, Walter Kennedy, and the rest of them."

"That's right," George said. "That's absolutely right."

"I'm telling you, there's nothing that makes the rich so furious as being mocked and insulted in the newspapers."

"Go on," George said. "Go on."

"All right. Now this is the plan." I was getting rather excited myself. I was leaning over the side of the bed, resting one hand on the little table, waving the other about in the air as I spoke. "We will set up immediately an organization and we will call it... what shall we call it... we will call it... let me see... we will call it 'Vengeance Is Mine Inc.'... How about that?"

"Peculiar name."

"It's biblical①. It's good. I like it. 'Vengeance Is Mine Inc.' It sounds fine. And we will have little cards printed which we will send to

---

① biblical or Biblical: *Adjective* of, relating to, or contained in the Bible (与《圣经》(有关)的;《圣经》中的(e. g. the biblical account of creation《圣经》中对创世的记述)

all our clients reminding them that they have been insulted and mortified in public and offering to punish the offender in consideration of① a sum of money. We will buy all the newspapers and read all the columnists and every day we will send out a dozen or more of our cards to prospective clients."

"It's marvellous!" George shouted. "It's terrific!"

"We shall be rich," I told him. "We shall be exceedingly wealthy in no time at all."

"We must start at once!"

I jumped out of bed, fetched a writing-pad and a pencil and ran back to bed again. "Now," I said, pulling my knees under the blankets and propping the writing-pad against them, "the first thing is to decide what we're going to say on the printed cards which we'll be sending to our clients," and I wrote, 'VENGEANCE IS MINE INC.' as a heading on the top of the sheet of paper. Then, with much care, I composed a finely phrased letter explaining the functions of the organization. It finished up with the following sentence: "*Therefore VENGEANCE IS MINE INC. will undertake, on your behalf and in absolute confidence, to administer suitable punishment to columnist and in this regard we respectfully submit to you a choice of methods (together with prices) for your consideration.*"

"What do you mean, 'a choice of methods'?" George said.

"We must give them a choice. We must think up a number of things... a number of different punishments. Number one will be..." and I wrote down, '1. *Punch him on the nose, once, hard.*' "What shall we charge for that?"

"Five hundred dollars," George said instantly.

---

① in consideration of: in return for; on account of 作为……的报答;作为对……的酬报;考虑到;顾及;由于(e. g. He paid them in consideration of their services. 他付他们钱以酬谢他们的服务。)

I wrote it down. "What's the next one?"

"Black his eye," George said.

I wrote it down, "2. Black his eye... MYM500."

"No!" George said. "I disagree with the price. It definitely requires more skill and timing to black an eye nicely than to punch a nose. It is a skilled job. It should be six hundred."

"OK," I said. "Six hundred. And what's the next one?"

"Both together, of course. The old one two." We were in George's territory now. This was right up his street①.

"Both together?"

"Absolutely. Punch his nose and black his eye. Eleven hundred dollars."

"There should be a reduction for taking the two," I said. "We'll make it a thousand."

"It's dirt cheap," George said. "They'll snap it up②."

"What's next?"

We were both silent now, concentrating fiercely. Three deep parallel grooves of skin appeared upon George's rather low sloping forehead. He began to scratch his scalp, slowly but very strongly. I looked away and tried to think of all the terrible things which people had done to other people. Finally, I got one, and with George watching the point of my

---

① (right) up one's street: (informal) well suited to one's tastes, interests, or abilities(非正式)对……口味的;符合……兴趣的;适合……能力的(e.g. This job would be right up your street. 这件工作会非常合你意的。)

② snap something up: quickly and eagerly buy or secure something that is in short supply or being sold cheaply 抢购(紧缺或廉价货)(e.g. All the tickets have been snapped up. 所有的票已被抢购一空。)

pencil moving over the paper, I wrote: '4. *Put a rattlesnake (with venom① extracted) on the floor of his car, by the pedals, when he parks it.*'

"Jesus Christ!" George whispered. "You want to kill him with fright!"

"Sure," I said.

"And where'd you get a rattlesnake, anyway?"

"Buy it. You can always buy them. How much shall we charge for that one?"

"Fifteen hundred dollars," George said firmly. I wrote it down.

"Now we need one more."

"Here it is," George said. "Kidnap him in a car, take all his clothes away except his underpants and his shoes and socks, then dump him out on Fifth Avenue in the rush hour." He smiled, a broad triumphant smile.

"We can't do that."

"Write it down. And charge two thousand five hundred bucks. You'd do it all right if old Womberg were to offer you that much."

"Yes," I said. "I suppose I would." And I wrote it down. "That's enough now," I added. "That gives them a wide choice."

"And where will we get the cards printed?" George asked.

"George Karnoffsky," I said. "Another George. He's a friend of mine. Runs a small printing shop down on Third Avenue. Does wedding invitations and things like that for all the big stores. He'll do it. I know he will."

"Then what are we waiting for?"

We both leapt out of bed and began to dress. "It's twelve o'clock,"

---

① venom: *Noun* [mass noun] poisonous fluid secreted by animals such as snakes and scorpions and typically injected into prey or aggressors by biting or stinging(毒蛇、蝎子等分泌的)毒液

I said. "If we hurry we'll catch him before he goes to lunch."

It was still snowing when we went out into the street and the snow was four or five inches thick on the sidewalk, but we covered the fourteen blocks to Karnoffsky's shop at a tremendous pace and we arrived there just as he was putting his coat on to go out.

"Claude!" he shouted. "Hi boy! How you been keeping," and he pumped my hand. He had a fat friendly face and a terrible nose with great wide-open nose-wings which overlapped his cheeks by at least an inch on either side. I greeted him and told him that we had come to discuss some most urgent business. He took off his coat and led us back into the office, then I began to tell him our plans and what we wanted him to do.

When I'd got about quarter way through my story, he started to roar with laughter and it was impossible for me to continue; so I cut it short and handed him the piece of paper with the stuff on it that we wanted him to print. And now, as he read it, his whole body began to shake with laughter and he kept slapping the desk with his hand and coughing and choking and roaring like someone crazy. We sat watching him. We didn't see anything particular to laugh about.

Finally he quietened down and he took out a handkerchief and made a great business about wiping his eyes. "Never laughed so much," he said weakly. "That's a great joke, that is. It's worth a lunch. Come on out and I'll give you lunch."

"Look," I said severely, "this isn't any joke. There is nothing to laugh at. You are witnessing the birth of a new and powerful organization..."

"Come on," he said and he began to laugh again. "Come on and have lunch."

"When can you get those cards printed?" I said. My voice was stern and businesslike. He paused and stared at us. "You mean...you really mean...you're serious about this thing?"

"Absolutely. You are witnessing the birth..."

"All right," he said, "all right," he stood up. "I think you're crazy and you'll get in trouble. Those boys like messing other people about①, but they don't much fancy being messed about themselves."

"When can you get them printed, and without any of your workers reading them?"

"For this," he answered gravely, "I will give up my lunch. I will set the type myself. It is the least I can do." He laughed again and the rims of his huge nostrils twitched with pleasure. "How many do you want?"

"A thousand—to start with, and envelopes."

"Come back at two o'clock," he said and I thanked him very much and as we went out we could hear his laughter rumbling down the passage into the back of the shop.

At exactly two o'clock we were back. George Karnoffsky was in his office and the first thing I saw as we went in was the high stack of printed cards on his desk in front of him. They were large cards, about twice the size of ordinary wedding or cocktail invitation-cards. "There you are," he said. "All ready for you." The fool was still laughing.

He handed us each a card and I examined mine carefully. It was a beautiful thing. He had obviously taken much trouble over it. The card itself was thick and stiff with narrow gold edging all the way around, and the letters of the heading were exceedingly elegant. I cannot reproduce it here in all its splendour, but I can at least show you how it read:

---

① mess someone about/around: (Brit. informal) cause someone inconvenience or problems, especially by acting unfairly or indecisively(英国英语非正式用法)给……制造麻烦

VENGEANCE IS MINE INC.

Dear·················

You have probably seen columnist ················'s slanderous① and unprovoked② attack upon your character in today's paper. It is an outrageous insinuation③, a deliberate distortion of the truth.

Are you yourself prepared to allow this miserable malice-monger④ to insult you in this manner?

The whole world knows that it is foreign⑤ to the nature of the American people to permit themselves to be insulted either in public or in pri-

---

① slanderous: *Adjective* (used of statements) harmful and often untrue; tending to discredit or malign 诽谤的；诋毁的；造谣中伤的(e. g. A man of moral integrity does not fear any slanderous attack. 人正不怕影子斜。)

② unprovoked: *Adjective* (of an attack, or a display of aggression or emotion) not caused by anything done or said (攻击、侵略或情感)无缘无故的(e. g. acts of unprovoked aggression 无缘无故的侵略行径)

③ insinuation: *Noun* an unpleasant hint or suggestion of something bad 影射；含沙射影(e. g. I've done nothing to deserve all your vicious insinuations. 我没有做任何值得你含沙射影的事情。)

④ monger: *Noun* a person promoting something undesirable or discreditable 挑起……的人

⑤ foreign: *Adjective* (foreign to) not belonging to or characteristic of 不属于……的；与……相悖的(e. g. Crime and brutality are foreign to our nature and our country. 犯罪和暴行与我们的本性和国家相背。)

vate without rising up in righteous indignation and demanding—nay①, exacting②—a just measure of retribution③.

On the other hand, it is only natural that a citizen of your standing④ and reputation will not wish personally to become further involved in this sordid⑤ petty affair, or indeed to have any direct contact whatsoever with this vile⑥ person.

How then are you to obtain satisfaction?

The answer is simple, VENGEANCE IS MINE INC. will obtain it for you. We will undertake, on your behalf and in absolute confidence, to administer individual punishment to columnist……………, and in this regard we respectfully submit to you a choice of methods (together with prices) for your consideration:

---

① nay: *Adverb* or rather; and more than that (used to emphasize a more appropriate word than one just used)（用以对已使用的言辞作更恰当的补充）说得更确切一点;不止如此(e. g. It will take months, nay years. 这会花上几个月乃至几年的时间。)

② exacting: *Adjective* making great demands on one's skill, attention, or other resources 苛求的;严厉的(e. g. living up to such exacting standards 达到如此苛刻的标准)

③ retribution: *Noun* [mass noun] punishment that is considered to be morally right and fully deserved 应得的惩罚;报应(e. g. Settlers drove the Navajo out of Arizona in retribution for their raids. 移民把纳瓦霍人赶出亚利桑那州,以报复他们的袭击。)

④ standing: *Noun* [mass noun] position, status, or reputation 地位;级别;名望(e. g. a man of high social standing 社会名望高的人)

⑤ sordid: *Adjective* involving ignoble actions and motives; arousing moral distaste and contempt 卑鄙的;令人不齿的(e. g. The story paints a sordid picture of bribes and scams. 这个故事刻画了一幅贿赂和阴谋的肮脏画面。)

⑥ vile: *Adjective* extremely unpleasant 可憎的;坏透的;极讨厌的(e. g. He has a vile temper. 他的脾气坏极了。)

1. Punch him on the nose, once, hard $500
2. Black his eye $600
3. Punch him on the nose and black his eye $1000
4. Introduce a rattlesnake (with venom extracted) into his car, on the floor by his pedals, when he parks it $1500
5. Kidnap him, take all his clothes away except his underpants, his shoes and socks, then dump him out on Fifth Ave. in the rush hour
$2500

This work executed by a professional.

If you desire to avail yourself of any of these offers, kindly reply to VENGEANCE IS MINE INC. at the address indicated upon the enclosed slip of paper. If it is practicable, you will be notified in advance of the place where the action will occur and of the time, so that you may, if you wish, watch the proceedings in person from a safe and anonymous distance.

No payment need be made until after your order has been satisfactorily executed, when an account will be rendered in the usual manner.

George Karnoffsky had done a beautiful job of printing.

"Claude," he said, "you like?"

"It's marvellous."

"It's the best I could do for you. It's like in the war when I would see soldiers going off perhaps to get killed and all the time I would want to be giving them things and doing things for them." He was beginning to laugh again, so I said, "We'd better be going now. Have you got large envelopes for these cards?"

"Everything is here. And you can pay me when the money starts coming in." That seemed to set him off① worse than ever and he collapsed into his chair, giggling like a fool. George and I hurried out of the shop into the street, into the cold snow-falling afternoon.

We almost ran the distance back to our room and on the way up I borrowed a Manhattan telephone directory from the public telephone in the hall. We found "Womberg, William S," without any trouble and while I read out the address—somewhere up in the East Nineties—George wrote it on one of the envelopes.

"Gimple, Mrs. Ella H," was also in the book and we addressed an envelope to her as well. "We'll just send to Womberg and Gimple today," I said. "We haven't really got started yet. Tomorrow we'll send a dozen."

"We'd better catch the next post," George said.

"We'll deliver them by hand," I said. "Now, at once. The sooner they get them the better. Tomorrow might be too late. They won't be half so angry tomorrow as they are today. People are apt to cool off through the night. See here," I said, "you go ahead and deliver those two cards right away. While you're doing that I'm going to snoop② around the town and try to find out something about the habits of Lionel Pantaloon. See you back here later in the evening..."

At about nine o'clock that evening I returned and found George lying on his bed smoking cigarettes and drinking coffee.

---

① set someone off: cause someone to start doing something, especially laughing or talking 使开始做(尤指使人发笑或议论)(e.g. Anything will set him off laughing. 任何事都能把他逗笑。)

② snoop: Verb [no obj.] investigate or look around furtively in an attempt to find out something, especially information about someone's private affairs 窥探;打探(某事,尤指隐私)(e.g. Your sister might find the ring if she goes snooping about. 如果你姐姐四处打探一下,也许会找到戒指。)

"I delivered them both," he said. "Just slipped them through the letter-boxes and rang the bells and beat it up the street. Womberg had a huge house, a huge white house. How did you get on?"

"I went to see a man I know who works in the sports section of the *Daily Mirror*. He told me all."

"What did he tell you?"

"He said Pantaloon's movements are more or less routine. He operates at night, but wherever he goes earlier in the evening, he *always*—and this is the important point—he *always* finishes up at the Penguin Club. He gets there round about midnight and stays until two or two-thirty. That's when his legmen[①] bring him all the dope[②]."

"That's all we want to know," George said happily.

"It's too easy."

"Money for old rope[③]."

There was a full bottle of blended whisky in the cupboard and George fetched it out. For the next two hours we sat upon our beds drinking the whisky and making wonderful and complicated plans for the development of our organization. By eleven o'clock we were employing a staff of fifty,

---

① legman: *Noun* a person employed to do simple tasks such as running errands or collecting information from outside their workplace(执行简单外出任务的)跑腿;外勤

② dope: *Noun* (informal) information about a subject, especially if not generally known(非正式)(尤指内幕的)消息(e.g. Our reviewer will give you the dope on hot spots around the town. 我们的评论家会告诉你城市周围娱乐场所的内幕消息。)

③ money for old rope or money for jam: (Brit. informal) money or reward earned for little or no effort(英国英语的非正式用法)容易赚的钱;不费吹灰之力的收益

第二章 冤冤相报 第二节 《复仇公司》Vengeance Is Mine Inc.

including twelve famous pugilists①, and our offices were in Rockefeller Center. Towards midnight we had obtained control over all columnists and were dictating their daily columns to them by telephone from our headquarters, taking care to insult and infuriate at least twenty rich persons in one part of the country or another every day. We were immensely wealthy and George had a British Bentley②, I had five Cadillacs③. George kept practising telephone talks with Lionel Pantaloon. "That you, Pantaloon?" "Yes, sir." "Well, listen here. I think your column stinks④ today. It's lousy." "I'm very sorry, sir. I'll try to do better tomorrow." "Damn right you'll do better, Pantaloon. Matter of fact we've been thinking about getting someone else to take over." "But please, please sir, just give me another chance." "OK, Pantaloon, but this is the last. And by the way, the boys are putting a rattlesnake in your car tonight, on behalf of Mr. Hiram C. King, the soap manufacturer. Mr. King will be watching from across the street so don't forget to act scared when you see it." "Yes, sir, of course, sir. I won't forget, sir..."

When we finally went to bed and the light was out, I could still hear George giving hell to Pantaloon on the telephone.

The next morning we were both woken up by the church clock on the corner striking nine. George got up and went to the door to get the papers and when he came back he was holding a letter in his hand.

① pugilist: Noun (dated or humorous) a boxer, especially a professional one (古旧或幽默的用法)(尤指职业的)拳击运动员;拳击手

② Bentley:一个著名汽车的品牌,通常译作"宾利"。

③ Cadillac:一个著名汽车的品牌,通常译作"凯迪拉克",也有人译作"卡迪拉克"。本书采用的是前一个翻译。

④ stink: Verb (informal) be very unpleasant, contemptible, or scandalous(非正式)讨厌透顶;坏透;糟透;名声臭(e.g. He thinks the values of the society in which he lives stink. 他认为他生活于其中的这个社会的价值观糟透了。)

"Open it!" I said.

He opened it and carefully unfolded a single sheet of thin notepaper.

"Read it!" I shouted.

He began to read it aloud, his voice low and serious at first but rising gradually to a high, almost hysterical shout of triumph as the full meaning of the letter was revealed to him. It said:

"*Your methods appear curiously unorthodox*[①]. *At the same time anything you do to that scoundrel has my approval. So go ahead. Start with Item 1, and if you are successful I'll be only too glad to give you an order to work right on through the list. Send the bill to me. William S. Womberg.*"

I recollect that in the excitement of the moment we did a kind of dance around the room in our pyjamas, praising Mr. Womberg in loud voices and shouting that we were rich. George turned somersaults on his bed and it is possible that I did the same.

"When shall we do it?" he said. "Tonight?"

I paused before replying. I refused to be rushed. The pages of history are filled with the names of great men who have come to grief by permitting themselves to make hasty decisions in the excitement of a moment. I put on my dressing-gown, lit a cigarette and began to pace up and down the room. "There is no hurry," I said. "Womberg's order can be dealt with in due course. But first of all we must send out today's cards."

I dressed quickly, we went out to the newsstand across the street, bought one copy of every daily paper there was and returned to our room.

---

① unorthodox: *Adjective* contrary to what is usual, traditional, or accepted; not orthodox 非传统的;非正统的;异端的(e.g. He frequently upset other scholars with his unorthodox views. 他那些反正统的看法经常令其他学者烦恼。)

The next two hours was spent in reading the columnists' columns, and in the end we had a list of eleven people—eight men and three women—all of whom had been insulted in one way or another by one of the columnists that morning. Things were going well. We were working smoothly. It took us only another half hour to look up the addresses of the insulted ones—two we couldn't find—and to address the envelopes.

In the afternoon we delivered them, and at about six in the evening we got back to our room, tired but triumphant. We made coffee and we fried hamburgers and we had supper in bed. Then we re-read Womberg's letter aloud to each other many many times.

"What's he doing he's giving us an order for six thousand one hundred dollars," George said. "Items 1 to 5 inclusive."

"It's not a bad beginning. Not bad for the first day. Six thousand a day works out at... let me see... it's nearly two million dollars a year, not counting Sundays. A million each. It's more than Betty Grable."

"We are very wealthy people," George said. He smiled, a slow and wondrous smile of pure contentment.

"In a day or two we will move to a suite of rooms at the St. Regis."

"I think the Waldorf," George said.

"All right, the Waldorf. And later on we might as well take a house."

"One like Womberg's?"

"All right. One like Womberg's. But first," I said, "we have work to do. Tomorrow we shall deal with Pantaloon. We will catch him as he comes out of the Penguin Club. At two-thirty a.m. we will be waiting for him, and when he comes out into the street you will step forward and punch him once, hard, right upon the point of the nose as per contract."

"It will be a pleasure," George said. "It will be a real pleasure. But how do we get away? Do we run?"

"We shall hire a car for an hour. We have just enough money left for that, and I shall be sitting at the wheel with the engine running, not ten yards away, and the door will be open and when you've punched him you'll just jump back into the car and we'll be gone."

"It is perfect. I shall punch him very hard." George paused. He clenched his right fist and examined his knuckles. Then he smiled again and he said slowly, "This nose of his, is it not possible that it will afterwards be so much blunted that it will no longer poke well into other people's business?"

"It is quite possible," I answered, and with that happy thought in our minds we switched out the lights and went early to sleep.

The next morning I was woken by a shout and I sat up and saw George standing at the foot of my bed in his pyjamas, waving his arms. "Look!" he shouted, "there are four! There are four!" I looked, and indeed there were four letters in his hand.

"Open them. Quickly, open them."

The first one he read aloud: "'Dear Vengeance Is Mine Inc., That's the best proposition I've had in years. Go right ahead and give Mr. Jacob Swinski the rattlesnake treatment (Item 4). But I'll be glad to pay double if you'll forget to extract the poison from its fangs①. Yours Gertrude Porter-Vandervelt. PS You'd better insure the snake. That guy's bite carries more poison than the rattler's.'"

George read the second one aloud: "'My cheque for MYM500 is made out and lies before me on my desk. The moment I receive proof that you have punched Lionel Pantaloon hard on the nose, it will be posted to you, I should prefer a fracture, if possible. Yours etc. Wilbur H. Gollogly.'"

George read the third one aloud: "'In my present frame of mind and

---

① fang: *Noun* the tooth of a venomous snake, by which poison is injected(毒蛇的)毒牙

against my better judgement, I am tempted to reply to your card and to request that you deposit that scoundrel Walter Kennedy upon Fifth Avenue dressed only in his underwear. I make the proviso① that there shall be snow on the ground at the time and that the temperature shall be sub-zero. H. Gresham.'"

The fourth one he also read aloud: "'*A good hard sock② on the nose for Pantaloon is worth five hundred of mine or anybody else's money. I should like to watch. Yours sincerely, Claudia Calthorpe Hines.*'"

George laid the letters down gently, carefully upon the bed. For a while there was silence. We stared at each other, too astonished, too happy to speak. I began to calculate the value of those four orders in terms of money.

"That's five thousand dollars worth," I said softly.

Upon George's face there was a huge bright grin. "Claude," he said, "should we not move now to the Waldorf?"

"Soon," I answered, "but at the moment we have no time for moving. We have not even time to send out fresh cards today. We must start to execute the orders we have in hand. We are overwhelmed with work."

"Should we not engage extra staff and enlarge our organization?"

"Later," I said. "Even for that there is no time today. Just think what we have to do. We have to put a rattlesnake in Jacob Swinski's car... we have to dump Walter Kennedy on Fifth Avenue in his underpants... we have to punch Pantaloon on the nose... let me see... yes, for three different people we have to punch Pantaloon..."

---

① proviso: *Noun* a condition attached to an agreement 附带条件;附文(e.g. He let his house with the proviso that his own staff should remain to run it. 他出租宅邸的一个附加条件是原有工作人员必须保留下来进行管理。)

② sock: *Noun* (informal) a hard blow(非正式)重重的一拳(e.g. a sock on the jaw 打在下巴上的一记重拳)

I stopped. I closed my eyes. I sat still. Again I became conscious of a small clear stream of inspiration flowing into the tissues of my brain. "I have it!" I shouted. "I have it! I have it! Three birds with one stone! Three customers with one punch!"

"How?"

"Don't you see? We only need to punch Pantaloon once and each of the three customers... Womberg, Gollogly and Claudia Hines... will think it's being done specially for him or her."

"Say it again." I said it again.

"It's brilliant."

"It's common-sense. And the same principle will apply to the others. The rattlesnake treatment and the others can wait until we have more orders. Perhaps in a few days we will have ten orders for rattlesnakes in Swinski's car. Then we will do them all in one go."

"It's wonderful."

"This evening then," I said, "we will handle Pantaloon. But first we must hire a car. Also we must send telegrams, one to Womberg, one to Gollogly and one to Claudia Hines, telling them where and when the punching will take place."

We dressed rapidly and went out.

In a dirty silent little garage down on East 9th Street we managed to hire a car, a 1934 Chevrolet①, eight dollars for the evening. We then sent three telegrams, each one identical and cunningly worded to conceal its true meaning from inquisitive people: *Hope to see you outside Penguin Club two-thirty a. m. Regards V. I. Mine.*

"There is one thing more," I said. "It is essential that you should be disguised. Pantaloon, or the doorman, for example, must not be able

---

① Bentley: 一个著名汽车的品牌，通常译作"雪佛兰"。

第二章 冤冤相报 第二节 《复仇公司》*Vengeance Is Mine Inc.*

to identify you afterwards. You must wear a false moustache."

"What about you?"

"Not necessary. I'll be sitting in the car. They won't see me."

We went to a children's toy-shop and we bought for George a magnificent black moustache, a thing with long pointed ends, waxed and stiff and shining, and when he held it up against his face he looked exactly like the Kaiser① of Germany. The man in the shop also sold us a tube of glue and he showed us how the moustache should be attached to the upper lip. "Going to have fun with the kids?" he asked, and George said, "Absolutely."

All was now ready, but there was a long time to wait. We had three dollars left between us and with this we bought a sandwich each and went to a movie. Then, at eleven o'clock that evening, we collected our car and in it we began to cruise slowly through the streets of New York waiting for the time to pass.

"You'd better put on your moustache so as you get used to it."

We pulled up under a street lamp and I squeezed some glue on to George's upper lip and fixed on the huge black hairy thing with its pointed ends. Then we drove on. It was cold in the car and outside it was beginning to snow again. I could see a few small snowflakes falling through the beams of the car-lights. George kept saying, "How hard shall I hit him?" and I kept answering, "Hit him as hard as you can, and on the nose. It must be on the nose because that is a part of the contract. Everything must be done right. Our clients may be watching."

At two in the morning we drove slowly past the entrance to the Penguin Club in order to survey the situation. "I will park there," I said,

---

① Kaiser: *Noun* (historical) the German Emperor, the Emperor of Austria, or the head of the Holy Roman Empire (历史上的用法)德国皇帝;奥地利皇帝;神圣罗马帝国皇帝

"just past the entrance in that patch of dark. But I will leave the door open for you."

We drove on. Then George said, "What does he look like? How do I know it's him?"

"Don't worry," I answered. "I've thought of that," and I took from my pocket a piece of paper and handed it to him. "You take this and fold it up small and give it to the doorman and tell him to see it gets to Pantaloon quickly. Act as though you are scared to death and in an awful hurry. It's a hundred to one that Pantaloon will come out. No columnist could resist that message."

On the paper I had written: *I am a worker in Soviet Consulate*[①] *Come to the door very quickly please I have something to tell but come quickly as I am in danger, I cannot come in to you.*

"You see," I said, "your moustache will make you look like a Russian. All Russians have big moustaches."

George took the paper and folded it up very small and held it in his fingers. It was nearly half past two in the morning now and we began to drive towards the Penguin Club.

"You all set?" I said.

"Yes."

"We're going in now. Here we come. I'll park just past the entrance... here. Hit him hard," I said, and George opened the door and got out of the car. I closed the door behind him but I leant over and kept my hand on the handle so I could open it again quick, and I let down the window so I could watch. I kept the engine ticking over.

I saw George walk swiftly up to the doorman who stood under the red

---

① consulate: *Noun* the place or building in which a consul's duties are carried out 领事馆;领事官邸

第二章 冤冤相报 第二节 《复仇公司》*Vengeance Is Mine Inc.*

and white canopy which stretched out over the sidewalk. I saw the doorman turn and look down at George and I didn't like the way he did it. He was a tall proud man dressed in a magenta①-coloured uniform with gold buttons and gold shoulders and a broad white stripe down each magenta trouser-leg. Also he wore white gloves and he stood there looking proudly down at George, frowning, pressing his lips together hard. He was looking at George's moustache and I thought Oh my God we have overdone it. We have over-disguised him. He's going to know it's false and he's going to take one of the long pointed ends in his fingers and he'll give it a tweak② and it'll come off. But he didn't. He was distracted by George's acting, for George was acting well. I could see him hopping about, clasping and unclasping his hands, swaying his body and shaking his head, and I could hear him saying, "Plees plees plees you must hurry. It is life and teth. Plees plees take it kvick to Mr. Pantaloon." His Russian accent was not like any accent I had heard before, but all the same there was a quality of real despair in his voice.

　　Finally, gravely, proudly, the doorman said, "Give me the note." George gave it to him and said, "Tank you, tank you, but say it is urgent," and the doorman disappeared inside. In a few moments he returned and said, "It's being delivered now." George paced nervously up and down. I waited, watching the door. Three or four minutes elapsed. George wrung his hands③ and said, "Vere is he? Vere is he? Plees to go and see if he is not coming!"

---

　　① magenta: *Noun* [mass noun] a light mauvish – crimson which is one of the primary subtractive colours, complementary to green 品红;洋红

　　② tweak: *Noun* a sharp twist or pull 扭;拧

　　③ wring one's hands: clasp and twist one's hands together as a gesture of great distress, especially when one is powerless to change the situation 苦恼地(或绝望地)绞拧双手

"What's the matter with you?" the doorman said. Now he was looking at George's moustache again.

"It is life and teth! Mr. Pantaloon can help! He must come!"

"Why don't you shut up," the doorman said, but he opened the door again and he poked his head inside and I heard him saying something to someone.

To George he said, "They say he's coming now."

A moment later the door opened and Pantaloon himself, small and dapper①, stepped out. He paused by the door, looking quickly from side to side like an inquisitive ferret②. The doorman touched his cap and pointed at George. I heard Pantaloon say, "Yes, what did you want?"

George said, "plees, dis vay a leetle so as novone can hear," and he led Pantaloon along the pavement, away from the doorman and towards the car.

"Come on, now," Pantaloon said. "What is it you want?"

Suddenly George shouted "Look!" and he pointed up the street. Pantaloon turned his head and as he did so George swung his right arm and he hit Pantaloon plumb③ on the point of the nose. I saw George leaning forward on the punch, all his weight behind it, and the whole of Pantaloon appeared somehow to lift slightly off the ground and to float back-

---

① dapper: *Adjective*（typically of a man）neat and trim in dress, appearance, or bearing(尤指男子)整洁的；衣冠楚楚的

② ferret: *Noun* a domesticated polecat used chiefly for catching rabbits. It is typically albino in coloration, but sometimes brown 白鼬；雪貂

③ plumb: *Adverb* [as sub-modifier]（N. Amer.）completely(北美英语)完全地；不折不扣地

wards for two or three feet until the fa?ade① of the Penguin Club stopped him. All this happened very quickly, and then George was in the car beside me and we were off and I could hear the doorman blowing a whistle behind us.

"We've done it!" George gasped. He was excited and out of breath. "I hit him good! Did you see how good I hit him!"

It was snowing hard now and I drove fast and made many sudden turnings and I knew no one would catch us in this snowstorm.

"Son of a bitch almost went through the wall I hit him so hard."

"Well done, George," I said. "Nice work, George."

"And did you see him lift? Did you see him lift right up off the ground?"

"Womberg will be pleased," I said.

"And Gollogly, and the Hines woman."

"They'll all be pleased," I said. "Watch the money coming in."

"There's a car behind us!" George shouted. "It's following us! It's right on our tail! Drive like mad!"

"Impossible," I said. "They couldn't have picked us up already. It's just another car going somewhere." I turned sharply to the right.

"He's still with us," George said. "Keep turning. We'll lose him soon."

"How the hell can we lose a police-car in a nineteen thirty-four Chev②," I said. "I'm going to stop."

"Keep going!" George shouted. "You're doing fine."

"I'm going to stop," I said. "It'll only make them mad if we go

---

① fa?ade or facade: *Noun* the face of a building, especially the principal front that looks on to a street or open space(尤指临街或正对空旷地的)建筑物正面

② Chev = Chevrolet

on."

George protested fiercely but I knew it was no good and I pulled in to the side of the road. The other car swerved out and went past us and skidded① to a standstill in front of us.

"Quick," George said. "Let's beat it." He had the door open and he was ready to run.

"Don't be a fool," I said. "Stay where you are. You can't get away now."

A voice from outside said, "All right boys, what's the hurry?"

"No hurry," I answered. "We're just going home."

"Yea?"

"Oh yes, we're just on our way home now."

The man poked his head in through the window on my side, and he looked at me, then at George, then at me again.

"It's a nasty night," George said. "We're just trying to reach home before the streets get all snowed up."

"Well," the man said, "you can take it easy. I just thought I'd like to give you this right away." He dropped a wad of banknotes② on to my lap. "I'm Gollogly," he added, "Wilbur H. Gollogly," and he stood out there in the snow grinning at us, stamping his feet and rubbing his hands to keep them warm. "I got your wire and I watched the whole thing from across the street. You did a fine job. I'm paying you boys

---

① skid: *Verb* [no obj.] (of a vehicle) slide, typically sideways or obliquely, on slippery ground or as a result of stopping or turning too quickly(尤指车辆因路滑、刹车或转弯过快而)侧滑;打滑;滑行(e.g. The taxi cab skidded to a halt. 出租车滑行了一段距离停了下来。)

② banknote: *Noun* a piece of paper money, constituting a central bank's promissory note to pay a stated sum to the bearer on demand(中央银行发行的)钞票;纸币

double. It was worth it. Funniest thing I ever seen. Goodbye boys. Watch your steps. They'll be after you now. Get out of town if I were you. Goodbye." And before we could say anything, he was gone.

When finally we got back to our room I started packing at once.

"You crazy?" George said. "We've only got to wait a few hours and we receive five hundred dollars each from Womberg and the Hines woman. Then we'll have two thousand altogether and we can go anywhere we want."

So we spent the next day waiting in our room and reading the papers, one of which had a whole column on the front page headed, "Brutal assault on famous columnist". But sure enough the late afternoon post brought us two letters and there was five hundred dollars in each.

And right now, at this moment, we are sitting in a Pullman① car, drinking Scotch whisky and heading south for a place where there is always sunshine and where the horses are running every day. We are immensely wealthy and George keeps saying that if we put the whole of our two thousand dollars on a horse at ten to one we shall make another twenty thousand and we will be able to retire. "We will have a house at Palm Beach②," he says, "and we will entertain upon a lavish③ scale. Beauti-

---

① Pullman: *Noun* [usu. as modifier] a railway carriage affording special comfort, typically with a lounge interior and meals service at the passengers' seats(尤指内装卧铺或座椅,并为顾客提供座位就餐服务的舒适型)普尔曼式车厢

② Palm Beach: a resort town in SE Florida, situated on an island just off the coast; pop. 9,810 (1990) 棕榈滩(佛罗里达东南旅游城镇,位于一个靠近海岸的岛上,1990年人口9,810。)

③ lavish: *Adjective* (of a person) very generous or extravagant(人)慷慨的;奢侈的(e.g. He was lavish with his hospitality. 他好客无度。)

ful socialites will loll① around the edge of our swimming pool sipping cool drinks, and after a while we will perhaps put another large sum of money upon another horse and we shall become wealthier still. Possibly we will become tired of Palm Beach and then we will move around in a leisurely manner among the playgrounds of the rich. Monte Carlo② and places like that. Like the Ali Khan③ and the Duke of Windsor④. We will become prominent members of the international set⑤ and film stars will smile at us and head-waiters will bow to us and perhaps, in time to come, perhaps we might even get ourselves mentioned in Lionel Pantaloon's column."

"That would be something," I said.

"Wouldn't it just," he answered happily. "Wouldn't that just be

---

① loll: Verb [no obj., with adverbial] sit, lie, or stand in a lazy, relaxed way 懒洋洋地坐(或躺、站)(e.g. The two girls lolled in their chairs. 两个女孩懒洋洋地坐在椅子上。)

② Monte Carlo: a resort in Monaco, forming one of the four communes of the principality; pop. 12,000 (1985). It is famous as a gambling resort and as the terminus of the annual Monte Carlo rally 蒙特卡洛(摩纳哥旅游胜地,该公国的四大行政区之一,1985年人口12,000;以赌博业和一年一度的蒙特卡洛汽车拉力赛最后一站著名。)

③ Ali Khan: Prince Ali Salman Aga Khan (1911—1960), known as Aly Khan was a son of Aga Khan III, the head of the Ismaili Muslims, and the father of Aga Khan IV. 阿里汗(1911—1960,他是伊斯玛仪派穆斯林领袖阿迦汗三世的儿子,阿迦汗四世的父亲。)

④ Duke of Windsor (1894—1972): King of England and Ireland in 1936; his marriage to Wallis Warfield Simpson created a constitutional crisis leading to his abdication 温莎公爵(1894—1972,他1936年任英格兰和爱尔兰的国王,迎娶辛普森夫人后退位。)

⑤ set: Noun the place or area in which filming is taking place or a play is performed(电影)摄影场;(戏剧)演出场(e.g. The magazine has interviews on set with top directors. 这家杂志在拍摄现场采访了大牌导演。)

something."

三、翻译探索

在主人公乔治戴上假胡子装扮俄罗斯人与门卫的那些对话的翻译中,本书的著者在风格对等方面做了一些尝试性的探索。除此之外,本篇小说翻译的障碍恐怕就是英美国家的一些文化背景知识了。

复仇公司

我醒来的时候,雪正飘落。

我判断外面正在飘雪,是因为屋子里有一种明亮的感觉,而且外面很安静,大街上没有传来嘈杂的脚步声,也没有汽车轮胎的碾压声,只能听见汽车引擎的声音。我抬起头,看见乔治穿着他那件绿色的晨衣在靠近窗户那儿,俯身煤油炉上方,正在煮咖啡呢。

"下雪了,"我说。

"很冷啊,"乔治回答。"真的很冷。"

我下了床,到屋外取来早晨的报纸。冷是无疑的,取完报纸,我就快速跑回,跳上床,静静地在铺盖底下躺了一会儿,同时将双手紧紧地夹在两腿之间取暖。

"没有信件吗?"乔治问。

"没有,没有信件。"

"看起来,老爷子似乎不会心甘情愿掏腰包了。"

"或许他认为,四百五足够一个月了,"我说。

"他从未到纽约来过,不知道这儿的生活开销。"

"你不应该一周内把钱都花光。"

乔治站了起来,看着我。"你的意思是,*我们*不应该把钱都花光吧。"

"说的没错,"我说,"是我们。"我开始看报纸。

现在,咖啡煮好了,乔治将咖啡壶拿了过来,放到我们床铺中间的小桌子上。"没有了钱,一个人就无法生活,"他说。"老爷子应该懂得这一点啊。"他连那件绿色的晨衣都没脱,钻回自己床中。我接着看报,跑马页看完,就看橄榄球页,然后开始看莱昂内尔·潘塔隆的专栏页,他是政治栏目和社会新闻栏目伟大的专栏作家。我总是阅读潘塔隆的文章,这一点。我跟全国其他两三千万公民没有什么不同。阅读他的文章已经成为我的习惯,甚至超越了习惯——他成为我早晨必不可少的一部分,就像是三杯咖啡或者刮脸一样必不可少。

"这个伙计真有胆量,"我说。

"谁?"

"这位莱昂内尔·潘塔隆啊。"

"他现在说什么了?"

"同样一套东西,就是他总说的那一套。同样的丑闻,总是一些关于有钱人的丑闻。你听听这一段:'……银行家威廉·S·沃姆伯格……在'企鹅俱乐部',被人看见跟美艳的新秀特蕾莎·威廉斯在一起……连续三天三夜不归宿……沃姆伯格太太在家,疼痛得很……要是老公在外跟威廉斯小姐一夜风流的话,这样的事任何一个人的妻子都会经历……'"

"那就是沃姆伯格的不对了,"乔治说。

"我想,这是个耻辱,"我说。"这类事情可能导致离婚。像这样的事情,潘塔隆怎么能脱得了干系呢?"

"他总干这样的事,他们都很怕他。可是,我要是威廉·S·沃姆伯格的话,"乔治说,"你知道我会做什么吗?我就会径直奔过去,照着这位莱昂内尔·潘塔隆的鼻子'砰'的一拳打过去。哇,处理这些家伙,这是唯一的办法。"

"沃姆伯格先生不可能那样去做。"

"为什么不能?"

"因为他上了年纪,"我回答。"沃姆伯格先生是位有尊严、受人尊敬的老头儿。他是这座城里很有名望的银行家,不可能去……"

接下来,计上心来。突然之间,这一想法不知从什么地方冒了出来。就在我跟乔治的话说到一半的时候,这个想法就冒出来了。我的话戛然而止,感觉到这个想法一下子涌进了我的大脑。于是,我保持安静状态,好让这个想法涌进来。它持续不断地涌进来,我还没来得及反应过来的时候,这个观点就成形了。整套计划——美妙绝伦、宏伟壮丽的计划——在我的头脑中清晰地勾画出来了。就在当时,我清楚,这个计划完美无缺。

我转过身,看见乔治盯着我,脸上露出一种惊奇的表情。"怎么了?"他问。"怎么回事儿?"

我保持冷静状态,伸出手给自己又倒了些咖啡,然后才开始说话。

"乔治,"我说,依然镇定自若。"我有个想法。现在,你仔仔细细听我说出来,因为我这个想法将使我们两个变成富人。我们现在都一文不名,对吧?"

"的确。"

"这位威廉·S·沃姆伯格,"我说,"今天早晨对莱昂内尔·潘塔隆很愤怒,你认为是这样吗?"

"愤怒!"乔治大声喊道。"愤怒!哇,他都快气疯了!"

"正是!他很想看到莱昂内尔·潘塔隆的鼻子给人'砰'地重击一下,你认为是这样的吗?"

"忒对啦,他很想。"

"现在,要是有人愿意代表他承担起拳击鼻子这个任务,而且干得卓有成效、谨慎周到,沃姆伯格先生就会准备付一大笔钱给这个人。告诉我,这事儿可能吗?"

乔治转过身看着我,然后,他轻轻地、小心翼翼地将咖啡杯放到桌子上,一丝笑容开始在他的脸上慢慢扩展开来。"我听明白了,"他说。"我懂你的想法了。"

"刚才那个只是我想法的一小部分。要是你阅读了潘塔隆这里的专栏内容的话,你就会看到,今天还有一个人受到了侮辱。"我拾起报纸。"有一位太太,名字叫埃拉·金普勒,是一个很有名望的上流社会人士,银行存款或许有一百万美元之多……"

"潘塔隆说她什么了?"

我又看了一眼报纸。"他暗示的是,"我回答,"她如何从自己朋友身上赚取钱财，靠的是举办轮盘赌晚会，自己充当银行角色借钱给他们。"

"金普勒真是咎由自取，"乔治说。"还有那个沃姆伯格。他们两个，金普勒和沃姆伯格。"他从床上坐直身体，等待着我继续往下说。

"现在，"我说，"我们今早总共有两个人对潘塔隆恨之入骨了。这两个人都极其渴望走出去，奔向他，照着他的鼻子来一拳，但是，他们两个谁都不敢亲自去做。你明白了吗？"

"绝对明白。"

"那么，对于莱昂内尔·潘塔隆，"我说，"我能说的就这么多啦。但是，不要忘记了，还有其他像他这样的人呢。除他之外，还有很多专栏作家把时间用在侮辱富有的名人这方面，如哈里·韦曼、克劳德·泰勒、雅各布·斯温斯基、沃尔特·肯尼迪等。"

"接着说，"乔治说道。"接着说。"

"好吧。现在计划是这样的。"我变得相当兴奋，俯身靠到床边，一只手放到那张小桌子上，另一只手随着我说话的节奏在空中乱舞。"我们要立刻成立一个机构，我们就称之为……该称呼什么呢……我们就称之为……容我想想啊……我们就称之为'复仇公司'……怎么样呢？"

"奇特的名字。"

"来自《圣经》。好名字，我喜欢。'复仇公司'——想复仇，就找我，听起来不错。我们要印出一些小卡片，将之分发给所有的客户，提醒他们说，他们当众受到了侮辱和伤害。然后，对他们提出，我们去惩罚冒犯者，他们付一笔钱作为报酬。我们要买来所有的报纸，每天要读完所有专栏作家的文章，然后，每天将卡片发出十来张给那些有可能成为我们客户的人。"

"太棒了！"乔治大喊道。"棒极了！"

"我们要有钱啦，"我对他说。"用不了多久，我们将特别富有。"

"我们必须马上行动！"

我跳下床，取来一本便签簿和一支铅笔，又跑回来上了床。"现在，"我边说，边将双膝缩回到毯子底下，将便签簿靠到膝盖上，"首先要做的就是，把要印制的卡片内容确定下来，好将它们分发给客户。"我顺手在顶部写下"复仇公司"四个大字作为这页纸的标题。然后，我慎重地写下几行措辞讲究的文字，对该机构的功能做了解释，最终成文如下："因此，复仇公司将代表你，以你绝对信任的方式承担起对专栏作家实施适当惩罚的任务。就这一方面而言，我们恭敬地呈递给你几种可以选择的方法（以及每种方法的报价），供你思考后作出选择。"

"你说的'几种可以选择的方法'是什么意思？"乔治问。

"我们必须给他们一个选择的机会。我们必须得想出一些东西——不同的惩罚措施。第一条是……"于是，我这样写道："1.拳击对方鼻子，打一次，使劲打。""这一条，我们收多少钱呢？"

"五百美元，"乔治迫不及待地说道。

我写了下来。"下一条呢？"

"把对方眼睛打青，"乔治说。

我写道："2.把对方眼睛打青……500美元。"

"不！"乔治说。"这个价我不同意。跟拳击鼻子比较起来，把对方眼睛打青，而且打得令人满意，肯定需要更多的技巧，而且，时机还得把握好。这是个技术活，应该值六百。"

"好，"我说。"六百就六百。下一条呢？"

"当然是两者的组合，前面那两个合二为一。"现在，这件事绝对是乔治的拿手好戏，十分符合他的口味。

"两者的组合？"

"绝对如此。拳击对方鼻子，同时将其眼睛打青，一千一百美元。"

"两者合在一起，应该少点儿，"我说。"我们就收一千得啦。"

"便宜透了，"乔治说。"这一条，他们会抢购一空的。"

"下一条呢？"

现在，我们两个都沉默下来，专心致志地使劲儿思考起来。乔治那低垂而倾斜的额头皮肤上皱起了三道深深的平行皱纹。他开始挠自己的头皮。挠得很慢,却十分用力。我将视线移开,尽量去想还有什么可怕的方法可以被人用来去惩罚他人。最终,我想到了一条,于是,乔治看着我的铅笔尖儿在纸上移动着,写下了这样一条:"4.*趁对方停车之际,将一条响尾蛇(毒液已经抽取出来)放入对方车内,放到脚踏板的附近。*"

"我的老天啊!"乔治低声说。"你要将对方吓死啊!"

"当然,"我说。

"不管怎样,你上哪儿去弄响尾蛇呢?"

"购买,总能买到的。这一条我们收多少钱呢?"

"一千五百美元,"乔治坚决地说道。我写了下来。

"现在,我们还需要再写一条。"

"有了,"乔治说。"将对方诱拐到车内,脱光所有的衣服,但不脱内裤、鞋和袜子。然后,在交通高峰期,将其丢出车外,丢到第五大街上。"说完,他微笑起来,嘴咧得很宽,一副大获全胜的样子。

"我们不能那样做。"

"写下来。要价两千五百块。要是年迈的沃姆伯格给你出这个价,你得照做不误。"

"是的,"我说。"我想我会做的。"随后,我把这条写了下来。"现在,这几条足够了,"我补充道。"他们有很大的选择余地了。"

"我们到哪儿去印制卡片呢?"乔治问。

"去乔治·卡尔诺夫斯基那儿印制,"我回答。"是另一个乔治,他是我的一个朋友,在第三大街往下的地方经营一家小型印刷店,为大型商店印制婚礼请帖之类的东西。他能印制。我知道他能印制。"

"那么,我们还等什么呢?"

我们两个都跳下床,开始穿衣服。"现在是十二点,"我说。"要是我们快点赶过去,他去吃午饭之前,我们能截住他。"

我们出门来到大街上的时候,天仍然下着雪。人行道上,积雪已有十一二厘米厚了。但是,我们却一阵疾走,走过十四个街区,来到了卡尔诺夫斯基的小店。到达那儿的时候,他正往身上披外衣准备出去呢。

"克劳德!"他喊道。"嗨,伙计!最近不错吧。"他握着我的手上下晃动着。他那张胖脸露出友好的表情,鼻子很吓人——鼻翼宽宽地伸张,跟两边面颊的一部分重叠起来,每边的重叠部分至少有两厘米半。我向他表示问候,告诉他我们来的目的是要讨论某些最为紧急的事情。他脱掉外衣,把我们领回到他的办公室。然后,我开始告诉他我们的计划,以及我们要他做些什么。

我说到大约四分之一的时候,他开始狂笑起来,笑得我不可能继续说下去。于是,我就长话短说,将那张纸递给他,上面写着我们想要他印刷的东西。现在,他一边读纸上的内容,一边开始大笑,笑得他整个身体都跟着震动起来。他用一只手不断拍打着书桌,狂笑得像一个疯子一般咳嗽着、噎着气。我们两个看着他在那儿狂笑,不明白有什么特别的地方令他如此笑个不停。

最后,他安静了下来,掏出一块手帕,郑重其事地擦起了眼睛。"从来没这么厉害地笑过,"他软弱无力地说道。"这个笑话很棒,的确很棒,值一顿午饭。跟我出去吧,我招待你俩吃午饭。"

"听着,"我严厉地说,"这事儿不是什么笑话,也没什么可笑的。你正在见证一个强大新机构的诞生,一个……"

"得了吧,"他说完,又开始大笑起来。"得了吧,吃午饭去吧。"

"那些卡片你什么时候能印好?"我问道。我的声音很严厉,一副公事公办的样子。

他暂停下来,盯着我们两个。"你的意思是……你的意思真的是……关于这件事,你是当真的吗?"

"绝对当真。你正在见证的是一个……"

"好吧,"他说,"好吧。"他站了起来。"我想你们俩疯了,会惹出麻烦的。那些家伙喜欢给他人制造麻烦,可是,他们却不想给自己找麻烦。"

"不能让你的工人看到卡片上的内容,这样的话,你什么时候能印好?"

"为了完成这件事儿,"他严肃地回答,"我午饭不吃了,亲自打字。这是我起码能够做到的。"他又大笑起来,笑得他那两只大大鼻孔的边缘抽动了起来。"想印多少？"

"先印一千份吧，还要信封。"

"两点钟回来取吧，"他说。我对他感谢一番，就走出门去。出门后，我们还能听到他的笑声沿着过道"嗡嗡"地传向店铺的后方。

两点整，我们两个回来取货。乔治·卡尔诺夫斯基坐在办公室里，首先映入我俩眼帘的是他前面高高摆放的那堆印制好的卡片，都是一些大张的卡片，是普通婚礼卡或者鸡尾酒会邀请卡的两倍大小。"给你们，"他说。"都为你们准备好了。"这个蠢货仍在哈哈大笑呢。

他给我们每人递来一张卡片，于是，我仔细审视着我手里的这张——印制得很漂亮。很显然，他在这上面花费了不少心思。卡片本身很厚、很硬，四周边缘装饰了窄窄的金边，信头的字母分外雅致。在这儿，卡片华丽的外观我无法再现，但是，我至少可以向你展示其中的内容：

复仇公司

亲爱的……………

在今天的报纸上，你或许已经看到了专栏作家………………对你人格的无理诽谤和恶意中伤。这是令人难以容忍的肮脏行径，是对事实有意的歪曲。

你准备容许这种无耻的、不怀好意的人渣以这种方式侮辱你吗？

全世界都了解的是，对他人公开的或者私底下的侮辱无动于衷，从不感到义愤填膺——不止如此，苛刻地说——甚至不采取一种正义的措施加以还击，这与美国人的本质背道而驰。

从另一个方面来说，作为一个公民，以你的名望和声誉，你是不会希望自己进一步卷入此类令人不齿的琐事中，或者说，真的不希望与这种卑鄙小人有任何形式的直接瓜葛。

那么，你怎么才能得到补偿呢？

答案很简单。**复仇公司**会为你谋求补偿。我们将代表你，以你绝对信任的方式承担起对专栏作家………………实施个体惩罚的任务。就这一方面而言，我们恭敬地呈递给你几种可以选择的方法

(以及每种方法的报价),供你思考后作出选择:

1. 拳击对方鼻子,打一次,使劲打 　　　　　　500 美元
2. 把对方眼睛打青 　　　　　　　　　　　　600 美元
3. 拳击对方鼻子,同时将其眼睛打青 　　　　1000 美元
4. 趁对方停车之际,将一条响尾蛇(毒液已经抽取出来)放入对方车内,放到脚踏板的附近 　　　　　　　　　　1500 美元
5. 将对方诱拐到车内,脱光所有的衣服,但不脱内裤、鞋和袜子。然后,在交通高峰期,将其丢出车外,丢到第五大街上 2500 美元

以上任务皆由专业人员完成。

要是你希望我们为你提供上述任何一项服务,烦请给**复仇公司**回信。回信地址见随信附上的纸条。要是可行的话,就会提前通知你实施行动的地点和时间。如果你愿意的话,我们这样做的时候,你就能亲自从一个安全的、不为人知的距离上看到全过程。

你订购的服务满意地得到实施后,付款即可。到时候,我们会提供给你一个常规的付款账户。

乔治·卡尔诺夫斯基的印制工作做得很漂亮。
"克劳德,"他说,"喜欢吗?"
"好极了。"
"我尽最大所能为你印制。这有点像在战时,看见士兵出发去作战,或许会送命,但自始至终,我都愿意给他们东西,为他们做事。"他又开始大笑起来,于是,我说:"我们最好现在就出发了。你有能装下这些卡片的大信封吗?"

"一切都准备好了。你们有钱进账的时候,付款给我吧。"这话似乎触动了他,令他笑得比任何时候更加厉害了。他瘫坐在椅子上,如傻子一般咯咯笑个不停。我和乔治匆忙离开,走到大街上,融入那个寒冷的、飘着雪花的下午。

· 243 ·

这段距离，我们几乎跑着回到了房间。上楼之前，我在前厅借了一本曼哈顿地区的公共电话簿。我们毫不费力地就从上面找到了"沃姆伯格，威廉·S"这个名字。我读地址——东九十大街某个繁华地段，乔治在其中一个信封上将地址写下来。

"金普勒，埃拉·H·太太"的名字也列在电话簿里，我们也给她写了封信。"今天，我们就发给沃姆伯格和金普勒这两个人，"我说。"我们还没有真正开张呢。明天我们要发出一打信件。"

"我们最好赶上下一次邮递时间，"乔治提醒道。

"我们要亲手送信，"我说。"现在，马上行动。他们越快收到就越好。明天或许太迟了，因为明天他们的愤怒情绪不会有今天的一半么强烈了。一夜过后，人的头脑会趋于冷静。听着，"我说，"你这就出发，立即递送这两张卡片。这期间，我到城四周打探一下，尽量查查莱昂内尔·潘塔隆的一些习惯什么的。晚上迟些时候，我们在这里碰面……"

那天晚上大约九点的时候，我返回，发现乔治躺在床上，抽着烟，喝着咖啡。

"两个我都送到了，"他说。"直接塞进了信筒，按完门铃，沿着大街溜掉。沃姆伯格家房子很大，大大的白色房子。你那边进行得怎么样？"

"我去见了一个我认识的人，他在《每日镜报》的体育栏目部工作。他把一切都告诉了我。"

"他都告诉你什么了？"

"他说，潘塔隆的行踪多多少少具有一定的常规性。他夜间出去活动，可是，不管晚上的早些时候他到什么地方去，他总是会——这一点很重要——他总是会在最后阶段到'企鹅俱乐部'去。大概午夜时分，他到达那里，一直待到两点或者两点半。其间，他的现场采访记者会陆续给他送来内幕消息。"

"那正是我们想要知道的，"乔治高兴地说。

"太容易了。"

"赚钱不费力。"

橱柜里有一整瓶混合型威士忌,乔治将其取出。接下来的两个小时时间里,我们两个坐在床上,一边喝着威士忌,一边为我们公司的发展谋划种种美妙而复杂的计划。到了十一点的时候,我们雇佣了五十名员工,其中包括十二名著名的职业拳击运动员,我们的办公室都设在洛克菲勒中心大厦。接近午夜时分,我们已经掌控了所有的专栏作家,从总部通过电话向他们口述每日栏目的内容,让他们确保每天侮辱或者激怒全国某些地区至少二十名富人。我们极其富有,乔治拥有一辆英国宾利车,我拥有五辆凯迪拉克。乔治还不断地练习打电话跟莱昂内尔·潘塔隆交谈。"那谁,是潘塔隆吗?""是的,先生。""那么,听好啦。我想,你今天的栏目讨厌透顶,简直令人作呕。""我很抱歉,先生。明天我会尽力做得更好。""你会做得更好,真该死,说得好听,潘塔隆。事实上,我们已经考虑让别人来接替你。""可是,拜托,拜托你,先生,再给我一次机会吧。""好吧,潘塔隆,这是最后一次啦。顺便说一下啊,今晚那些伙计代表海勒姆·C·金先生——肥皂制造商,要在你的车里放一条响尾蛇。金先生要从对面大街观看,所以,看到蛇的时候,你别忘了,要作出惊恐的举动。""是的,先生,当然,先生。我不会忘记的,先生……"

我们最终上床熄灯的时候,我还能听见乔治在电话里训斥潘塔隆。

第二天早晨,角落处教堂的钟敲响了九点,我们两个都被吵醒了。乔治起床,出门取报纸。回来时,他手里握着一封信。

"打开!"我说。

他打开信封,将里面的一页薄薄的便笺纸谨小慎微地展开。

"读一读!"我喊道。

他开始朗读起来。起先,他的声音很低、很严肃,而当整封信的内容在他眼前展现出来的时候,他的声音逐渐升高,发出了胜利的呼喊,几乎到了歇斯底里的地步。信是这样写的:

"你们的方法看起来离奇古怪、不合正统,但与此同时,不管你们对那个混蛋实施哪一项,我都不反对。因此,只管去行动吧。就从第一条开始。要是成功的话,我会十分乐意给你们再下订单,让你们顺着那份清单继续往下实施。账单寄给我。威廉·S·沃姆伯格。"

我记得,在那令人兴奋的时刻,我们两个穿着宽松的睡衣裤绕着屋子竟然跳起了某种舞蹈,边跳边大声称赞沃姆伯格先生,同时大喊我们要有钱了。乔治在床上翻起了跟头,要是可能的话,我也真想跟着翻几个跟斗。

"我们什么时候行动?"他问。"今晚吗?"

我暂停下来,没有回答。我不愿意做事匆忙草率。一页页历史写满了伟大人物的名字,这些人由于在令人兴奋时刻做出了草率的决定而遭受痛苦。我穿上晨衣,点燃一支香烟,开始沿着屋子来回踱步。"莫急,"我说。"沃姆伯格的订单在适当的时候再处理。我们首先要做的,就是要把今天的卡片发出去。"

我快速穿好衣服,出门走到大街对面的报摊,将那里所有种类的日报都买来一份,然后返回房间。接下来的两个小时时间里,我们就阅读专栏作家的专栏文章,最终我们列出一份十一个人的清单——八男三女,所有人那天早晨都被其中一位专栏作家以这样或那样的方式侮辱过。事情进展得很顺利,我们的工作也畅通无阻。我们只用了半个小时的时间就将受辱之人的地址查找出来,并写好了信封。但是,其中两位的地址没有查到。

那天下午,我们出去投递信件。大约晚上六点的时候,我们回到屋子,疲乏不堪但却欢欣鼓舞。煮完咖啡,煎完汉堡,拿到床上吃起了晚饭。然后,我们彼此都朗读了沃姆伯格先生的那封信,读了好多好多遍。

"他所做的,就是给我们下了一份订单,价值六千一百美元的订单,"乔治说。"第1—5条服务都包含在内。"

"开头不赖,第一天生意不赖。一天六千美元,算起来是……让我算算……一年将近两百万美元,星期天没有计算在内。每人一百万啊,比贝蒂·格拉布尔挣得还多。"

"我们是很富有的人了,"乔治说。他微笑起来——奇异的笑容慢慢地浮现出来,一副完全心满意足的样子。

"一两天之内,我们就能搬进圣里吉斯的套房里居住了。"

"我想应该搬进沃尔多夫,"乔治说。

"好吧,沃尔多夫。以后,我们或许会买下一座房子。"

"像沃姆伯格家那样的房子?"

"好吧,像沃姆伯格家那样的房子。但是,首先,"我说,"我们有工作要做。明天我们要对付潘塔隆。他从企鹅俱乐部出来之际,我们将他堵住。凌晨两点半的时候,我们等着他。他出来走到大街上的时候,你跨步向前,按照每份合同上写的那样,正对着他的鼻子尖拳击一次,狠狠地击打。"

"乐事一桩,"乔治说。"真的是乐事一桩。可是,我们如何逃离?跑吗?"

"我们租一个小时的车,剩下的钱足够租车了。我发动起引擎,坐在方向盘前,停在离你九十多米的地方,车门不关。你一打完,跳回到车上,我们就逃之夭夭。"

"好极了。我要狠狠地打他一下。"乔治暂停下来。他攥紧右拳,仔细查看每一个关节。然后,他又微笑起来,慢慢说道:"他的那只鼻子,打完后会变得扁平,是不是再也不会有棱角去嗅探别人的事情了呢?"

"很有这个可能,"我回答。我们心怀这样的想法关上灯,早早上床睡觉了。

第二天早晨,一声喊叫将我吵醒。我坐起身,看见乔治穿着宽松的睡衣裤站在我的床脚,挥舞着双臂。"看啊!"他喊道。"四封信!四封信啊!"我看了看,他的手里的确举着四封信。

"都打开。快点,都打开。"

他把第一封朗读了出来:"'亲爱的复仇公司:你们提出的是多年以来我所见过的最好的建议。去执行吧,往雅各布·斯温斯基的车里放响尾蛇(第4条)。但是,要是你们忘记将毒牙里的毒液取出来的话,我会很乐意付双倍的价钱。格特鲁德·波特-范德维尔特敬上。附言:你们最好给蛇投保,因为那个家伙咬一口的毒性要比响尾蛇咬一口的毒性强。'"

乔治将第二封朗读了出来:"'我那张500美元支票已经开好,放在我面前的桌子上。只要一看到证据,表明你们使劲拳击了莱昂内尔·潘塔隆的鼻子,我就把支票邮寄给你们。可能的话,我更喜欢他的鼻子骨折。威尔伯·H·戈洛格里虔诚敬上。'"

乔治把第三封朗读了出来:"'以我目前的心绪来看,与我认为理智的情感相反的是,我受到了诱惑,对你们的卡片作出回复,请求你们将那个混蛋沃尔特·肯尼迪丢到第五大街上,只给他留下一条内裤穿。我的附带条件是,当时地面上应该有雪,温度为零下。H·格雷沙姆。'"

他也将第四封信朗读了出来:"'在潘塔隆的鼻子上狠狠地打上一记重拳,不管是我还是其他人都认为付出五百美元是值得的。我想亲自观看。你诚挚的克劳迪娅·卡尔索普·海因斯敬上。'"

乔治将这几封信轻轻放下,小心地放到床上。有那么一会儿的时间,房间里静悄悄的。我们两个你盯着我看,我盯着你看,吃惊地说不出话来,高兴地说不出话来。我开始计算起那四笔订单会值多少钱了。

"价值五千美元,"我轻轻地说。

乔治宽宽地咧开了嘴,脸上露出欢快的笑容。"克劳德,"他说,"我们现在不应该搬到沃尔多夫去住吗?"

"就快了,"我回答,"可是,目前我们没有搬家的时间,甚至没有递送新卡片的时间。我们必须去执行手头已有订单发出的命令。我们将埋头于工作之中。"

"我们是否应该多雇佣几名员工、扩大公司的规模呢?"

"以后吧,"我说。"今天,就算要扩大规模,我们也没有时间去做了,就想想我们必须得做的事情吧。我们必须得往雅各布?斯温斯基的车里放响尾蛇……必须得把只穿着内裤的沃尔特·肯尼迪丢到第五大街上……必须得拳击潘塔隆的鼻子……让我看看啊……对了,我们得为三个不同的客户分别拳击潘塔隆的鼻子。"

我停了下来,闭上了眼睛,一动不动地坐着。我又一次意识到,一小股清澈的灵感之溪流淌进我的大脑组织。"有啦!"我喊道。"有啦! 有了啦! 一石击三鸟! 一拳为三人!"

"怎么做?"

"难道你没看出来吗?我们只需拳击潘塔隆一次,三位客户中的每一位……沃姆伯格、戈洛格里、克劳迪娅·海因斯……都会认为这是特地为他或她而做的。"

"再说一遍。"于是,我又说了一遍。

"妙极了。"

"常识性的东西,而且,同样的原则也可以应用到其他几条。响尾蛇订单和其他订单可以等到我们接到更多的订单后再做决定。或许再等几天,我们就会有十份订单都要求往斯温斯基的车里放响尾蛇。到那时候,我们就一次性完成所有订单。"

"太棒了。"

"那么,今天晚上,"我说,"我们就去对付潘塔隆。但是首先,我们必须租一辆车,也必须给沃姆伯格、戈洛格里、克劳迪娅·海因斯每人分别发一封电报,告诉他们击打的时间和地点。"

我们飞快穿上衣服,走出门去。

我们设法在东第九大街一家寂静的、脏兮兮的小汽修厂租了一辆车,是一辆1934年产的雪佛兰牌车,一晚上的租金是八美元。然后,我们发出三封电报,每一封都是一样的内容,巧妙的措辞将真实的意图隐藏了起来,以免有好奇的人会追根究底:"凌晨两点半,希望在企鹅俱乐部外见到你。复仇公司谨致问候。"

"还有一件事儿,"我说。"你应该化装,这很重要。比方说,一定不要让潘塔隆或者门卫以后认出你来。你必须得戴上假胡子。"

"你呢?"

"没有那个必要。我就坐在车里,他们不会看见我。"

我们去了一家儿童玩具店,给乔治买了个很棒的黑胡子。胡子上了蜡,又坚挺又闪亮,胡稍部分又长又尖。他将胡子举到脸前,看起来跟神圣罗马帝国的皇帝像极了。店里的伙计也卖给我们一管胶水,告诉我们如何将胡子粘到上嘴唇上。"要去跟孩子嬉戏玩耍?"乔治回答:"完全正确。"

现在,一切准备妥当,但是,要等待很长时间。我们身上总共只剩下三美元,我们用这点钱一人买了份三明治夹心面包,看了场电影。接着,在那天晚上十一点的时候,我们将车取来,开着车慢慢地在纽约的各条大街上巡行,消磨时间。

"你最好戴上胡子,适应一下。"

在一盏街灯下,我们将车停靠好。我把一些胶水挤出来,涂到乔治的上嘴唇上,将大黑胡子固定住,胡稍部分又长又尖。然后,我们继续驾车。车内很冷,外面又下起雪来。通过车灯的光柱,我能看到一些小雪花飘落。乔治不断地问:"打他该打多重?"我不断地回答:"尽可能重地去打,打到鼻子上。一定要打到鼻子上,因为那是合同规定的一部分。一切都要处理妥当,我们的客户或许正在看着呢。"

凌晨两点的时候,我们开着车慢慢经过企鹅俱乐部大门口,目的是想勘查一下实际情况。"我要把车停在那儿,"我说,"就是过了大门口以后那块黑色的区域。但是,车门我会为你开着。"

我们继续往前开。接着,乔治说:"他长什么样?我怎么知道要打的就是他?"

"不要担心,"我说。"这个问题,我已经想过了。"我从衣兜里掏出一张纸片,递给他。"这个你拿着,折叠成一小块儿,交给门卫。对门卫说,要确保将字条快速交给潘塔隆。做的时候,你要装出怕得要死的样子,而且要显得特别匆忙。有100:1的可能就是,潘塔隆会出来的。没有哪个专栏作家能够抵制得了纸条上内容的诱惑。"

我在纸条上写的是:"我是苏联领事馆的工作人员。请速到门口来,我有事要告诉你,但是,请你快点来,我有危险,无法进来找你。"

"你知道,"我说,"你的胡子令你看起来像俄罗斯人,所有俄罗斯人都留大胡子。"

乔治拿起纸条,将其折叠成很小的形状,夹到指缝间。现在,几乎要到凌晨两点半了,于是,我们开始向企鹅俱乐部方向开去。

"你都准备好了吗?"我问。

"是的。"

"我们现在要到位了。好了,我把车停在刚过大门口的地方……就这儿。使劲打他一下,"我说。乔治打开车门,下了车。我随后关车门,但趴在门上,一只手放到把手上,以便能够再次迅速将门打开。我摇下车窗,好看个清楚,同时让引擎"嗒嗒"地响着。

我看见乔治迅速走到门卫那儿,门卫站在红白相间的顶棚下,那个顶棚一直延伸到人行道上。我看见那个门卫转身,俯视着乔治,我不喜欢门卫这样看人的方式。门卫是位高个子男子,很傲慢的样子,穿着一身洋红色的制服,制服上缝着金色扣子,镶着金色肩部,沿着每只洋红色裤腿向下,分别镶嵌着一条白色的宽线条。他还戴了副白手套。只见他站在那儿,傲慢地俯视着乔治,皱着眉头,双唇紧紧合到一起,眼睛看着乔治的胡子。我想,哦,天呐,胡子弄得有些做作,化装有些过分了。他会弄明白那胡子是假的,会用手指夹住其中一处又长又尖的胡稍部分,只需一揪,胡子就会脱落。但是,他没有那么做。乔治的表演分散了他的注意力,演技很棒。我能够看到乔治左右跳跃,十指交叉握紧又松开,摇摆着身体,晃动着脑袋,听见他说:"庆庆庆你务必快些,介事儿生屎攸关。庆庆庆你里克拿给潘塔隆先生。"他的俄罗斯口音我以前从未听到过,但自始至终,他的声音里含有一种真正绝望的腔调。

最终,门卫严肃而傲慢地说:"把纸条给我。"乔治把纸条给了他,说道:"斜斜你,斜斜你,但告诉对方,情况很紧急。"门卫走了进去,消失不见。没过多大工夫,他回来了,说道:"现在,有人送进去了。"乔治来回踱步,紧张兮兮的。我眼盯着门口,等待着。三四分钟的时间过去了。乔治绞拧着双手,问道:"他在那离?他在那离?庆求你去看看,他来了没有!"

"你是怎么回事啊?"门卫说。现在,他又看向乔治的胡子。

"介事儿生屎攸关!潘塔隆先生能帮得上!他必须得来!"

"你为什么不闭上嘴!"门卫说完,又一次打开门,把头伸进去,我听见他跟里面的人说了些什么。

然后,他对乔治说:"他们说,他现在就要出来了。"

过了一会儿,门开了,个头矮小、穿戴整洁的潘塔隆跨出门外。他在靠门的地方暂停下来,眼睛快速从一侧扫向另一侧,就像一只好奇的白鼬。门卫碰了碰潘塔隆的帽子,指了指乔治。我听见潘塔隆说:"是我,你要干什么?"

乔治说:"白托,往介边一店儿,默让憃人听见。"他引着潘塔隆沿着人行道走去,离开了门卫,向我们车停的方向走。

"快说,现在,"潘塔隆说。"你想要干什么?"

突然之间,潘塔隆喊道:"看!"他指向大街上方。潘塔隆随即转头。就在这当儿,乔治抡起右胳膊,不偏不倚正好击打到潘塔隆的鼻尖部位。我看见乔治身体前倾,猛地一击,所有力气都随着拳头砸了过去。毫不费力,潘塔隆整个人就被轻轻抛起,离开了地面,向后飘移了一米多,撞到了企鹅俱乐部房子的前脸。这一切就发生在瞬间,迅雷不及掩耳,乔治随即跳进车里,坐到我旁边,我们随即开车离开。我听见门卫在我们身后吹着哨子。

"我们做到了!"乔治喘着气说。他情绪激动,上气不接下气。"我打得利索!你看到我打得多么利索了吗?"

现在,雪下大了。我开得很快,多次急转弯。于是,我清楚,在这样的暴风雪之中,没有人会追上我们。

"我击打得太重了,这个狗娘养的几乎穿墙而过了。"

"打得好,乔治,"我说。"干得漂亮,乔治。"

"你看见他离开地面了吗?你看见他垂直向上离开地面了吗?"

"沃姆伯格会很开心的,"我说。

"戈洛格里,还有那个叫海因斯的女子也会很开心的。"

"他们都会很开心的,"我说。"就看着钱滚滚而来吧。"

"后面有一辆车!"乔治喊道。"正跟着我们!紧紧尾随而来!疯一般行驶!"

"不可能!"我说。"他们不可能跟上我们的。刚好是另一辆车要去什么地方吧。"我向右来了个急转弯。

"他还紧追不舍,"乔治说。"不断转弯,很快就会把他甩掉。"

"我们这辆 1934 年的雪佛兰怎么能甩掉一辆警车,"我说。"我要停下。"

"继续开!"乔治大喊。"你开得不错。"

"我要停下,"我说。"继续开只能惹得他们疯狂追赶。"

第二章 冤冤相报 第二节 《复仇公司》Vengeance Is Mine Inc.

乔治激烈地反对,但是我知道继续开毫无用处,于是,我驶向路边停靠。后面那辆随即超过,开到我们前方滑行而止。

"快,"乔治说。"我们快溜。"他打开了门,拔腿要跑。

"不要犯傻!"我说。"原地待好。现在跑也跑不掉的。"

车外传来一个人的声音:"好了,伙计们,怎么这么着急?"

"没有着急,"我回答。"我们只是赶着回家。"

"是吗?"

"哦,是的。我们现在正在回家的路上。"

这名男子从我坐着的一侧将头从窗户探了进来,先看了看我,再看看乔治,接着又看了看我。

"令人讨厌的夜晚,"乔治说。"趁大街还没有完全被雪覆盖,我们只是想尽快赶回家。"

"噢,"这名男子说,"你们放轻松些。我只是寻思,我要把这个立即交给你们。"他随手将一沓钞票扔到我的膝盖上。"我叫戈洛格里,"他又补充道,"威尔伯·H·戈洛格里。"他站在车外的雪地里,咧开嘴冲着我们笑,同时跺着脚、搓着手来取暖。"我收到了你们的电报,在大街对面看到了整个过程。干得好,我给你们俩双倍报酬,值这个价。这是我看到过最有意思的事儿。再见,伙计们。当心点儿,他们现在会尾随而来。我要是你们的话,我就离开这座城镇。再见。"我们还没来得急说什么,他就消失不见了。

最终,我们回到了房间。一回到房间,我就立刻开始打包装箱。

"你疯了?"乔治说。"我们只需再等几个小时,就能从沃姆伯格和海因斯那个女子那儿分别收到五百美元。然后,我们拥有钱的总数就达两千,我们可以想去哪儿就去哪儿。"

因此,接下来的一天,我们待在房间里,等待着,读着报纸,其中一份报纸头版整个栏目刊登的是一篇题为"著名专栏作家遭到野蛮的暴力攻击"的文章。当然,下午的邮件中有两封信,每封信里有五百美元。

就在现在,就在此时此刻,我们坐在一辆挂有普尔曼式车厢的列车里,喝着苏格兰威士忌,向一个充满阳光、每天都有跑马赛的地方驶去。我们极其富有,乔治一个劲儿说,要是我们将所有的两千美元全部押到一匹赔率为十比一的马身上,我们就会再拥有两万美元,就能退休了。"我们会在棕榈滩拥有一座房子,"他说,"慷慨地款待客人。上流社会的名人会懒洋洋地躺在我们游泳池边上,小口喝着凉爽的饮料。稍过一会儿,我们或许将另外一大笔钱投到另一匹马身上,我们将会更加富有。或许,我们会厌倦棕榈滩,然后闲散地在富人地盘搬来搬去,如蒙特卡洛等地,过着像阿里汗王子和温莎公爵一样的生活。我们将成为国际电影摄影场的显赫成员,影星会冲我们微笑,服务生领班会向我们鞠躬。或许,在即将到来的时间里,莱昂内尔·潘塔隆甚至或许在他的栏目里提到我们。"

"那或许会非同寻常,"我说。

"岂止是,"他高兴地说。"岂止是非同寻常。"

第三章 意味深长

安徒生(Hans Christian Andersen)的童话《夜莺》(The Nightingale)讲的是一只会唱歌的夜莺和皇帝的故事,安徒生把这个故事的背景设在古代中国的某个朝代。最开始的时候,这只夜莺在乡间唱歌,皇帝听了它的歌唱就喜欢上它那美妙的歌声。于是,皇帝就把它带到了皇宫,让它住进金笼子,每日都听它歌唱。后来,有人献给皇帝一个镶满宝石的机械夜莺,这只夜莺同样能唱出美妙的歌声,而且不知疲倦。那只真夜莺无奈地飞出皇宫,再次融入美丽的大自然。一年过去了,突然有一天,这只人造夜莺坏掉,再也无法歌唱了。五年过去了,皇帝病倒了,突然想起了那只会唱歌的真夜莺……安徒生的这个童话故事可谓意味深长、耐人寻味。

在《伊索寓言》(Aesop's Fables)中,乌龟苦练飞行本领,意欲飞上蓝天。一天,乌龟看见老鹰在空中飞翔,便仰头祈求老鹰教他飞行本领。老鹰劝告乌龟说,任凭它怎么努力学习飞行,终究是不可能飞起来的。可是,乌龟不肯放弃,再三恳求,老鹰无奈,抓起乌龟,飞到高空,然后将其松开,只见"乌龟像一只折了翅膀的鸟歪歪斜斜地往下跌,越跌越快,不偏不倚,正好跌在一块大青石上,摔得粉碎"(安晓峰等译,2001:78)。《伊索寓言》中的这个乌龟和老鹰的故事亦可谓意味深长、耐人寻味。

类似上述作品,正如宋代程颢、程颐兄弟俩读《论语》时所言:"某自十七八读《论语》,当时已晓文义,读之愈久,但觉意味深长。读《论语》,有读了后全然无事者;有读了后,其中得一两句喜者;有读了后,知好之者;有读了后,直有不知手之舞之足之蹈之者。"①

在英国作家罗尔德·达尔的笔下,这样的作品也可见到。《熏制奶酪》中,飞行员比普不堪忍受老鼠成灾这个事实,买来了捕鼠夹、熏制奶酪等东西,但却将它们粘到了天花板上,招来众老鼠的嘲笑……在与《熏制奶酪》极其相似的另一部作品《倒立之鼠》中,一位名叫拉邦的87岁老人,对家中老鼠成灾的事实,也不堪忍受,于是买来捕鼠夹、奶酪等东西粘到了天花板上,同样招来老鼠的嘲笑,结果同样出人意料。达尔的这两个故事,情节虽然几乎相同,但寓意的倾向却有所不同。

《蛇毒解药》中,在孟加拉的乡村地区,哈里·波普认为自己的被窝里钻进了一条金环蛇,于是,当地医生甘德贝被紧急招来。然而,甘德贝医生到来后,哈里的出言不逊以及甘德贝医生的一举一动,则预示着故事的结局意味深长、耐人寻味——正如上面提到的宋代程颢、程颐在《河南程氏遗书》中所言:"读之愈久,但觉意味深长。"

第一节 《熏制奶酪》Smoked Cheese

罗尔德·达尔的《熏制奶酪》(Smoked Cheese)首次发表在美国《大西洋月刊》(Atlantic Monthly)1945年12月号上。顺便说一下,"《大西洋月刊》是一本高雅的杂志,发表的文章包含对时事进行分析等内容。人们认为这本杂志比流行度更高、用"事实"说话的《星期六晚邮报》要高出好几个层次"(The Atlantic Monthly was a sophisti-

---

① 此语典出《河南程氏遗书》卷19中的《伊川先生语五·杨遵道录》,转引自杨海文发表于《中华读书报》2014年2月12日第15版"国学"栏目的文章《朱熹﹤读论语孟子法﹥溯源》,稍加更改。

第三章 意味深长 第一节 《熏制奶酪》Smoked Cheese

cated magazine that included current events analysis, considered several grades above the more popularistic [sic] *Saturday Evening Post* and their "factual" stories)①。

一、原作导读

这篇小说篇幅很短,带有童话性质,但不乏幽默的笔触和精彩的描写。主人公是飞行员比普。

快乐的比普唯一的烦恼就是家里老鼠成灾。为此,他上街买来捕鼠夹、熏制奶酪等东西,但却违反常规,将这些东西粘到了天花板上。当天晚上出洞的老鼠纷纷嘲笑他的愚蠢行为,但他不为所动,仍然我行我素:

他拿起一把椅子,将黏合剂涂到四条腿的底部,然后将其倒着粘到了天花板上,粘到了靠近捕鼠夹的位置上。屋子里的桌子、收音机、台灯,他也如法炮制。他甚至还在天花板那儿粘上了一小块地毯。

He took a chair and put glue on the bottom of its legs and stuck it upside down to the ceiling, near the mousetraps. He did the same with the table, the radio set, and the lamp. He even put a little carpet up there.

第二天晚上,老鼠出洞后被眼前的情景弄迷糊了,纷纷倒立……比普早晨起来,发现满地都是死老鼠。

"啊哈,"他说着,拍了拍双手。"啊哈。我就知道,它们会去够熏制奶酪吃的。"

---

① 这段叙述由本书著者译自"罗尔德·达尔粉丝网"(Roald Dahl Fans),具体可参见克里斯廷·霍华德(Kristine Howard)创建并维护的网站"Roald Dahl Fans.com",网址为:http://www.roalddahlfans.com/。

"Ah-ha," he said, and he clapped his hands. "Ah-ha. I knew they'd go for smoked cheese."

二、原作释读

这部小说篇幅短小,具有寓言性质,意味深长。阅读中,要注意体会主人公比普和老鼠不同的想法,可谓各具意蕴。

Smoked① Cheese②

Not so very long ago there lived a pilot whose name was Bipou. He was very poor and he lived all alone in a small house in a small village; but he was happy.

The only thing that bothered him was mice; his house was infested③ with mice. Now Bipou thought nothing at all of mice, because they lived even further below the ground than non-flyers. And the mice multiplied and multiplied④ until there came a time when he could stand it no longer.

"This is too much," Bipou said, and he laughed and went out into

---

① smoked: *Adjective* (used especially of meats and fish) dried and cured by hanging in wood smoke 熏制的(e. g. Smoked salmon—what a treat! 熏大马哈鱼——馐馔之福啊!)

② 本部小说的原文出自克里斯廷·霍华德(Kristine Howard)创建并维护的网站"Roald Dahl Fans. com",网址为:http://www. roalddahlfans. com/。

③ infest: *Verb* [with obj.] (usu. as "be infested") (of insects or animals) be present (in a place or site) in large numbers, typically so as to cause damage or disease(昆虫或动物)大批出没于;侵扰(e. g. The house is infested with cockroaches. 这座房子蟑螂成灾。)

④ multiply: *Verb* [no obj.] (of an animal or other organism) increase in number by reproducing(动物或其他有机体)繁殖;增殖(e. g. Hot weather multiplied the bacteria in milk rapidly. 炎热的天气使牛奶中的细菌迅速繁殖。)

the village and bought some mousetraps① and some smoked cheese and a lot of glue.

When he got home, he put the glue on the underneath of the mousetraps and then stuck them to the ceiling. Then he baited② them carefully with pieces of smoked cheese and set them to go off.

That night when the mice came out of their holes and saw the mousetraps, they began laughing fit to burst③. They walked around on the floor, nudging④ each other and pointing up at the ceiling and giggling. After all, it was so silly, mousetraps on the ceiling.

When Bipou came down the next morning and saw that there were no mice caught in the traps, he smiled but didn't say anything.

He took a chair and put glue on the bottom of its legs and stuck it upside down to the ceiling, near the mousetraps. He did the same with the table, the radio set, and the lamp. He even put a little carpet up there.

The next night when the mice came out of their holes they were still

---

① mousetrap: *Noun* a trap for catching and usually killing mice, especially one with a spring bar which snaps down on to the mouse when it touches a piece of cheese or other bait attached to the mechanism 捕鼠器;捕鼠夹

② bait: *Verb* put bait on (a hook) or in (a trap, net, or fishing area) to entice fish or animals as prey 装饵于;做饵;上饵(e. g. They bait the mousetrap with stale cheese. 他们用变质的乳酪作捕鼠夹的诱饵。)

③ fit to burst: If someone is fit to burst with an emotion or a feeling, it is very strong inside them(笑的)几乎要爆炸(e. g. The children were fit to burst with excitement. 孩子们兴奋地几乎笑破了肚皮。)

④ nudge: *Verb* [with obj.] prod (someone) gently with one's elbow in order to draw their attention to something 用肘轻触(某人以引起注意)(e. g. People were nudging each other and pointing at me. 人们用肘互相触碰对方,并对我指指点点。)

joking and laughing about what they had seen the night before. But when they looked up at the ceiling, they stopped laughing very suddenly.

"Good gracious me!" said one. "Look up there. There's the floor!"

"Heavens above!" said another. "We must be standing on the ceiling!"

"I'm beginning to feel a little giddy," said another.

"All the blood's going to my head," said another.

"This is awful," said the oldest mouse of all. "This is awful. We must do something about this at once."

"I've got it," said a mouse who had a face like a politician and bushy eyebrows like Mr. John L. Lewis's[①]. "I know what we'll do." (He was a very clever mouse.) "We'll all stand on our heads; then, at any rate, we'll be the right way up."

So they all stood on their heads, and after a long time, one by one, they died from a rush of blood to the brain.

When Bipou came down the next morning, the floor was covered with dead mice.

"Ah-ha," he said, and he clapped his hands. "Ah-ha. I knew they'd go for smoked cheese."

---

① John Llewellyn Lewis (1880—1969): He was U. S. labor leader. He headed the United Mine Workers 1920—1960 and organized the Committee for Industrial Organization 1935, which became the Congress of Industrial Organizations (CIO). He served as its president until 1940. 约翰·卢埃林·刘易斯(1880—1969,曾任美国工党领袖,1920—1960年间任美国矿工联合会主席。1935年,他组建了美国产业工会联合会的前身——产业组织委员会,并任主席,1940年卸任。)

三、翻译探索

本篇小说短小精悍,具有寓言性质,翻译起来难度不大,可在"雅"上多做探索。

熏制奶酪

不算是很久以前吧,有一个名叫比普的飞行员独自一个人生活着。他很穷,居住在一个小村子里的一座小房子中,但是,他却很快乐。

唯一令他烦恼的就是老鼠,他家的房子里老鼠成了灾。但现在,他根本不用去考虑老鼠的事情,因为那些老鼠生活在地下,比那些没长翅膀的住的地方还要深。可是,老鼠繁殖了又繁殖,直到有一天,他再也无法忍受他们繁殖的速度了。

"这也忒多了,"比普说。说完,他大笑起来,走进村子,买回几只捕鼠夹、一些熏制奶酪以及很多的黏合剂。

回到家,他将黏合剂抹到所有的捕鼠夹底部,将捕鼠夹粘到天花板上,然后在上面仔细地将一块块奶酪作为诱饵放好,并将捕鼠夹支好。

当天晚上,那些老鼠走出洞穴,看到了捕鼠夹,就开始大笑,笑破了肚皮。它们绕着地板走动,互相触碰对方,向上指着天花板,咯咯吱吱笑个不停。毕竟,这样做也太愚蠢了——竟把捕鼠夹支在天花板上。

第二天早晨,比普下楼,当他看到夹子上一个老鼠也没有捕到时,他只是微微一笑,但什么都没有说。

他拿起一把椅子,将黏合剂涂到椅子四条腿的底部,然后将椅子倒着粘到了天花板上,粘到了靠近捕鼠夹的位置上。屋子里的桌子、收音机、台灯,他也如法炮制。他甚至还在天花板那儿粘上了一小块地毯。

第二天夜晚,老鼠走出洞穴时依然有说有笑,嘲笑着昨晚它们目睹的情景。但是,抬起头看向天花板时,它们的欢笑声却戛然而止。

"我的老天啊!"其中一只说道。"抬头看那儿,那儿有地面啊!"

"老天在上呀!"另一只说道。"我们现在一定是站在天花板上了!"

"我开始感觉有点眩晕了,"另一只说道。

"所有的血液都涌向我的脑袋了,"另一只附和道。

"这很糟糕,"最年长的一只说。"这很糟糕。我们必须立刻采取点什么措施。"

"我有主意了,"一只老鼠说道。这只老鼠长着一张政客的面孔,眉毛浓密,就像美国矿工联合会主席约翰·L·刘易斯先生的眉毛。"我知道我们要做什么了。"(这是一只很聪明的老鼠)"我们都倒立,那么,不管怎么说,我们的生活方式就都正过来了。"

因此,它们都倒立起来。过了很长时间,它们一只接一只地死去,因为血液涌入了大脑。

第二天早晨比普下楼时,地板上尽是些死老鼠。

"啊哈,"他说着,拍了拍双手。"啊哈。我就知道,它们会去够熏制的奶酪吃的。"

第二节 《倒立之鼠》The Upsidedown Mice

罗尔德·达尔的《倒立之鼠》(The Upsidedown Mice)被收录在大不列颠海鹦图书公司 1974 年出版的《海鹦年度最佳作品选》(Puffin Annual Number One)一书中。

有意思的是,达尔的这篇带有童话性质短篇小说的情节跟本章第一节,也就是上一节《熏制奶酪》的情节简直是"如出一辙",这说明作家罗尔德·达尔善于充分利用类似的故事情节来循环制造故事,这一点从达尔其他作品中不难发现。举个例子来说,罗尔德·达尔乡村故事"克劳德的狗"(Claud's Dog)系列中的一篇——《世界冠军》(The Champion of the World)①,其情节后来竟成为《世界冠军丹尼》(Danny the Champion of the World)一书的主线。

当然,本节讨论的《倒立之鼠》跟上一节讨论过的《熏制乳酪》还是存在细微差别的。例如,在《倒立之鼠》中,粘到天花板上的是电视机,而在《熏制奶酪》中,粘到天花板上的则是收音机;故事的结局也有所不同,《熏制奶酪》的结局幽默,意味深长,而《倒立之鼠》的结局,则是说教式的,也颇耐人寻味。

一、原作导读

这篇小说篇幅很短,带有童话性质,但不乏幽默的笔触和精彩的描写。主人公是78岁的老人拉邦。

过着平静生活的拉邦,突然有一天对家中成灾的老鼠忍无可忍了。于是,他买来老鼠夹、乳酪等东西,但他并没有把这些东西放置到地面上来捕捉老鼠,而是将它们粘到了天花板上。当天晚上,老鼠纷纷出洞,因为他的这一行为而笑得前仰后合。第二天早晨,拉邦发现一个老鼠都没有捕到,但却不动声色,继续他我行我素的行为:

他拿起一把椅子,将其四条腿的底部涂上黏合剂,把椅子倒过来粘到了天花板上,粘到了靠近捕鼠夹的位置上。房间里的桌子、电视机、台灯,他也如法炮制。他将房间里的一切都倒着粘到了天花板上,甚至还把一小块地毯也粘了上去。

He took a chair and put glue on the bottom of its legs and stuck it upsidedown to the ceiling, near the mousetraps. He did the same with the table, the television set and the lamp. He took everything that was on

---

① 关于《世界冠军》这部短篇小说是否属于达尔乡村故事"克劳德的狗"(Claud's Dog)系列,存在着争议。本书的说法基于"DAHL, R. The Best of Roald Dahl . London: Penguin Books Ltd., 2006"。因为在这本书中,《世界冠军》被列到"克劳德的狗"系列的最后一篇。关于《世界冠军》,读者可参阅《罗尔德·达尔短篇故事品读及汉译探索(第4卷)》第三章第二节。

the floor and stuck it upsidedown on the ceiling. He even put a little carpet up there.

第二天晚上,老鼠照例纷纷出洞,但目睹天花板上的情景时,它们却慌了手脚,不知如何是好。于是,一个年长的、显得很有智慧的老鼠站了出来:

"我知道我们要做什么了,"上了年纪的那只老鼠说道。"我们大家都倒立,那么,无论如何,我们的生活方式就正过来了。"
"I know what we'll do," said the very senior mouse. "We'll all stand on our heads, then anyway we'll be the right way up."

故事的最后,作家罗尔德·达尔站了出来,总结道:

因此,要记住的是:

无论何时这个世界看起来多么严重地颠倒过来,你都一定要将双脚牢牢地踩到地面上。
So the thing to remember is this:
Whenever the world seems to be terribly upsidedown, make sure you keep your feet firmly on the ground.

二、原作释读

这篇小说跟本章上一节的《熏制奶酪》如出一辙,从中可以看出作家罗尔德·达尔非凡的讲故事功力。不同的是,在本篇小说的结尾,达尔站了出来,道出了其中的寓意。这种做法类似于很多寓言作家的做法。阅读中,读者应注意体会两部"孪生"小说在情节上的细微差异。

The Upsidedown[①] Mice[②]

Once upon a time there lived an old man of 87 whose name was Labon. All his life he had been a quiet and peaceful person. He was very poor and very happy.

When Labon discovered that he had mice in his house, he did not at first bother himself greatly about it. But the mice multiplied. They kept right on multiplying and finally there came a time when he could stand it no longer.

"This is too much," he said. "This really is going a bit too far." He hobbled[③] out of the house and down the road to a shop where he bought himself some mousetraps, a piece of cheese and some glue.

When he got home, he put the glue on the underneath of the mousetraps and stuck them to the ceiling. Then he baited them carefully with pieces of cheese and set them to go off.

That night when the mice came out of their holes and saw the mousetraps on the ceiling, they thought it a tremendous joke. They walked around on the floor, nudging each other and pointing up with their front paws and roaring with laughter. After all it was pretty silly, mousetraps on the ceiling.

---

① upsidedown or upside down: *Adverb & Adjective* having the part that is usually at the top turned to be at the bottom 颠倒着;倒转着(e. g. The sloth spends most of its time hanging upside down from the branches. 树懒大部分时间里都是倒挂在树枝上。)

② 本部小说的原文出自克里斯廷·霍华德(Kristine Howard)创建并维护的网站"Roald Dahl Fans. com",网址为:http://www.roalddahlfans.com/。

③ hobble: *Verb* [no obj. , with adverbial of direction] walk in an awkward way, typically because of pain from an injury 蹒跚;(尤指因为伤痛)跛行(e. g. He was hobbling around on crutches. 他拄着拐杖跛行。)

When Labon came down the next morning and saw that there were no mice caught in the traps, he smiled but said nothing.

He took a chair and put glue on the bottom of its legs and stuck it upsidedown to the ceiling, near the mousetraps. He did the same with the table, the television set and the lamp. He took everything that was on the floor and stuck it upsidedown on the ceiling. He even put a little carpet up there.

The next night when the mice came out of their holes they were still joking and laughing about what they had seen the night before. But now, when they looked up at the ceiling, they stopped laughing very suddenly.

"Good gracious me!" cried one. "Look up there! There's the floor!"

"Heavens above!" shouted another. "We must be standing on the ceiling."

"I'm beginning to feel a little giddy," said another.

"All the blood's going to my head," said another.

"This is terrible!" said a very senior mouse with long whiskers. "This is really terrible! We must do something about it at once."

"I shall faint if I have to stand on my head any longer!" shouted a young mouse.

"Me too!"

"I can't stand it!"

"Save us! Do something somebody, quick!"

"I know what we'll do," said the very senior mouse. "We'll all stand on our heads, then anyway we'll be the right way up."

Obediently, they all stood on their heads, and after a long time, one by one, they fainted from a rush of blood to their brains.

When Labon came down the next morning the floor was littered① with mice. Quickly he gathered them up and popped them all in a basket.

So the thing to remember is this:

Whenever the world seems to be terribly upsidedown, make sure you keep your feet firmly on the ground.

三、翻译探索

与上一节中的小说一样，本篇小说的翻译难度不大，但要注意体会对话的口气，并在翻译中以不同的翻译手法精确加以再现。

倒立之鼠

从前有一位 87 岁的老人，名字叫拉邦。一生之中，他一直很安静、很平和。他很穷，却很快乐。

拉邦发现家中有老鼠，起先他自己并没有感觉有多大的烦恼，但是，老鼠不断繁殖，一个劲儿繁殖。最终有一天，他再也无法忍受了。

"这也忒多了，"他说。"这真是有点太过分了。"他蹒跚地走出家门，沿着马路走到一家商店。在那儿，他买了几只捕鼠夹、一块奶酪以及一些黏合剂。

回到家，他将所有的捕鼠夹底部都抹上黏合剂，将捕鼠夹粘到天花板上。然后，他仔细将一块块奶酪作为诱饵摆放好，并且将捕鼠夹支好。

当天夜晚，那些老鼠走出洞穴，看见了天花板上的捕鼠夹。它们当时想，这真是一个天大的笑话。于是，它们绕着地板闲荡，相互触碰着对方，前爪向上指着，前仰后合地放声大笑起来。毕竟，那是一个极其愚蠢的行为——竟将捕鼠夹支在天花板上。

---

① litter: Verb [with obj. and adverbial] (usu. as "be littered") leave (rubbish or a number of objects) lying untidily in a place 乱扔；乱丢（e.g. There was broken glass littered about. 打碎的玻璃杯乱丢在那儿。）

第二天早晨,拉邦下楼看到夹子上没有捕到一只老鼠,他微微一笑,但什么都没有说。

他拿起一把椅子,将其四条腿的底部涂上黏合剂,把椅子倒过来粘到了天花板上,粘到了靠近捕鼠夹的位置。房间里的桌子、电视机、台灯,他也如法炮制。他将房间里的一切都倒着粘到了天花板上,甚至还把一小块地毯也粘了上去。

第二天夜里,那些老鼠从洞穴出来,仍然有说有笑,拿昨晚所看到的景象开着玩笑。但是现在,当它们抬起头看向天花板时,欢笑声就戛然而止了。

"我的老天呐!"其中一只叫道。"看那上边啊!上面有地面!"

"老天在上啊!"另一只喊道。"我们大家现在一定是站在天花板上了。"

"我开始感觉有点眩晕了,"另一只说道。

"所有的血液都涌入我的脑袋了,"另一只说。

"这太糟糕了!"一只长着长长胡须的、年纪很大的老鼠说。"这真是太糟糕了!我们必须立即采取点什么措施。"

"如果再这么样多倒立一会儿,我就会昏倒!"一只年轻的老鼠说道。

"我也一样!"

"我受不了啦!"

"救救我们!有谁站出来做点什么,快啊!"

"我知道我们要做什么了,"上了年纪的那只老鼠说道。"我们大家都倒立,那么,无论如何,我们的生活方式就正过来了。"

它们都顺从地倒立起来。过了很长时间,它们一个接一个地昏了过去,因为血液涌入了大脑。

第二天早晨拉邦下楼时发现老鼠横七竖八地躺在地板上。于是,他快速将它们收集起来,抛入一只篮子。

因此,要记住的是:

无论何时这个世界看起来多么严重地颠倒过来,你都一定要将双脚牢牢地踩到地面上。

第三章 意味深长 第三节 《蛇毒解药》Poison

第三节 《蛇毒解药》Poison

罗尔德·达尔的《蛇毒解药》(*Poison*)首次发表在《科利尔周刊》(*Collier's Weekly*,也有人译作《柯里尔》《科里尔》或《柯莱尔斯》)1950年6月3日出版的那一期上。后来,这个故事又收录到《罗尔德·达尔短篇故事集锦》(*The Collected Short Stories of Roald Dahl*)、《如你之人》(*Someone like You*)、《五部畅销书集》(*5 Bestsellers*)、《完全出人意料故事集》(*Completely Unexpected Tales*)、《更多出人意料故事集》(*More Tales of the Unexpected*)、《后续出人意料故事集》(*Further Tales of the Unexpected*)、《罗尔德·达尔选集》(*The Roald Dahl Omnibus*)以及《罗尔德·达尔二十九篇成人故事集》(*Twenty Nine Kisses from Roald Dahl*)等书中。

此外,这部小说在收音机系列剧《逃脱》(*Escape*)的第133集(Episode 133)中播出,播出时间是1950年7月28日。这部小说还被改编成电视系列剧——分别是1958年10月5日播映的《阿尔弗雷德·希区柯克出品短剧选》(*Alfred Hitchcock Presents*)中第118集(Episode 118),以及1980年3月29日播映的《出乎意料的故事集》(*Tales of the Unexpected*)第二部中的第5集(Episode 2.5),可见其影响力之大。

对于罗尔德·达尔《蛇毒解药》的解读往往存在着某些偏差,克里斯廷·霍华德(Kristine Howard)认为,"在整个阅读过程中,你会认为故事的主要冲突在人和哈里·波普腹部的金环蛇之间。但是,读到最后几个段落,你就会意识到,达尔真正的目的是要揭示种族主义:哈里·波普在自己的生命受到威胁的时候,会心甘情愿去忍受当地医生甘德贝的行为,可是,一旦甘德贝医生敢对白人提出质疑,哈里的本色就露了出来。这部小说也是制造紧张感和悬念方面的杰作"(The entire time you're reading it, you think that the main conflict is between the men and the krait on Harry's stomach. It's only in the last few paragraphs, though, that you realize that Dahl's real point is about racism. Harry Pope is perfectly willing to tolerate Dr. Ganderbai as long as his life is in danger, but as soon as Ganderbai dares to question the white man, Harry lets his true colors show. The story is also a masterpiece of tension and suspense)[①]。

一、原作导读

这是罗尔德·达尔最著名的短篇小说之一,以第一人称"我"(名字叫"廷伯·伍兹")的视角展开,但叙述者"我"是"隐身"的,起到了"纽带"或者"桥梁"的作用,可以看成作家达尔本人的化身。

廷伯·伍兹回到住处发现同伴哈里·波普躺在床上,行为怪异——小声说话,而且满身是汗。哈里告诉廷伯,一条有剧毒的金环蛇爬上了床,躺在他肚子上盖着的床单下面。廷伯从厨房取来一把刀,一旦毒蛇咬到哈里,便将哈里皮肤切开,吸出里面的毒液,但哈里却催促廷伯喊医生过来。

当地医生甘德贝如约而至。医生当即做出决定,给哈里注射免疫血清。只见"甘德贝医生从包里拿出一块红色的橡胶管,将管子的一头向上一滑,绕到了哈里的二头肌上,然后,将管子紧紧系上一个扣"(Ganderbai took a piece of red rubber tubing from his bag and slid one end up and around Harry's biceps; then he tied the tubing tight with a knot),开始给哈里注射免疫血清。哈里努力坚持着,保持着不动的姿势,也尽量控制自己不去咳嗽。

注射完血清,来到卧室外面,医生对廷伯说,免疫血清不能保证哈里是绝对安全的,还得向毒蛇所在的地方施用一种叫作氯仿的麻醉剂。这个过程花了很长的时间,最后,医生和廷伯慢慢地将床单从哈里的身体上移开,却不见毒蛇的踪影。

---

① 这段叙述由本书著者译自"罗尔德·达尔粉丝网"(Roald Dahl Fans),具体可参见克里斯廷·霍华德(Kristine Howard)创建并维护的网站"Roald Dahl Fans.com",网址为:http://www.roalddahlfans.com/。

第三章　意味深长　第三节　《蛇毒解药》Poison

"别动,"甘德贝说道。"别动,波普先生。"然后,他就在哈里身体的边缘、双腿的底部四处察看。

"我们一定得小心,"他说。"蛇不一定会钻到什么地方去,有可能钻进睡裤裆儿呢。"

"Don't move," Ganderbai said, "don't move, Mr. Pope"; and he began to peer around along the side of Harry's body and under his legs.

"We must be careful," he said. "It may be anywhere. It could be up the leg of his pyjamas."

闻听此言,哈里从床上跳了起来,力图将毒蛇抖落掉……但是,哈里没有被咬,毒蛇也不见踪影。

"波普先生,你当然是十分肯定开始的时候看到过蛇吗?"甘德贝的声音里带有一种讥讽的腔调,而这种腔调在一般场合里他从没有表露过。"波普先生,难道你不认为,你或许有可能是在做梦吗?"

"Mr. Pope, you are of course quite sure you saw it in the first place?" There was a note of sarcasm in Ganderbai's voice that he would never have employed in ordinary circumstances. "You don't think you might possibly have been dreaming, do you, Mr. Pope?"

甘德贝医生的质疑惹恼了先前还言听计从的哈里·波普:

"你是说,我在撒谎吗?"他喊道。
甘德贝一动不动站着,眼睛看着哈里。哈里在床上向前迈出一步,双眼发出了亮光。
"嘿,你这只下水道脏毛老鼠,你这个小印度佬!"
"闭嘴,哈里!"我说。
"你这肮脏的、黑乎乎的——"
"哈里!"我叫道。"闭嘴,哈里!"他的话语糟糕透顶。
"Are you telling me I'm a liar?" he shouted.

Ganderbai remained absolutely still, watching Harry. Harry took a pace forward on the bed and there was a shining look in his eyes.

"Why, you dirty little Hindu sewer rat!"

"Shut up, Harry!" I said.

"You dirty black—"

"Harry!" I called. "Shut up, Harry!" It was terrible the things he was saying.

面对哈里的出言不逊,甘德贝一声未吱,走出了房间。廷伯追了出去,尽量打圆场,安慰医生:

"你工作做得很出色,"我说。"你能来,十分感谢。"

"他所需要的,就是好好休个假,"他安静地说,眼睛并没有看着我。然后,他发动引擎,驾车而去。

"You did a wonderful job," I said. "Thank you very much for coming."

"All he needs is a good holiday," he said quietly, without looking at me, then he started the engine and drove off.

二、原作释读

在这篇小说里,达尔再次"卖弄"了一些医学方面的知识,应理解好这方面的表达。在了解一些医学知识的基础上,对本篇小说的结尾就会有一个清晰的理解或想象了。

Poison[①]

It must have been around midnight when I drove home, and as I approached the gates of the bungalow[②] I switched off the headlamps of the car so the beam wouldn't swing in through the window of the side bedroom and wake Harry Pope. But I needn't have bothered. Coming up the drive I noticed his light was still on, so he was awake anyway unless perhaps he'd dropped off while reading.

I parked the car and went up the five steps to the balcony, counting each step carefully in the dark so I wouldn't take an extra one which wasn't there when I got to the top. I crossed the balcony, pushed through the screen doors into the house itself and switched on the light in the hall. I went across to the door of Harry's room, opened it quietly, and looked in.

He was lying on the bed and I could see he was awake. But he didn't move. He didn't even turn his head towards me, but I heard him say, "Timber, Timber, come here."

He spoke slowly, whispering each word carefully, separately, and I pushed the door right open and started to go quickly across the room.

"Stop, wait a moment, Timber." I could hardly hear what he was saying. He seemed to be straining enormously to get the words out. "What's the matter, Harry?"

"Sshhh!" he whispered. "Sshhh! For God's sake don't make a noise. Take your shoes off before you come nearer. *Please* do as I say,

---

① 本部小说原文出自 "DAHL, R. *The Collected Short Stories of Roald Dahl*. London: Penguin Books Ltd., 1992"。

② bungalow: *Noun* a low house having only one storey or, in some cases, upper rooms set in the roof, typically with dormer windows 独层的孟加拉式的小住宅; 平房

Timber."

The way he was speaking reminded me of George Barling after he got shot in the stomach when he stood leaning against a crate① containing a spare aeroplane engine, holding both hands on his stomach and saying things about the German pilot in just the same hoarse straining half whisper Harry was using now.

"Quickly, Timber, but take your shoes off first."

I couldn't understand about taking off the shoes but I figured that if he was as ill as he sounded I'd better humour② him, so I bent down and removed the shoes and left them in the middle of the floor. Then I went over to his bed.

"Don't touch the bed! For God's sake don't touch the bed!" He was still speaking like he'd been shot in the stomach and I could see him lying there on his back with a single sheet covering three-quarters of his body. He was wearing a pair of pyjamas③ with blue, brown, and white stripes, and he was sweating terribly. It was a hot night and I was sweating a little myself, but not like Harry. His whole face was wet and the

---

① crate: *Noun* a slatted wooden case used for transporting goods(运输货物的)板条箱(e.g. a crate of bananas 一箱香蕉)

② humour or humor: *Verb* [with obj.] comply with the wishes of (someone) in order to keep them content, however unreasonable such wishes might be 纵容;迁就;迎合(e.g. She was always humouring him to prevent trouble. 她总是迁就他以防止麻烦)

③ pyjamas or pajamas: *Plural Noun* a suit of loose trousers and jacket for sleeping in 睡衣裤

pillow around his head was sodden① with moisture. It looked like a bad go② of malaria③ to me.

"What is it, Harry?"

"A krait④," he said.

"A *krait*! Oh, my God! Where'd it bite you? How long ago?"

"Shut up," he whispered.

"Listen, Harry," I said, and I leaned forward and touched his shoulder. "We've got to be quick. Come on now, quickly, tell me where it bit you." He was lying there very still and tense as though he was holding on to himself hard because of sharp pain.

"I haven't been bitten," he whispered. "Not yet. It's on my stomach. Lying there asleep."

I took a quick pace backwards, I couldn't help it, and I stared at his stomach or rather at the sheet that covered it. The sheet was rumpled⑤ in several places and it was impossible to tell if there was anything underneath.

"You don't really mean there's a krait lying on your stomach now?"

"I swear it."

"How did it get there?" I shouldn't have asked the question because

---

① sodden: *Adjective* saturated with liquid, especially water; soaked through 湿漉漉的；湿透的(e.g. His clothes were sodden. 他的衣服湿透了。)

② go: *Noun* (Chiefly Brit.) an attack of illness(主要为英国英语用法)(疾病)发作(e.g. He's had this nasty go of dysentery. 他得过如此讨厌的痢疾。)

③ malaria: *Noun* The parasite belongs to the genus Plasmodium (phylum Sporozoa) and is transmitted by female mosquitoes of the genus Anopheles. 疟疾

④ krait: *Noun* a highly venomous Asian snake of the cobra family 环蛇

⑤ rumple: *Verb* [withobj.] [usu. as adj. rumpled] give a creased, ruffled, or dishevelled appearance to 弄皱；压皱；弄乱

it was easy to see he wasn't fooling. I should have told him to keep quiet.

"I was reading," Harry said, and he spoke very slowly, taking each word in turn and speaking it carefully so as not to move the muscles of his stomach. "Lying on my back reading and I felt something on my chest, behind the book. Sort of tickling[①]. Then out of the corner of my eye saw this little krait sliding over my pyjamas. Small, about ten inches. Knew I mustn't move. Couldn't have anyway. Lay there watching it. Thought it would go over the top of the sheet." Harry paused and was silent for a few moments. His eyes looked down along his body towards the place where the sheet covered his stomach, and I could see he was watching to make sure his whispering wasn't disturbing the thing that lay there.

"There was a fold in the sheet," he said, speaking more slowly than ever now and so softly I had to lean close to hear him. "See it, it's still there. It went under that. I could feel it through my pyjamas, moving on my stomach. Then it stopped moving and now it's lying there in the warmth. Probably asleep. I've been waiting for you." He raised his eyes and looked at me.

"How long ago?"

"Hours," he whispered. "Hours and bloody hours and hours. I can't keep still much longer. I've been wanting to cough."

There was not much doubt about the truth of Harry's story. As a matter of fact it wasn't a surprising thing for a krait to do. They hang around people's houses and they go for the warm places. The surprising thing was that Harry hadn't been bitten. The bite is quite deadly except sometimes when you catch it at once and they kill a fair number of people

---

[①] tickle: *Verb* [no obj.] (of a part of the body) give a sensation similar to that caused by being touched in this way(身体部位)有痒感;觉得痒

each year in Bengal①, mostly in the villages.

"All right, Harry," I said, and now I was whispering too. "Don't move and don't talk any more unless you have to. You know it won't bite unless it's frightened. We'll fix it in no time."

I went softly out of the room in my stocking feet and fetched a small sharp knife from the kitchen. I put it in my trouser pocket ready to use instantly in case something went wrong while we were still thinking out a plan. If Harry coughed or moved or did something to frighten the krait and got bitten, I was going to be ready to cut the bitten place and try to suck the venom② out. I came back to the bedroom and Harry was still lying very quiet and sweating all over his face. His eyes followed me as I moved across the room to his bed and I could see he was wondering what I'd been up to. I stood beside him, trying to think of the best thing to do.

"Harry," I said, and now when I spoke I put my mouth almost on his ear so I wouldn't have to raise my voice above the softest whisper, "I think the best thing to do is for me to draw the sheet back very, very gently. Then we could have a look first. I think I could do that without disturbing it."

"Don't be a damn fool." There was no expression in his voice. He

---

① Bengal: *Noun* a region in the north-east of the Indian subcontinent, containing the Ganges and Brahmaputra River deltas. In 1947 the province was divided into West Bengal, which has remained a state of India, and East Bengal, now Bangladesh. 孟加拉(印度次大陆东北部地区,包括恒河和布拉马普特拉河三角洲;1947年分为东西两部分,西孟加拉现仍为印度的一个邦,东孟加拉现为孟加拉国。)

② venom: *Noun* [mass noun] poisonous fluid secreted by animals such as snakes and scorpions and typically injected into prey or aggressors by biting or stinging(毒蛇、蝎子等分泌的)毒液

spoke each word too slowly, too carefully, and too softly for that. The expression was in the eyes and around the corners of the mouth.

"Why not?"

"The light would frighten him. It's dark under there now."

"Then how about whipping the sheet back quick and brushing it off before it had time to strike?"

"Why don't you get a doctor?" Harry said. The way he looked at me told me I should have thought of that myself in the first place.

"A doctor. Of course. That's it. I'll get Ganderbai."

I tiptoed out to the hail, looked up Ganderbai's number in the book, lifted the phone and told the operator to hurry.

"Dr. Ganderbai," I said. "This is Timber Woods."

"Hello, Mr. Woods. You not in bed yet?"

"Look, could you come round at once? And bring serum[①]—for a krait bite."

"Who's been bitten?" The question came so sharply it was like a small explosion in my ear.

"No one. No one yet. But Harry Pope's in bed and he's got one lying on his stomach asleep under the sheet lying on his stomach."

For about three seconds there was silence on the line. Then speaking slowly, not like an explosion now but slowly, precisely, Ganderbai said, "Tell him to keep quite still. He is not to move or to talk. Do you understand?"

"Of course."

"I'll come at once!" He rang off and I went back to the bedroom. Harry's eyes watched me as I walked across to his bed.

---

① serum: Noun the blood serum of an animal, used especially to provide immunity to a pathogen or toxin by inoculation or as a diagnostic agent 免疫血清

"Ganderbai's coming. He said for you to lie still."

"What in God's name does he think I'm doing!"

"Look, Harry, he said no talking. Absolutely no talking. Either of us."

"Why don't you shut up then?" When he said this one side of his mouth started twitching with rapid little downward movements that continued for a while after he finished speaking. I took out my handkerchief and very gently I wiped the sweat off his face and neck, and I could feel the slight twitching of the muscle—the one he used for smiling—as my fingers passed over it with the handkerchief.

I slipped out to the kitchen, got some ice from the ice-box, rolled it up in a napkin, and began to crush it small. That business of the mouth, I didn't like that. Or the way he talked, either. I carried the ice pack to the bedroom and laid it across Harry's forehead.

"Keep you cool."

He screwed up his eyes and drew breath sharply through his teeth. "Take it away," he whispered. "Make me cough." His smiling-muscle began to twitch again.

The beam of a headlamp shone through the window as Ganderbai's car swung around to the front of the bungalow. I went out to meet him, holding the ice pack with both hands.

"How is it?" Ganderbai asked, but he didn't stop to talk; he walked on past me across the balcony and through the screen doors into the hall. "Where is he? Which room?"

He put his bag down on a chair in the hall and followed me into Harry's room. He was wearing soft-soled bedroom slippers and he walked across the floor noiselessly, delicately, like a careful cat. Harry watched him out of the sides of his eyes. When Ganderbai reached the bed he looked down at Harry and smiled, confident and reassuring, nodding his head to tell Harry it was a simple matter and he was not to worry but just to leave it to Dr. Ganderbai. Then he turned and went back to the hall and I followed him.

"First thing is to try and get some of the serum into him," he said, and he opened his bag and started to make preparations. "Intravenously①. But I must do it neatly. Don't want to make him flinch②."

We went into the kitchen and he sterilized a needle. He had a hypodermic③ syringe④ in one hand and a small bottle in the other and he stuck the needle through the rubber top and began drawing a pale yellow liquid up into the syringe by pulling out the plunger⑤. Then he handed the syringe to me.

"Hold that till I ask for it."

He picked up the bag and together we returned to the room. Harry's eyes were bright now and wide open. Ganderbai bent over Harry and very cautiously, like a man handling sixteenth-century lace, he rolled up the pyjama sleeve to the elbow without moving the arm. I noticed he stood well away from the bed.

He whispered, "I'm going to give you an injection. Serum. Just a

---

① intravenous: *Adjective* existing or taking place within, or administered into, a vein or veins 静脉内的;静脉内发的;静脉的

② flinch: *Verb* [no obj.] make a quick, nervous movement of the face or body as an instinctive reaction to fear or pain(因害怕或疼痛而)退缩;畏缩(e.g. She flinched at the acidity in his voice. 他尖刻的话音令她畏缩。)

③ hypodermic: *Adjective* (of a needle or syringe) used to inject a drug or other substance beneath the skin(针或注射器)用于皮下注射的

④ syringe: *Noun* (Medicine) a tube with a nozzle and piston or bulb for sucking in and ejecting liquid in a thin stream, used for cleaning wounds or body cavities, or fitted with a hollow needle for injecting or withdrawing fluids(医学)注射器

⑤ plunger: *Noun* a part of a device or mechanism that works with a plunging or thrusting movement 柱塞;活塞

prick but try not to move. Don't tighten your stomach muscles. Let them go limp."

Harry looked at the syringe.

Ganderbai took a piece of red rubber tubing① from his bag and slid one end up and around Harry's biceps②; then he tied the tubing tight with a knot. He sponged a small area of the bare forearm with alcohol, handed the swab③ to me and took the syringe from my hand. He held it up to the light, squinting④ at the calibrations⑤, squirting out some of the yellow fluid. I stood beside him, watching. Harry was watching too and sweating all over his face so it shone like it was smeared⑥ thick with face cream melting on his skin and running down on to the pillow.

I could see the blue vein on the inside of Harry's forearm, swollen

---

① tubing: *Noun* [mass noun] a length or lengths of metal, plastic, glass, etc., in tubular form 一截(金属、塑料、玻璃等)管子(e.g. Use the plastic tubing to siphon the beer into the bottles. 用这根塑料管把啤酒虹吸进瓶子里。)

② biceps: *Noun* a large muscle in the upper arm which turns the hand to face palm uppermost and flexes the arm and forearm 肱二头肌(e.g. He clenched his fist and exhibited his bulging biceps. 他攥紧拳头，露出突起的臂部肌肉。)

③ swab: *Noun* an absorbent pad or piece of material used in surgery and medicine for cleaning wounds, applying medication, or taking specimens 拭子；药签

④ squint: *Verb* [no obj.] look at someone or something with one or both eyes partly closed in an attempt to see more clearly or as a reaction to strong light(为了能看清楚或由于强光而)眯着眼看(e.g. The bright sun made them squint. 明亮的阳光使他们眯起眼来。)

⑤ calibration: *Noun* [count noun] each of a set of graduations on an instrument 刻度

⑥ smear: *Verb* [with obj.] coat or mark (something) messily or carelessly with a greasy or sticky substance(用油或黏性物质随便胡乱)涂抹(某物)(e.g. His face was smeared with dirt. 他的脸上涂满了泥。)

now because of the tourniquet①, and then I saw the needle above the vein, Ganderbai holding the syringe almost flat against the arm, sliding the needle in sideways through the skin into the blue vein, sliding it slowly but so firmly it went in smooth as into cheese. Harry looked at the ceiling and closed his eyes and opened them again, but he didn't move.

When it was finished Ganderbai leaned forward putting his mouth close to Harry's ear. "Now you'll be all right even if you are bitten. But don't move. Please don't move. I'll be back in a moment."

He picked up his bag and went out to the hall and I followed.

"Is he safe now?" I asked.

"No."

"How safe is he?"

The little Indian doctor stood there in the hall rubbing his lower lip.

"It must give him some protection, mustn't it?" I asked.

He turned away and walked to the screen doors that led on to the verandah②. I thought he was going through them, but he stopped this side of the doors and stood looking out into the night.

"Isn't the serum very good?" I asked.

"Unfortunately not," he answered without turning round. "It might save him. It might not. I am trying to think of something else to do."

"Shall we draw the sheet back and brush it off before it has any time to strike?"

"Never! We are not entitled to take a risk." He spoke sharply and his voice was pitched a little higher than usual.

"We can't very well leave him lying there," I said. "He's getting

---

① tourniquet: *Noun* a device for stopping the flow of blood through an artery, typically by compressing a limb with a cord or tight bandage 止血带;压脉器

② verandah or veranda: *Noun* a roofed platform along the outside of a house, level with the ground floor 游廊;走廊;阳台

nervous."

"Please! Please!" he said, turning round, holding both hands up in the air. "Not so fast, please. This is not a matter to rush into bald-headed." He wiped his forehead with his handkerchief and stood there, frowning, nibbling his lip.

"You see," he said at last. "There is a way to do this. You know what we must do—we must administer an anaesthetic to the creature where it lies."

It was a splendid idea.

"It is not safe," he continued, "because a snake is cold blooded and anaesthetic does not work so well or so quick with such animals, but it is better than any other thing to do. We could use ether①... chloroform②..." He was speaking slowly and trying to think the thing out while he talked.

"Which shall we use?"

"Chloroform," he said suddenly. "Ordinary chloroform. That is best. Now quick!" He took my arm and pulled me towards the balcony. "Drive to my house! By the time you get there I will have waked up my boy on the telephone and he will show you my poisons cupboard. Here is the key of the cupboard. Take a bottle of chloroform. It has an orange label and the name is printed on it. I stay here in case anything happens. Be quick now, hurry! No, no, you don't need your shoes!"

I drove fast and in about fifteen minutes I was back with the bottle of chloroform. Ganderbai came out of Harry's room and met me in the hall.

---

① ether: *Noun* [mass noun] (Chemistry) a pleasant-smelling colourless volatile liquid that is highly flammable. It is used as an anaesthetic and as a solvent or intermediate in industrial processes(化学)乙醚

② chloroform: *Noun* [mass noun] a colourless, volatile, sweet-smelling liquid used as a solvent and formerly as a general anaesthetic 氯仿

"You got it?" he said. "Good, good. I've just been telling him what we are going to do. But now we must hurry. It is not easy for him in there like that all this time. I am afraid he might move."

He went back to the bedroom and I followed, carrying the bottle carefully with both hands. Harry was lying on the bed in precisely the same position as before with the sweat pouring down his cheeks. His face was white and wet. He turned his eyes towards me and I smiled at him and nodded confidently. He continued to look at me. I raised my thumb, giving him the okay signal. He closed his eyes. Ganderbai was squatting down by the bed, and on the floor beside him was the hollow rubber tube that he had previously used as a tourniquet, and he'd got a small paper funnel① fitted into one end of the tube.

He began to pull a little piece of sheet out from under the mattress. He was working directly in line with Harry's stomach, about eighteen inches from it, and I watched his fingers as they tugged gently at the edge of the sheet. He worked so slowly it was almost impossible to discern any movement either in his fingers or in the sheet that was being pulled.

Finally he succeeded in making an opening under the sheet and he took the rubber tube and inserted one end of it in the opening so that it would slide under the sheet along the mattress towards Harry's body. I do not know how long it took him to slide that tube in a few inches. It may have been twenty minutes, it may have been forty. I never once saw the tube move. I knew it was going in because the visible part of it grew shorter, but I doubted that the krait could have felt even the slightest vibration. Ganderbai himself was sweating now, large pearls of sweat standing out all over his forehead and along his upper lip. But his hands

---

① funnel: *Noun* a tube or pipe that is wide at the top and narrow at the bottom, used for guiding liquid or powder into a small opening 漏斗

were steady and I noticed that his eyes were watching, not the tube in his hands, but the area of crumpled sheet above Harry's stomach.

Without looking up, he held out a hand to me for the chloroform. I twisted out the ground-glass① stopper and put the whole bottle right into his hand, not letting go until I was sure he had a good hold on it. Then he jerked his head for me to come closer and he whispered, "Tell him I'm going to soak the mattress and that it will be very cold under his body. He must be ready for that and he must not move. Tell him now."

I bent over Harry and passed on the message.

"Why doesn't he get on with it?" Harry said.

"He's going to now, Harry. But it'll feel very cold, so be ready for it."

"Oh, God Almighty, get on, get on!" For the first time he raised his voice, and Ganderbai glanced up sharply, watched him for a few seconds, then went back to his business.

Ganderbai poured a few drops of chloroform into the paper funnel and waited while it ran down the tube. Then he poured some more. Then he waited again, and the heavy sickening② smell of chloroform spread out all over the room bringing with it faint unpleasant memories of white-coated nurses and white surgeons standing in a white room around a long white table. Ganderbai was pouring steadily now and I could see the heavy vapour of the chloroform swirling slowly like smoke above the paper funnel. He paused, held the bottle up to the light, poured one more funnelful and handed the bottle back to me. Slowly he drew out the rubber

---

① ground-glass or ground glass: *Noun* [mass noun] glass with a smooth ground surface that renders it non-transparent while retaining its translucency 毛玻璃;磨砂玻璃

② sickening: *Adjective* causing or liable to cause a feeling of nausea or disgust 引起呕吐的;令人厌恶的(e.g. a sickening stench of blood 令人恶心的血腥味)

tube from under the sheet; then he stood up.

The strain of inserting the tube and pouring the chloroform must have been great, and I recollect that when Ganderbai turned and whispered to me, his voice was small and tired. "We'll give it fifteen minutes. Just to be safe."

I leaned over to tell Harry, "We're going to give it fifteen minutes, just to be safe. But it's probably done for already."

"Then why for God's sake don't you look and see!" Again he spoke loudly and Ganderbai sprang round, his small brown face suddenly very angry. He had almost pure black eyes and he stared at Harry and Harry's smiling-muscle started to twitch. I took my handkerchief and wiped his wet face, trying to stroke his forehead a little for comfort as I did so. Then we stood and waited beside the bed, Ganderbai watching Harry's face all the time in a curious intense manner. The little Indian was concentrating all his will power on keeping Harry quiet. He never once took his eyes from the patient and although he made no sound, he seemed somehow to be shouting at him all the time, saying: Now listen, you've got to listen, you're not going to go spoiling this now, d'you hear me; and Harry lay there twitching his mouth, sweating, closing his eyes, opening them, looking at me, at the sheet, at the ceiling, at me again, but never at Ganderbai. Yet somehow Ganderbai was holding him. The smell of chloroform was oppressive and it made me feel sick, but I couldn't leave the room now. I had the feeling someone was blowing up a huge balloon and I could see it was going to burst, but I couldn't look away.

At length Ganderbai turned and nodded and I knew he was ready to proceed. "You go over to one side of the bed," he said. "We will each take one side of the sheet and draw it back together, but very slowly, please, and very quietly."

"Keep still now, Harry," I said and I went around to the other side of the bed and took hold of the sheet. Ganderbai stood opposite me, and together we began to draw back the sheet, lifting it up clear of Harry's body, taking it back very slowly, both of us standing well away but at the same time bending forward, trying to peer underneath it. The smell of chloroform was awful. I remember trying to hold my breath and when I couldn't do that any longer I tried to breathe shallow so the stuff wouldn't get into my lungs.

The whole of Harry's chest was visible now, or rather the striped pyjama top which covered it, and then I saw the white cord of his pyjama trousers, neatly tied in a bow. A little farther and I saw a button, a mother-of-pearl① button, and that was something I had never had on my pyjamas, a fly button, let alone a mother-of-pearl one. This Harry, I thought, he is very refined. It is odd how one sometimes has frivolous② thoughts at exciting moments, and I distinctly remember thinking about Harry being very refined when I saw that button.

Apart from the button there was nothing on his stomach.

We pulled the sheet back faster then, and when we had uncovered his legs and feet we let the sheet drop over the end of the bed on to the floor.

"Don't move," Ganderbai said, "don't move, Mr. Pope"; and he began to peer around along the side of Harry's body and under his legs.

"We must be careful," he said. "It may be anywhere. It could be up the leg of his pyjamas."

When Ganderbai said this, Harry quickly raised his head from the

---

① mother-of-pearl: *Noun* [mass noun] a smooth shining iridescent substance forming the inner layer of the shell of some molluscs, especially oysters and abalones, used in ornamentation(尤指牡蛎、鲍鱼中的)珠母层;(螺钿)亮贝壳

② frivolous: *Adjective* not having any serious purpose or value 无严肃目的的;无意义的;无价值的(e. g. rules to stop frivolous law suits 制止为琐事打官司的规章)

pillow and looked down at his legs. It was the first time he had moved. Then suddenly he jumped up, stood on his bed and shook his legs one after the other violently in the air. At that moment we both thought he had been bitten and Ganderbai was already reaching down into his bag for a scalpel and a tourniquet when Harry ceased his caperings① and stood still and looked down at the mattress he was standing on and shouted, "It's not there!"

Ganderbai straightened up and for a moment he too looked at the mattress; then he looked up at Harry. Harry was all right. He hadn't been bitten and now he wasn't going to get bitten and he wasn't going to be killed and everything was fine. But that didn't seem to make anyone feel any better.

"Mr. Pope, you are of course quite sure you saw it in the first place?" There was a note of sarcasm② in Ganderbai's voice that he would never have employed in ordinary circumstances. "You don't think you might possibly have been dreaming, do you, Mr. Pope?" The way Ganderbai was looking at Harry, I realized that the sarcasm was not seriously intended. He was only easing up a bit after the strain.

Harry stood on his bed in his striped pyjamas, glaring③ at Ganderbai, and the colour began to spread out all over his cheeks.

"Are you telling me I'm a liar?" he shouted.

---

① caper: *Verb* [no obj., with adverbial of direction] skip or dance about in a lively or playful way 蹦蹦跳跳;雀跃(e.g. Children were capering about the room. 孩子们在房间里蹦来跳去。)

② sarcasm: *Noun* [mass noun] the use of irony to mock or convey contempt 讽刺;挖苦;嘲笑(e.g. She didn't like the note of sarcasm in his voice. 她不喜欢他话音中挖苦的腔调。)

③ glare: *Verb* [no obj.] stare in an angry or fierce way 怒目而视;瞪眼看(e.g. She glared at him, her cheeks flushing. 她瞪着他,两腮涨得通红。)

Ganderbai remained absolutely still, watching Harry. Harry took a pace forward on the bed and there was a shining look in his eyes.

"Why, you dirty little Hindu① sewer rat!"

"Shut up, Harry!" I said.

"You dirty black——"

"Harry!" I called. "Shut up, Harry!" It was terrible the things he was saying.

Ganderbai went out of the room as though neither of us was there and I followed him and put my arm around his shoulder as he walked across the hall and out on to the balcony.

"Don't you listen to Harry," I said. "This thing's made him so he doesn't know what he's saying."

We went down the steps from the balcony to the drive and across the drive in the darkness to where his old Morris car was parked. He opened the door and got in.

"You did a wonderful job," I said. "Thank you very much for coming."

"All he needs is a good holiday," he said quietly, without looking at me, then he started the engine and drove off.

三、翻译探索

本篇小说的翻译中,主要障碍是医学方面的一些词汇,同时还要准确、形象地传达小说中那位印度医生行医时的一些专业性的行为。

蛇毒解药

我开车到家的时候,一定是午夜时分了。接近平房大门时,我关

---

① Hindu: *Adjective* of or relating to Hindus or Hinduism(与)印度教(或教徒)(有关)的

掉了车前灯,因此,灯柱就不会晃来晃去、射进侧面卧室的窗户,将哈里·波普晃醒。但是,我没有必要操这个心,因为驶上私家车道的时候,我注意到他房间里还亮着灯,所以不管怎么说,他还没有入睡——除非看书的时候,或许会不知不觉地睡着。

我停好车,迈上五级台阶,到了露台。黑暗中,我每迈上一级台阶,就数一个数,不敢马虎。这样,就不用到了顶部还多迈一级,而实际上已经没有台阶了。我穿过露台,推开纱门,进入房子,打开了门厅的灯。我走过去,走到哈里房间的门前,悄悄推开门,向里面观瞧。

他躺在床上,我看得出,他没有睡着,但却没有动弹,甚至没有转头看我一眼。我听见他说:"廷伯,廷伯,到这儿来。"

他说话速度很慢,声音很低,一个字、一个字很小心地往外蹦。我将门完全推开,开始快速穿过了屋子。

"停,等一下,廷伯。"我几乎听不见他说的是什么,他似乎使出了浑身的力气才将那几个词说出来。

"哈里,怎么了?"

"嘘!"他低声耳语。"嘘,看在上帝的分上,别出声。靠近之前,脱下鞋。拜托,哈里,照我说的做。"

他说话的样子让我想起了乔治·巴林。当时,他腹部中弹,双手捂着腹部,倚着板条箱站立着,板条箱里装的是备用的飞机引擎。他嘴里说的是一些关于那个德国飞行员的事情,声音嘶哑,近乎耳语,使出了浑身的力气,那样子跟哈里现在的样子完全相同。

"廷伯,快点,但是,先把鞋脱掉。"

我不明白脱鞋的原因,但是,他的声音听起来好像身体不舒服。我寻思着,要是那样的话,我最好迁就他一下。于是,我弯腰脱下鞋,将鞋放到地板中央。然后,我走过去,走到他的床边。

"不要碰床!看在上帝的分上,不要碰床!"他说起话来,仍然好像腹部中弹似的。我看见他仰卧在那儿,身上就盖了一条被单,被单盖住了他身体的四分之三。他穿了一套睡衣裤,上面有蓝色、棕色和白色的条纹。晚上很热,哈里汗出得很厉害,我也出了一点汗,但不像他出得那么厉害。他的脸都湿了,头部周围的枕头被汗水浸得湿漉漉的。在我看来,那情景就像是疟疾严重发作。

"哈里,怎么回事儿?"

"有一条金环蛇,"他说。

"金环蛇!噢,我的天呐!咬到你什么部位了?多久以前咬的?"

"闭嘴,"他小声说。

"听着,哈里,"我说着,倚身向前,触摸他的肩膀。"我们必须得快些。现在,快啊,快些告诉我它咬到你什么地方了。"他一动不动躺在那儿,绷紧了神经,就好像因为剧烈的疼痛而咬紧牙关,全身绷得紧紧的。

"还没有咬到我,"他低声说。"还没咬。它在我的肚子上,躺在那儿睡着了。"

我快速后退了一步,情不自禁要后退。我盯向他的肚子,或者更确切地说,盯向盖在肚子上的那片被单,被单上有好几处起了皱褶。辨别出被单下面是否有东西,是不可能的事情。

"现在,你说,你的肚子上躺着一条金环蛇,不是当真的吧?"

"当真,我发誓。"

"它怎么爬到那里的?"我真不该这样问,因为很明显看得出,他没有开玩笑的意思。我本应该告诉他要保持安静状态的。

"我当时在看书,"哈里回答,语速很慢,一个字、一个字十分谨慎地说出来,生怕牵动腹部的肌肉。"仰卧着看书,感觉胸部——就在书的后面——有东西,有点发痒。然后,从眼角处,看见这条小金环蛇在睡衣上滑动,很小,约有二十五厘米长。我知道,一定不能动弹,死也不能动弹。我躺在那儿看着它,心想,它会爬到被单上面来的。"哈里暂停下来,好一会儿没有说话。他的双眼沿着自己的身体看过去,看向腹部盖着被单的地方。我看得出,他时刻注意着,以确保自己的低声耳语别惊扰了躺在那儿的那个东西。

"被单里有一个褶,"他说。现在,他说话的速度更慢了,声音很是轻微,我不得不贴近才能听见。"看看它,还在那儿,就在那底下。我可以感觉到,它穿过了睡衣,移到了我的肚子上。然后,它停下。现在,它正暖呼呼地躺在那儿,或许睡着了。我一直在等你回来。"他抬起眼睛，看了看我。

"多久以前的事儿？"

"数小时了，"他低声说道。"数小时，不知多少小时，很多小时了。这样一动不动地待着，我保持不了多久。我一直想咳嗽来着。"

哈里所讲述的经历的真实性，没有过多可以怀疑的。事实上，金环蛇做出的并不是令人惊奇的事情。这些毒蛇在人们的房前屋后爬来爬去，寻找温暖的安身之所。令人惊奇的事情是，哈里竟然没有被咬到。被它咬到是相当致命的事情，除非有的时候，你能立刻将它捉住。在孟加拉，特别在乡村地区，每年有相当多的一部分人死于金环蛇之口。

"好吧，哈里，"我说。现在，我的声音也放低了。"不要动弹，万不得已不要说话。你知道，除非受到惊吓，否则它不会主动咬人。我们要立刻将它搞定。"

我脚上穿着袜子悄悄地走出了房间，从厨房取来一把尖尖的小刀，将其放进我的裤兜里，以备应急之用。之所以这样做，就是因为我们还在思考着对策，怕思考过程中出现什么差错。要是哈里咳嗽、动弹，或者做出什么事情惊吓了金环蛇而被咬了的话，我就会时刻准备好，切开被咬部位，尽力将里面的毒液吸出来。我返回卧室，发现哈里仍然安静地躺在那儿，满脸是汗，我穿过房间，走到他的床前而移动着，他的双眼也一直跟着我在移动。我看得出，他心里纳闷：我到底要做些什么。我站在他的旁边，尽量要想出最佳的对策。

"哈里，"我说。现在我说话的时候，嘴几乎贴到他的耳朵上，以确保说话的声音不要高过最轻微的耳语声。"我想，最佳的行动方案就是，我把这条被单很轻微、很轻微往后拉，然后，我就能先看看是怎么回事。我想，我能做到，不会惊扰到它。"

"别他妈的犯傻了。"他的声音里听不出任何的表情，因为每一个字他说的都特别缓慢、特别谨慎、特别轻微。只有从眼里和嘴角处能看到他的表情。

"为什么不能那样呢？"

"灯光会吓着它。现在，那底下是黑的。"

第三章　意味深长　第三节　《蛇毒解药》Poison

"那么,一下子猛地将被单扯开,趁它来不及咬的当儿,将它划拉掉,怎么样?"

"你为什么就不能找个医生过来?"哈里问道。他看我的那种表情就是向我表明:我本应该首先想到那一点的。

"找医生。当然。正是。我这就去找甘德贝"

我踮起脚尖儿走到门厅,在号码簿里查到了甘德贝的电话号码,然后拾起话机,催促接线员快点接通。

"甘德贝医生,"我说。"我是廷伯·伍兹。"

"你好,伍兹先生。你还没有入睡吗?"

"听着,你能马上来一下吗? 带上免疫血清——治金环蛇的咬伤。"

"谁被蛇咬了?"这个问题提得太尖锐,就像一小枚炸弹在我耳畔炸响。

"没有谁被咬,还没有。但是,哈里·波普躺在床上,腹部躺着一条蛇——就在盖着肚子的被单下面睡着了。"

有大约三秒钟的时间,电话里静悄悄的。接下来,传来缓慢的说话声,跟刚才爆炸般的声响不一样了,只听得甘德贝缓慢地、准确无误地说道:"告诉他一动也别动,不能动弹,也不能说话。你明白了吗?"

"当然明白。"

"我这就来!"他随即挂断了电话,我则走回卧室。哈里的双眼始终看着我,随着我穿过房间走到床前。

"甘德贝马上就来。他说,你要安静地躺着。"

"天呐,他认为我还能四处乱动啊!"

"听着,哈里,他说,不能说话,绝对不能说话,你我都不能说话。"

"那你怎么不闭上嘴?"说这话的时候,他嘴角的一侧开始急速向下快速抽动起来。说完了话,还继续抽动了一会儿。我把我自己的手绢掏出来,很是轻微地擦拭他脸上和脖子上的汗水。擦拭的时候,我用手指压着手绢从他皮肤表面滑过,感觉到他以前用来微笑的那部分肌肉在轻微地抽搐。

我奔入厨房,从冰箱里取出一些冰块,放入餐巾里卷好,然后压成小块。他嘴角抽搐的样子,我不喜欢。他说话的方式,我也不喜欢。我将碎冰包拿进卧室,横放在哈里的前额上。

"让你保持凉爽用的。"

他鼓起眼睛,通过牙齿急剧地呼着气。"拿走,"他低声说。"会让我咳嗽的。"他的那部分微笑用的肌肉开始抽搐起来。

甘德贝的车拐到平房正面的时候,车头灯的光柱透过窗户射进房内。我双手握着冰包出去迎接他。

"情况怎样?"甘德贝问道,但他并没有停下脚步,而是经过我之后一直往前走,越过露台,穿过纱门,进入了门厅。"他在哪儿?哪个房间?"

他将包放到门厅里的一把椅子上,跟着我进入哈里的房间。他脚下穿的是家用的软底拖鞋,小心谨慎地走过地板时悄无声息,就像一只谨小慎微的猫一般。哈里斜着眼睛看着他。甘德贝走到床前,低头看着哈里,信心十足又颇令人宽心地微笑着,点着头对哈里说,这种情况处理起来很简单,你不要担心,一切都交给甘德贝医生我好啦。然后,他转过身,走回门厅。我紧随其后。

"首先要做的,就是尽量将一些免疫血清给他注射进去,"他说着,打开带来的包,开始准备起来。"静脉注射,但是,我必须干净利落地注射。不能让他因疼痛而畏缩、动弹。"

我们走进厨房后,他将一根针做了消毒处理。然后,一只手拿着皮下注射器,另一只手拿着小瓶子,将针头穿过瓶子的橡胶盖,向上拉动活塞,往注射器里吸进一种暗黄色的液体。吸完后,他将注射器递给了我。

"拿好了,我一要,就给我。"

他拿起包后,我们俩一起返回卧室。现在,哈里的双眼明亮起来,睁得很大。甘德贝俯身哈里上方,十分小心地将哈里的睡衣袖子卷到了胳膊肘处,就像考古时处理十六世纪的衣服蕾丝花边似的,但是,并没有移动哈里的胳膊。我注意到,他是站在离床很远的地方操作的。

第三章　意味深长　第三节　《蛇毒解药》Poison

他低声耳语:"我要给你打一针,打免疫血清。就有一点儿刺痛感,但是,尽量不要动。不要绷紧腹部肌肉,要让那部分肌肉松弛下来。"

哈里看了看注射器。

甘德贝从包里拿出一块红色的橡胶管,将管子的一头向上一滑,绕到了哈里的二头肌上,然后,将管子紧紧系上一个扣。他用棉球蘸上酒精,在哈里裸露前臂的一小块区域上擦拭着,随即将擦拭完的药签递给我,并从我手中接过了注射器。他将注射器冲着灯光举起,眯起眼睛看着上面的刻度,将里面的药水喷射出一些。我站在他旁边,观看着。哈里也在观看着,满脸淌着汗水,脸上闪闪发亮,就好像涂抹上一层厚厚的面霜、面霜在脸部皮肤上融化、流淌到了枕头上。

我能够看得见哈里前臂皮肤下蓝蓝的静脉管,因为绑上了止血橡胶管,现在已经鼓胀起来。接着,我看见针头放到了静脉管上面。甘德贝握着注射器,几乎与哈里的胳膊齐平,从一侧滑动针头,刺破皮肤,穿入蓝蓝的静脉管。针头慢慢地滑入,但滑入得十分稳定,就像滑入奶酪一样顺畅无阻。哈里看了看天花板,闭上眼睛,又睁开了眼睛,但没有动。

注射完,甘德贝俯身向前,嘴贴近哈里的耳朵。"现在,你没事儿了,即使蛇咬到了你。但是,不要动。请不要移动。我去去就来。"

他拿起包,走出屋子,来到了门厅。我紧随其后。

"他现在安全了吗?"我问。

"不安全。"

"安全性有多大呢?"

这位小个子印度医生站在门厅那儿,手摩擦下嘴唇。

"这一针一定会起到保护作用,对不对?"我问。

他转身去,走向纱门,那道纱门直通晒台。我还以为他会穿过纱门走出去,但是,却在纱门里边停下,站在那儿,透过纱门看着外面的夜色。

"难道免疫血清不是很好吗?"我问。

"不幸的是,不是很好,"他头也不回地回答。"或许会挽救他,或许挽救不了他。我在想有没有别的法子可用。"

"趁它还没有咬人的时候,我们将被单往后拽,然后把它划拉掉,可以吗?"

"千万别!我们没有权利冒险。"他说起话来很尖锐,声调也比平常抬高了一点点。

"我们不能让他在那儿躺很长时间的,"我说。"他紧张着呢。"

"拜托!拜托!"他说道,人也转过身来,双手举到了空中。"拜托,不要如此操之过急。这不是着急的事儿,急得头发掉光了也没用。"他用手绢擦干额头,站在那儿,皱着眉头,轻轻咬着嘴唇。

"你知道,"他最终说道。"有一种方法可用。你知道,我们必须得这么做——必须得向这东西躺着的地方施用麻醉剂。"

这个想法很妙啊。

"不太安全,"他继续说,"蛇是冷血动物,麻醉药不会很好地起作用,或者说,对这样的动物不会快速起作用,但是,这方法比所有的方法都要好。我们可以使用乙醚……氯仿……"他说得很慢,力图边说边能想出所要说的内容。

"我们要用哪一种?"

"氯仿,"他突然说道。"很常见的氯仿,那是最好的。现在,赶快!"他抓起我的胳膊,将我拉向露台。"开车去我家!你到达之前,我就会打电话叫醒我的儿子,他会告诉你我放置有毒药物的橱柜在什么地方。给你,橱柜的钥匙。拿出一瓶氯仿,瓶子上有一枚橘黄色的标签,药名就印在标签上。我待在这儿,以防万一。现在要快,赶紧!不,不,你不用穿鞋了!"

我开得很快,不到十五分钟,就带着那瓶氯仿回来了。甘德贝从哈里的房间走出来,到门厅接我。"拿到了吗?"他问。"好,不错。刚才已经告诉你,我们要做的是什么,可是现在,我们必须得抓紧。他自始至终那样待着,不很容易的。我担心他或许会动弹。"

他回到了卧室,我双手小心谨慎地拿着药瓶,跟随其后。哈里躺在床上,姿势跟先前的一模一样,汗水顺着脸颊往下流淌。他的脸很白,湿乎乎的。他转动眼睛看着我,我冲他微笑着,并且信心十足地点了点头。他继续看着我,我则竖起大拇指,冲他做出"OK"的手势。接着,他闭上了眼睛。甘德贝在床边蹲下,身边的地板上放着那根他方才止血用的中空橡胶管,管子的一端插入一只他用纸做的小漏斗。

他开始从床垫底下将被单往外抽出一点点。抽的时候,他跟哈里的腹部保持平行的状态,离腹部约四十五厘米。我看着他的手指轻轻拉着被单的边缘,拉得十分缓慢,慢到几乎不可能觉察到他手指的移动,也觉察不到被单被拉开。

最终,他成功地从被单下拉开一条缝隙,于是,他拿起橡胶管,将其一端插入缝隙中,以便使橡胶管在被单底下沿着床垫滑向哈里的身体。他将管子往里滑动几厘米,用去多少时间,我不知道——或许二十分钟,或许四十分钟。我从未看到管子移动过,但我知道,管子在向里面滑动,因为管子露在外面的可见部分越来越短。至于金环蛇能否觉察到哪怕最轻微的震动,我持怀疑态度。现在,就连甘德贝也出汗了——整个前额,还有上唇部位,生出珍珠般大小的汗珠。可是,他的双手平稳如初,双眼一直在看,不是看自己的双手,而是看哈里腹部上方起皱的区域。

他头也不抬,把一只手伸向我,向我要氯仿。我拧开磨砂玻璃瓶塞,将整个瓶子放入他的手中,但是,直到确定他已经稳稳地接住了瓶子,我才放手。接着,他猛地冲我一摆头,让我靠近些,低声说:"告诉他,我要将床垫浸上药剂。这样,他的身底下就会很冷。他一定得做好准备,千万别动。现在就告诉他。"

我俯身哈里上方,将消息传给了他。

"他怎么不赶紧去做?"哈里说。

"他这就要开始进行,哈里。但是,会感觉很冷的,因此,要做好准备。"

"噢,老天爷啊,加紧,加紧!"这是他第一次提高了嗓音,弄得甘德贝一下子抬起头,看了他好几秒钟的时间,然后才接着往下进行。

甘德贝向纸质漏斗里倒入几滴氯仿。等液体沿管子流完,又倒入一些,然后又等了一会儿。氯仿浓烈的气味在整个房间弥漫开来,令人呕吐,使人模糊记起那个令人不快的场景:白色房间里一张白色的长桌子周围站着白衣外科医生,还有白衣护士。现在,甘德贝倒得很平稳了,我可以看见纸漏斗上方,浓烈的氯仿气雾,如同烟雾一般,慢慢地打着旋儿。他暂停一下,冲着灯光举起了瓶子,又倒满一漏斗,然后将瓶子递回给我。他从被单底下慢慢地将橡胶管抽出,然后,站起身来。

插进胶管时的紧张程度,还有倒入氯仿时的紧张程度,一定是相当大的,因为我记得甘德贝转过身、低声跟我说话的时候,他的声音很小,显得很疲劳。"我们等上十五分钟的时间,就是为了安全起见。"

我俯身哈里上方说:"我们要等上十五分钟的时间,就是为了安全起见。可是,或许已经搞定了。"

"那么,看在老天的分上,你们为什么不看看、瞧瞧?"他又一次大声说话,弄得甘德贝跳转身来,他那张棕色的小脸突然间变得怒容满面。甘德贝的双眼几乎是纯黑色的,直勾勾盯着哈里,盯得哈里脸上微笑用的那部分肌肉开始抽搐起来。我掏出自己的手绢,擦了擦他那湿漉漉的脸,尽量轻轻抚摸他的额头,以示安慰。

接着,我们两个站在床边,等待着。甘德贝一副怪异而专注的样子,始终观察着哈里的脸。这位个子矮小的印度人,一门心思想要哈里保持安静状态,一刻也没有将眼睛从病人身上移开。尽管他没有发出声音来,但不知怎么的,似乎一刻也没有停止对他喊叫:现在听着,你必须得听好,你现在可不要将一切毁于一旦,听到我的话了吧。哈里躺在那儿,嘴角抽搐着,出汗不止,闭上眼睛,睁开眼睛,看看我,看看被单,看看天花板,又看看我,但是,从来没看见甘德贝。然而,不知怎么的,甘德贝始终控制着他。氯仿的气味令人压抑难耐,也令我感到恶心,但是现在,我不能离开房间。我感觉,有人正将一只大大的气球吹得鼓鼓的。我也看得出,这只气球就要爆裂,但是,我就是不能把脸转过去看。

最终,他转过身,点了点头。于是,我知道,他要准备往下进行了。"你走到床的一边,"他吩咐道。"我们每人抓住被单的一边,一齐往后拉,但是要慢慢地拉。拜托,要静悄悄地拉。"

"现在,挺住别动,哈里,"我说。然后,我绕到床的另一边,握住了被单。甘德贝站在我对面。我们两个要开始一齐往后拉被单,先将被单抬起,不使其碰到哈里的身体,然后很缓慢地往后拉。拉的时候,我们都站在一定远的距离上,但与此同时,都弯腰向前,眼睛都往被单下面瞥。氯仿的气味很难闻,我记得当时我尽量屏住呼吸。实在忍受不了,我就浅浅地呼吸,以免将这种东西吸入肺部。

现在,可以看到哈里整个胸部了,或者准确地说,可以看见盖在胸部的、印有条纹图案的睡衣了。接下来,我看到了他睡裤上的白色带子,整整齐齐打成一个蝴蝶结。蝴蝶结稍远一点的地方,我看到了一枚纽扣,而且是一枚珠母扣。我的睡衣裤上连一个普通的扣子都没有,更别说是珠母扣了。这个哈里,我想呢,很有品味。一个人在兴奋之际,有时候会有一些琐碎的想法,这一点很奇怪。我清清楚楚记得,看到那枚纽扣,我当时想的是,哈里是一个很有品味的人。

除了那枚纽扣,哈里的腹部就什么都没有了。

然后,我们加快了速度,往后拉被单。腿和脚都露出来后,我们就将被单翻过床尾,扔到地板上。

"别动,"甘德贝说道。"别动,波普先生。"然后,他就在哈里身体的边缘、双腿的底部四处察看。

"我们一定得小心,"他说。"蛇不一定会钻到什么地方去,有可能钻进睡裤裆儿呢。"

听到甘德贝的这句话,哈里一下子从枕头上抬起了头,往下看了看自己的双腿。这还是他第一次动弹呢。然后,突然之间,他跳了起来,站在床上,猛烈地往空中晃腿,晃完一只,再晃另一只。就在那时,我们俩都认为他被蛇咬上了。于是,甘德贝做好了准备,从包里掏出手术刀和止血带。恰恰此时,哈里停止了晃荡,安静地站好,低头看了看自己站立的床垫,喊道:"不在那儿啊!"

甘德贝直起腰身,就在那转瞬之间,也看了看床垫,然后抬头看了看哈里。哈里安然无恙,没有被咬,而且现在,也不会被咬了,也没有生命危险了,一切都很好。可问题是,这一切似乎并没有令谁感觉更好一些。

"波普先生,你当然是十分肯定开始的时候看到过蛇吗?"甘德贝的声音里带有一种讥讽的腔调,而这种腔调在一般场合里他从没有表露过。"波普先生,难道你不认为,你或许有可能是在做梦吗?"从甘德贝看哈里的样子,我意识到,他不是存心要讽刺哈里,只不过是在紧张过后,一块石头落了地、轻松起来罢了。

哈里穿着一身带有条纹的睡衣裤站在床上,整个脸颊也开始泛出色彩,对着甘德贝怒目而视。

"你是说,我在撒谎吗?"他喊道。

甘德贝一动不动站着,眼睛看着哈里。哈里在床上向前迈出一步,双眼发出了亮光。

"嘿,你这只下水道脏毛老鼠,你这个小印度佬!"

"闭嘴,哈里!"我说。

"你这肮脏的、黑乎乎的——"

"哈里!"我叫道。"闭嘴,哈里!"他的话语糟糕透顶。

甘德贝走出房间,就好像我跟哈里谁都不存在似的。我紧跟其后,一只手搭拢在他的肩膀上,穿过门厅,走到了露台上。

"你不要听哈里信口胡言,"我安慰他。"蛇这件事把他搞得不知道自己说些什么啦。"

我们两个从露台上走下台阶,走上私家车道。黑暗中,我们穿过车道,走到了他停放老莫里斯车的地方。他打开车门,上了车。

"你工作做得很出色,"我说。"你能来,十分感谢。"

"他所需要的,就是好好休个假,"他安静地说,眼睛并没有看着我。然后,他发动引擎,驾车而去。

参考文献

[1] DAHL R. The Wonderful Story of Henry Sugar and Six More [M]. London：Penguin Books Ltd. , 2002.

[2] DAHL R. The best of Roald Dahl [M]. London：Penguin Books Ltd. , 2006.

[3] DAHL R. The Collected Short Stories of Roald Dahl [M]. London：Penguin Books Ltd. , 1992.

[4] 陈钰. 畸形精神世界的工笔画家——谈罗尔德·达尔的小说创作特色[J]. 外国文学研究, 1985(4)：66 - 69.

[5] 金山软件. 金山词霸 2009 牛津版[CP]. 北京：北京金山软件有限公司, 2008.

[6] 刘卫东. 意识流文学综述[J]. 安徽文学, 2009(5)：95.

[7] 屈光. 中国古典诗词中的意识流[J]. 中国社会科学, 2000(5)：155 - 156.

[8] 吴锡民. "意识流"流入中国现代文坛论[J]. 外国文学研究, 2002(4)：110 - 111.

[9] 新华社译名室. 世界人名翻译大辞典[M]. 北京：中国对外翻译出版公司, 2007.

［10］ 曾艳兵. 意识流:从西方"流"到中国[J]. 文艺理论与批评, 2004(01):120.

［11］ 周定国. 世界地名翻译大辞典[M]. 北京:中国出版集团,中国对外翻译出版公司, 2008.

后　记

  我们对罗尔德·达尔"非儿童类"短篇故事（小说）进行研究和翻译已经持续了四个年头了。其间，因教学和其他科研的缘由，有所间断，但多数时间是在研读和翻译达尔的这部分短篇小说中度过的。所研读、翻译的达尔这部分短篇作品共计六十篇。

  在研究和翻译罗尔德·达尔这部分作品过程中，历尽了艰辛，特别是在翻译过程中，不时会遇到这样或那样的"坎坷"。达尔在写作过程中，时常会"卖弄"自己所掌握的某些专业方面的知识，如葡萄酒、收藏、音乐、医学等，这就逼着译者硬着头皮去熟悉相应的知识。另外，达尔还偶尔会"显摆"一下自己英语之外的词汇，如法语、拉丁语等，这对于译者来说，未免有些"捉襟见肘"了——有的词，任凭怎么查也不得结果。达尔原文中的某一段有时会罗列出若干的专有名词，本着一丝不苟的研究态度，翻译过程中译者对它们均一一查证——哪怕对其中某些表达已经相当熟悉了。对于这样的"坎坷"，下笔前会来回踱步、反复思量、仔细斟酌，正如鲁迅先生在译完《死魂灵》谈到翻译时所言："我向来总以为翻译比创作容易，因为至少是无须构想。但到真的一译，就会遇着难关，譬如一个名词或动词，写不出，创作时候可以回避，翻译上却不成，也还得想，一直弄到头昏眼花，好像在脑子里面摸一个急于要开箱子的钥匙，却没有。"（鲁迅《"题未定"草·且介亭杂文二集》）

在研究和翻译罗尔德·达尔的这部分作品过程中,还会遇到语言及文化差异方面的"绊脚石",处理起来颇费脑筋,正如严复在他翻译的《天演论》(译例言)中所言:"新理踵出,名目纷繁,索之中文,渺不可得,即有牵合,终嫌参差,译者遇此,独有自具衡量,即义定名。"另外,在翻译中对于查询无果的地方,也得认真加以思考,甚至经过了很长时间才"创造性"地下笔定论,可谓"一名之立,旬月踟蹰。我罪我知,是存明哲"(严复《译例言》)。由此可见,译事之难,不亚于李太白笔下的"蜀道之难,难于上青天"了!

幸运的是,在对罗尔德·达尔这些"非儿童类"短篇小说进行研究和翻译过程中,我们得到了许多朋友和同事热情的帮助和有力的支持,感激之情无以言表。

对罗尔德·达尔短篇小说的研究和翻译源于英国朋友马礼(他的英文原名叫"Jonathan Rackham",时任渤海大学外籍英语教师)2009年赠送给著者的一本书,书名叫《罗尔德·达尔小说精品集》(*The Best of Roald Dahl*)。在阅读这本书的过程中,得到了启发,萌生了要研究并翻译作家罗尔德·达尔"非儿童类"短篇小说的念头。我们于2010年9月开始动笔,从此一发而不可收。在对原文理解过程中所遇到的难题,得到了马礼耐心而细致的解答,甚至在他回到英国后,还继续通过电子邮件、越洋电话等方式给予我们热情的解答。在此,衷心感谢好友兼同行的马礼,感谢他的热情帮助!

译文从初稿到成稿,虽经数次校正和修改,仍然存在不少问题。此时,我们的学长兼兄长又兼同事和朋友的刘恩东先生及时伸出了援助之手,对最终的成稿在"忠实"的基础上进行了"通顺"方面的梳理。刘恩东先生虽身为渤海大学英语教师,但是,其汉语功力不可小觑,令吾等外语研究者难以望其项背,特别是他古汉语的功力,甚至超出很多古汉语的专业研究者。有了我们兄长对书稿的梳理和理顺,毛坯一样的成稿方焕发出光彩。兄长对书稿的修改,虽然有时只

后　记

是增填一个字，或者是删除一个词，但却救译文于"水火"之中。可以说，没有兄长对书稿的理顺，名为"成稿"的译文只能如同一个咿呀学语、走路不稳的婴儿。在此，衷心感谢刘恩东先生，感谢他辛苦的付出！

研究伊始，一个偶然的机会，我们搜索到克里斯廷·霍华德（Kristine Howard）创建并维护的网站"罗尔德·达尔粉丝网"（Roald Dahl Fans.com），并就罗尔德·达尔有关问题联系过霍华德女士，收到了她及时的回复。整个研究也因霍华德女士的网站而受益匪浅。在此，衷心感谢克里斯廷·霍华德女士，感谢她在网站里所提供的全面而翔实的资料！

同时，我们十分感谢渤海大学外语教研部和渤海大学外国语学院领导和同事给予我们热情的帮助和有力的支持！十分感谢哈尔滨工业大学出版社田新华在出版方面提供的有力支持！同时感谢为本书的出版而忙碌的所有编辑人员和工作人员！同时，我们十分感谢为本研究提供帮助的所有朋友和同仁！

当然，由于时间和能力所限，错误在所难免，还望读者赐教、斧正，并多提宝贵意见。

对罗尔德·达尔"非儿童类"短篇故事（小说）研究、翻译所成之书，难免泛泛而论，甚至是流于平庸，但是，我们本着扎实做学问、做学问如做人的思想，从起点出发，稳扎稳打，力戒浮躁之风，勿求好高骛远。

记得《礼记·中庸》里有言："君子之道，譬如行远，必自迩，譬如登高，必自卑。"愿以此语共勉。

闫宝华　王永胜
2015 年初夏于渤海大学